Vocal Apparitions

PRINCETON STUDIES IN OPERA

CAROLYN ABBATE AND ROGER PARKER

SERIES EDITORS

Vocal Apparitions

THE ATTRACTION OF CINEMA TO OPERA

MICHAL GROVER-FRIEDLANDER

PRINCETON UNIVERSITY PRESS

PRINCETON AND OXFORD

Copyright ©2005 by Princeton University Press

Published by Princeton University Press, 41 William Street, Princeton, New Jersey 08540

In the United Kingdom: Princeton University Press, 3 Market Place,
Woodstock, Oxfordshire OX20 1SY

All Rights Reserved

Library of Congress Cataloging-in-Publication Data
Grover-Friedlander, Michal.
Vocal apparitions : the attraction of cinema to opera / Michal Grover-Friedlander.
p.   cm. — (Princeton studies in opera)
Includes bibliographical references and index.
ISBN 0-691-12008-0 (alk. paper)
1. Motion pictures and opera.   2. Voice in motion pictures.   3. Music—Philosophy and
aesthetics.   I. Title.   II. Series.

ML2100.G76 2005
791.43'657—dc22   2004018107

British Library Cataloging-in-Publication Data is available

This book has been composed in Galliard

Printed on acid-free paper. ∞

pup.princeton.edu

Printed in the United States of America

1   3   5   7   9   10   8   6   4   2

With all my love

To Eli, Elam, and Omer all at once

CONTENTS

❧

ILLUSTRATIONS

◢◣◢

Figures

Musical Examples

ACKNOWLEDGMENTS

VOCAL APPARITIONS would be something of a miraculous apparition had it not been for the presence and repeated gestures of friendship and encouragement from some very special people. Nothing I say here can capture the depth of their inspiration and the range of their impact. First among these friends and scholars is Carolyn Abbate. I have never met someone as unique or as generous. Her daring and radical scholarship has drastically altered the study of music, fundamentally challenging the ways we think of things heard and seen. Whatever sensitivity I show about the aesthetics of opera and cinema can be traced to the teachings of Stanley Cavell. His wondrous ways of personalizing the philosophical freed me to think about works I deeply care about. Allan Keiler, my teacher and mentor from a more distant past, started me off on opera. The ways he taught me to think rigorously about music helped me through the many intricacies of this book.

I was fortunate to be in an extraordinary environment while writing my book, spending an extended sabbatical at Princeton University. Stefanie Stcharos was an exceptional research assistant. Her resourcefulness and thoroughness were unmatched. I also want to thank Wayne Heisler for his imaginative assistance during the final stages of writing. Zsofia Surjan and Paula Matthews of the music library at Princeton University were remarkable in their ability to locate everything and anything.

My gratitude also goes to Fred Appel, my editor at Princeton University Press, who has been patient, considerate, and helpful all through. The readers he chose for my book, Mary Ann Smart and David Levin, were impressive in their engaged responses, thoughtful suggestions, and insightful comments. I also thank Roger Parker for his acute and sensitive observations and unquestioned support throughout.

The field of opera and cinema would not have been as distinguished without the scholarship of Marcia Citron, nor as fascinating and dynamic without the original work done by Jeongwon Joe and Rose Theresa. It would also not have been as fun.

My colleagues in the musicology department at Tel Aviv University have created, against all odds, an intellectual and friendly environment in times of political and cultural despair. Much of the material for this book originated in courses I taught. Exceptionally talented students from the musicology department and the interdisciplinary program in the arts at Tel Aviv University helped me elucidate my ideas and turned writing into an exciting journey.

I would also like to acknowledge with appreciation my dear friends Vered, Margalit, and Osnat for the crucial place of their friendship in the process of writing. With Vered Lev Kenaan I have worked wonderfully together, learning enormously from her creative thought and scholarship, and from our friendship.

My deepest thanks go to my parents, exemplary in their courage to battle and overcome grave illness. I am always aware that they are unequivocally there for me at all times and in all conditions. I cannot think of the book without the love of Eli Friedlander and his love of books. Only he could have agreed to read, reread and re-reread everything I have written, helping me become readable. Nor can I think of the world of this book without the parallel one invented by Omer and Elam, my magical twin boys, as they go off on imaginary quests to save the world. I dedicate my book to them.

Vocal Apparitions

INTRODUCTION

THIS BOOK is about cinema's attraction to the operatic voice: not about any and all points of contact between cinema and opera but rather about films that thematize the power that opera has over film—thematize, so to speak, their own "pull" toward opera. I explore cinema's acknowledgment of opera's power over it and account for this extreme attraction to opera. If a film is not driven by opera or does not wish, in its infatuation and obsession, to become operatic, if it does not risk its own "cinematicness" in being so haunted by opera, it does not figure in this book.

Starting with questions about the inner elaboration of the space of opera, I ask what happens when that space is projected onto the medium of film. My emphasis is on what specifically occurs when what is aesthetically essential about one medium is transposed into the aesthetic field of the other. It is not the case that each medium—opera or film—loses what is characteristic about it in this transformation. Instead, the transformation reveals the specificity of each, in ways that a consideration of opera or film on its own terms cannot. Paradoxically, cinema at times can be more "operatic" than opera itself, thus capturing something essential that escapes opera's self-understanding.

I deal with opera as a *medium,* on par with the medium of cinema, rather than as a musical genre or style comparable with, say, the symphony or the concerto. My investigation of cinema's relation to opera is to be distinguished from historical accounts of the influence of opera on cinema or of operatic music on film music. I do not outline continuities between the two media or discuss the development of genres across them (for instance, the melodrama of opera as finding a renewed life in Hollywood melodramas). Nor am I concerned with analogies of themes, actions, or characters, although those are always part of the picture. Operas appear within plots of films; characters go to the opera, listen to it, and are absorbed or overwhelmed by it, as we ourselves often are when viewing and listening to opera.

But if those instances are to be elaborated in relation to the guiding thread of the book, it is not by merely asking about the relation between the plot of the film and that of the embedded opera, or by treating the music of the opera as part of the film's music (operatic music as background film music is almost "too much," overdetermined). This is true of filmed operas as well: the attraction that opera holds for cinema does not express itself in what would initially seem to be the obvious case of filmed opera productions. Indeed, the most important, even avant-garde filmed operas emphasize the impossibility of a straightforward and direct transformation of the operatic into the cinematic, or of the vocal into the visual.[1]

The fundamental point is always how all these cases of film's interaction with opera teach us something about the exchange between the two media, and how the transformation of one medium into the other may reveal unanticipated or previously unarticulated characteristics of each. The particular cases thus teach us something essential about the two media in question.

For precisely this reason, I am most interested in individual cases where the affinity between opera and film is extreme and extravagant, since true attraction is never moderate. These are often cases where opera—true to its nature—makes contact with film in unique conditions, under special circumstances, or in unexpected places. These extreme cases delimit the boundaries of the possibilities for film's involvement with opera.

This book assumes a conception of opera that ties together all six chapters. First and foremost, the chapters share a premise about the foundation of opera in a notion of *voice*. Voice is thus a common theme, yet I have not tried to cite or construct some common theoretical framework that could subsume and organize all the works I discuss. Any theoretical framework must be consequential to the interpretation of the works themselves, not something assumed or imported beforehand. My own idiosyncratic view of the nature of opera and of cinema, in particular the importance I assign to the singing voice and to the voice as a more abstract idea, does inform my approach. Yet I have tried to allow it to emerge from the material: the voice of opera in silent film (chapter 1), an impossible striving for the perfect image of song (chapter 3), opera on the phone (chapter 5), and a journey of the bodily remains of opera (chapter 6). It is my hope that, viewed in this way, my operatic films will reveal something about the relation of opera and film that is available neither in the abstract nor by way of theoretical accounts alone.

The title *Vocal Apparitions: The Attraction of Cinema to Opera* is meant to intimate a paradoxical linkage. First, "attraction" is meant, deliberately, to anthropomorphize film and opera, to imply transgression, to suggest that films deal with opera as an object of desire that may also be perilous to their autonomy or strict cinematic identity. But in coining that title, I wanted as well to problematize the notion that there is some continuous passage or smooth, predictable transition (either historically or within any given film) between opera and cinema. The linkage between cinema and opera should be taken as improbable or paradoxical, not natural; we should not assume that one melodramatic genre naturally and inevitably calls out to another and is answered in kind.

The title is also meant to suggest a series of *passages* or transformations. First among these is the passage between the *vocal* and the *visual*, both within each medium and in film's appropriations of opera. The idea of a vocal apparition unites the spectral with the acoustic; in my view, the interaction of these two domains always involves a critical negotiation, and not just in the more obvious case of film. Voice and image are uneasily related within opera. But "apparition" also alludes to the specific case where film calls up images whose origin lies, so to speak, beyond the medium of film. These images are imported into film by way of a hidden power that belongs to opera—they are the spectral remnants of the immaterial, invisible operatic voice.

Another passage implied by the idea of the apparition is the passage between death and life. One of my claims is that cinema inherits opera, as it were, reincarnating it. Thus scenes and images of opera in cinema refer to a past existence, a dead ancestor. At the same time, they *mask* these reminders of mortality; they both divert us from and draw our attention to the uncanny presence of death. And paradoxically, at the same time, by lavishly staging the human voice with its implications of life and presence, opera in cinema holds out a promise of revival.

Four premises delineate my understanding of opera. The first premise is that the aesthetic foundation of opera is the operatic voice. Opera's voices and, with them, *the idea* of the operatic voice are unique to its world; the medium conceives of itself through its voices. This premise assumes a notion of song and singing that is characteristic of Italian opera and less so of other national genres. Though I do not wish to insist on or argue for the point, my view is that all opera—including nineteenth-century French and German opera, twentieth- and twenty-first-century opera—carries some trace of an "Italian" notion of song.

By an "Italian notion of song," I do not refer to some style of singing (such as bel canto) or even to the general point that melodious singing is an important aesthetic criterion in opera. What I mean is something quite different: opera that engenders a state in which one is always listening in anticipation of, or listening toward, a place where one knows beautiful singing will take place. The Italian notion of song produces the condition of always waiting for "beautiful moments" of singing. This is a kind of ecstatic listening, and it specifically acknowledges operatic singing as an activity bordering on the superhuman. Such singing is transcendent on the one hand yet always under the threat of appearing ridiculous on the other, being both miraculous and continually available for parody.

Such beautiful moments do not have any fixed aesthetic manifestation.

They could figure as outbursts of coloratura, as improvisation, as continuous and smooth legato articulation, as singing to the limits of breath, or as an expression of "dramatic truth." These beautiful moments could yield the high note, the long note, the darkest note, and the most lyrical note. But in all cases, it is the special state of listening in anticipation of these moments that is crucial and accounts for their meaning. All opera has such moments.

These beautiful moments are objects of desire and anticipation; however, they are also ephemeral. Thus the state of anticipation brings with it a simultaneous consciousness of mortality. Moments of beautiful singing are always already being mourned, since one knows that they will have gone by at the very moment they appear. Put in its most paradoxical form: they are gone before they are there. There is a sense of no return connected to those beautiful moments, and, ultimately, their power over the listener depends on this programmed loss.

By raising the issue of mortality, I am intimating the second premise that conditions my understanding of opera. This is that death is immanent in the operatic voice. There are several accounts of death as a phenomenon in opera, and not just simply from the overobvious perspective of the libretto and the plot. Catherine Clément, Michel Poizat, Slavoj Žižek, and Carolyn Abbate, to name only a few, have various perspectives on this theme.

Clément provocatively claimed that singing itself seems to kill the heroines of opera. In her interpretation of opera's cultural work, these repeated deaths—the "undoing of women" in opera—are a symptom of female victimization in general. Our investment in this victimization ensures that opera will continue to be enjoyed. We are doubly deceived by the beautiful music, for it not only gives voice to and even causes these deaths but also encourages us to overlook or become amorally complicit in the murderous plot. Thus though the plots wallow in female death scenes, singing and music are also guilty—or even guiltier. They mask the horror of opera's excessive female mortality. Clément envisions a future for opera wherein women sing and are finally *permitted to die* for good. Violetta expires one last time, and *La traviata* is never performed again, for this is preferable to the forced immortality of infinitely repeated deaths.[2]

In theorizing opera's attraction to death, Michel Poizat downplays the role of operatic plot while endorsing Clément's correlation between voice and death. For Poizat, the various characters' deaths mirror a trajectory that is, in the abstract, immanent in the idea of the operatic voice as such. Voice, in Poizat's view, is a spectrum, a continuum whose "high" extreme is a sound beyond singing (melos) and beyond signification: the cry, the shriek, the scream, fading out into after-echoes and silence. The "low" extreme of the voice is logos: a logical, minimally inflected, and unsung speech. For Poizat, operatic voice, in being drawn into melodious singing, is always impelled toward the high extreme in an unattainable quest for a transcendent point that does not exist. Thus operatic narratives that prescribe death for their characters allegorize the tendency of voice to reach for its own high extreme. Thus in staging death, opera stages its fundamental vocality. For Poizat, opera's essence resides in moments in which listener and singer alike lose themselves in the singer's voice, dissolving in what becomes sheer voice, a vocal object. He writes: "In opera, the voice does not express the text—that is what theatre is for; the text expresses the voice . . . it is not because the dramatic logic of the libretto has led the female character to her death that she cries out at that moment; it is because a logic of vocal jouissance is at work and is driving at the cry that the dramatic conditions necessary for its occurrence are created, demanding a death, for example."[3]

Slavoj Žižek, concentrating mainly on Wagner, interprets opera as being about a subject unable to die, about longing for peace in death. Žižek imports the Lacanian—some might say horror-movie—motif of "two deaths" and existence "between two deaths," the first being the biological death, and the second, dying in peace "with . . . accounts settled and with no symbolic debt haunting his or her memory."[4] Between the two deaths is a state of eternal longing and unfulfilled desire. It is here that Žižek locates the exemplary Wagnerian horror as he sees it: the threat of existing as an undead monster. For Abbate, however, death in Wagner's operas is a Utopian moment in which the opera seems to displace the authorial voice quite radically, replacing it with a voice that has no source from within the plot. Death thus also allows a form of operatic immortality. Heroines remain in music after their death, in something resembling a sonorous form.[5]

As an addendum to these theories about death in opera, I formulate my third premise, which is more specific and yet makes a rather pan-historical critical claim about mortality and operatic voice. Operatic deaths replay the medium's primal "Orphic death," by which I mean not the death of Orpheus (which was, in fact, seldom included in librettos) but a more complicated system or structure implicit in the myth. Citing the Orpheus myth as a master operatic figure is, of course, hardly unprecedented. As Wayne Koestenbaum put it, "Every opera revives Orpheus, the art form's genesis."[6] The very persistence with which critics and historians return to this master trope should, itself, be seen as significant. We should note how curious it is that the founding myth of the "birth of opera" via the narrative of Orpheus has persisted for so long, despite grave reservations concerning its historical accuracy. An accounting of the actual invention of opera, the precedents of opera, and its development after 1600 has long gone beyond Orpheus. Yet the sense of a miraculous birth persists—in other words, opera's "philosophical" and fabulous lineage, as opposed to its actual and "pragmatic" lineage, persists even in light of contradictory evidence.[7]

And so, the founding myth: the death of Eurydice, the transformation of Orpheus's loss into music that attempts to overcome death. Initially, Orpheus is successful in bringing back the dead Eurydice. But Orpheus's success is ultimately also the story of his failure to sustain Eurydice's revival. What is striking in the myth is that song's power manifests itself in the first instance as the *possibility of passage* between death and life, indeed, as the power to bring the world to life or back to life. But if we turn this on its head, we see the corollary: without facing mortality and separation, without experiencing the pain that can create song, one brings death into one's life. A world without song is itself dead.

But there should be reservations about any such ecstatic claim, reservations already intimated in my first premise, about opera, voice, and song. It is inherently impossible to sustain the ecstatic power of song. Singing, "Italian song," is always anticipated as subject to inevitable mortality. Singing is a way station on the voice's inevitable trajectory toward cries and silence. And, in the Orpheus myth, song opens only a *temporary passage* between worlds, and it is unable to make the upper world a permanent home for someone who inhabits the netherworld. The slip back into old ways of experiencing the world is the temptation figured in Orpheus's need to gaze backward at Eurydice. But, more important, he cannot sustain, or make permanent, a miraculous phenomenon based on and in song. Any such phenomenon is transient, ephemeral, and without the reassurance of actual presence. Orpheus is tempted to look back at Eurydice and to relate to her in the way that must bring her renewed death.

In the myth, a distinction is established between a song that revives (but is transient) and a gaze that kills (and is permanent). According to Stanley Cavell, this duality has to do with "the expressive capacity of song: ecstasy over the absolute success of its expressiveness in recalling the world, as if bringing it back to life; melancholia over its inability to sustain the world, which may be put as an expression of the absolute inexpressiveness of the voice, of its failure to make itself heard, to become intelligible—evidently a mad state."[8]

What I mean by "Orphic death" as a premise about opera, then, is the complete structure suggested by the myth. Song revives the dead, but that revival is overturned by a gesture that is not acoustic (song) but visual (looking back). The myth of Orpheus is first and foremost about the power of Orpheus's voice. But a curious power it is, since Orpheus cannot sustain it and loses whatever this power achieves. Perhaps Clément's formulation that singing in opera "kills" is possible only if we first assume that the voice has the power *to revive*; yet this power is fragile. Song, it would seem, is too easily overcome, and the puzzle is not why Orpheus turned around but rather why song's power to revive is overturned and canceled so easily by only one quick glance. "Orphic death" thus hints that the spectral, the visual, or the optical is able to bring about the total collapse of whatever has been achieved by the vocal or the acoustic.

That this model is critical to any consideration of cinema and opera should be stressed in no uncertain terms. Even simply taken at face value, the model indicates that "the visual" might summarize the impossibility of ever completing a passage and thus stands for an interruption, a rude break in the death-to-life motion that song continually attempts to achieve but cannot.

Finally, it is important to acknowledge opera's "Orphic" basis—in my particular sense of "Orphic death"—if only to distinguish its aesthetic foundation from the many other myths about the power of voice, the miraculous effects of voice, and so forth. For instance, the myth of Ulysses and the Sirens (to cite another paradigmatic myth about voice) deals with voice as an enchanting force capable of waylaying the senses. There have been contrary readings of this myth: Kafka, troubled by the idea that Ulysses overcomes the power of the Sirens' singing, explains that the Sirens, offended by Ulysses, did not sing at all; it is only their silence that Ulysses withstood.[9] But the Sirens, in either case, are not very good as a model for the origination of operatic song, since their song kills its listeners. Neither can Ulysses be opera's ideal mythical listener, since, if anything, he allegorizes the capacity to resist song by whatever means possible, and opera is about neither withstanding the power of song nor refusing to listen. On the contrary, from the listener's point of view, opera involves abandoning oneself to song, anticipating its beautiful singing, longing for the intimations of a miraculous passage inherent in that singing, at the same time knowing that the singing will come to an end.

My fourth premise follows on the notion of an "Orphic death" of song itself within opera, the idea that song is abbreviated or terminated by a visual intervention. The relation between the vocal and the visual, the passage toward death or away from it: these are themes internal to opera; yet, as I have argued, they are not independent themes, unrelated to one another. The myth of Orpheus shows visuality entering the picture in the case of a primal operatic death. But I want to turn the screw one last time and say that it is not quite the gaze that causes death. Rather, the idea of mortality or impermanence is already called for by the frailty of song, by its incapacity to *sustain* life, or by its passing and ephemeral nature.

According to this formulation, opera's repeated murders within its plots, which for Poizat echo the voice tending toward its own unraveling at the "high" extreme, are, with that unraveling, a reference to what initiated operatic singing in the first place—the Utopian attempt to overcome death with song and the belief (as Cavell put it) that song will revive the world, which end in the inevitable failure of those attempts and their revival, the repeated hope invested in song. The promise to bring back what is dead is supplanted by a more profound, less ecstatic acknowledgment that what is ephemeral and passing is also what can return. The gesture of endless dying signifies the failure of death to hold sway. The repetition of song questions the finality of death, introducing a dimension of immortality. The repetition becomes its own conversion and a correction. In opera what cannot truly be internalized is this power to resurrect, and the constant resurgence provides for the medium's immortalization.

One can, therefore, phrase a counterargument to Clément—whose distaste for turning death into a Utopian metaphor is so patent—in the following terms. Opera's endless repetitions of the structure of singing and dying restate the originating act of Orpheus's revival of Eurydice through song while also reinscribing the failure to sustain life—which is also opera's own. Through its sheer mortality and human frailty, the operatic voice wills what is beyond the human: the reversal of death. The possibility opened by loss is one where singing reverses death. Thus, against Clément's conclusion that the death of heroines attests to women's problematic positioning within opera, we might say that death in fact hands over to the operatic heroine the ultimate power of song. In apparently dying Eurydice's death, the heroine is endowed with the power opera longs for: that granted to Orpheus. Finally, it is symptomatic that opera tends to delegate the biggest moment of Italian song to the heroine at her fatal apotheosis. If the soprano's death song is the prototypical beautiful moment in opera, this is not simply because, as Clément suggests, the most regressive or horrifying plot element demands the most persuasive musical cover-up. As I have intimated, what goes on at such moments is far more complex and may well be the first entry point that cinema found in opera when it was first felled by opera's seductive gaze.

❧

This book is divided into three parts, each with two chapters. Each part has a particular local color and a singular inner unity, but there are also important thematic connections running through the different parts. The first part, "Silent Voices," begins with the last decade of silent film. Its two chapters trace film's attempts to visualize the voices of opera while forgoing its sounds. On the whole, silent film was attracted to opera in both obvious and paradoxical ways—in an obvious way in that an operatic voice may have seemed an ideal compensation for the absence of sound; in a paradoxical way in that it is unclear how an operatic voice would be represented in a silent genre. And yet, it is precisely silent film that depicts something essential about opera: silence, muteness, and the disintegration of language are at the core of the operatic voice.

The film interpreted in chapter 1, the 1925 silent version of *The Phantom of the Opera,* portrays an obsession with opera, primarily the obsession of the central character in the film, the Phantom, but also that of the film itself. *The Phantom of the Opera* attempts at all costs to express the conditions of voice in opera by way of the cinematic image. The film is haunted by the operatic voice and makes its singing "audible" by revealing this voice's power to take over the images of cinema. Ultimately, cinema substitutes for opera. The Phantom, as he comes to signify the operatic in the film, dies an operatic death. His death pulls down the cinematic figure, the one that took over opera, and allows the operatic figure of the prima donna to live but requires her to relinquish her powers of song to obtain that cinematic happiness. In *The Phantom of the Opera*, it suffices to see the operatic voice in order to hear it. This provides the first fundamental interpretation of the interplay between the vocal and the visual and of the passage between opera's vocality and cinema's visuality.

The Marx Brothers' film, *A Night at the Opera* (1935), is the main focus of chapter 2. Though not a silent film, *A Night at the Opera* invokes silent film by thematizing film's attraction to opera. In their extravagant display of the disintegration of speech, the Marx Brothers show their inheritance of silent burlesque but, more important, their sense of the uneasy relation between operatic music (perhaps even music in general) and discursive meaning. In translating operatic manners into their own mode of being, the Marx Brothers subvert opera's tragic fate, allowing for a cinematic happy ending for one of the Italian repertory's most melodramatically deadly operatic works. In effect, the Marx Brothers rescue the film's operatic twin plot of *Il trovatore* by avoiding a repetition of its unhappy end. The happy ending made possible by the film overrides the threat implicit in that tragic opera. In the process, however, the film carefully conceals the origins of its own happy ending, which restages a famous death scene: the now-united lovers (a star soprano and an aspiring tenor) joyously celebrate their triumph and future marital bliss by singing what, in Verdi's *Il trovatore*, is a last premortem duet.

Considered together, the two chapters put forth the claim that something about silent film's way of presenting the operatic voice without sounding it is essential for understanding a more general relation between opera and film. Moreover, both films show that in engaging with the operatic voice, they must also share opera's preoccupation with death as an outcome of the journey of the operatic voice. The Phantom dies operatically; the Marx Brothers cunningly, willingly, and cheerfully "mishear" the operatic death and avoid its fate.

The second part of the book, "Visions of Voices," considers what occurs when cinema absorbs opera in its entirety in the form of filmed opera. Chapter 3, "*Otello*'s One Voice," and 4, "*Falstaff*'s Free Voice," center on Verdi's last operas and two unusual and (some would say) problematic cinematic realizations: Franco Zeffirelli's *Otello* and Götz Friedrich's *Falstaff*. Part 2 is the most explicit in arguing that the tensions between the vocal and the visual are inherent to the medium of opera prior to any consideration of its relation to cinema. *Otello* and *Falstaff* represent opposite notions of the relation of the vocal to the visual in opera (notoriously, in the case of *Otello*, "optical proof" is at odds with the truth expressed ineffably through Desdemona's voice). The cinematic productions enter this picture as secondary reorderings of a vocal-visual dyad that has already been foregrounded by the operas themselves. Taken together, these two chapters claim that a successful cinematic production of opera is necessarily a radical interpretation of relations that occur within the opera itself. A straightforward transposition of opera into film would neither be cinematic nor operatic.

In these chapters, the complex relationship of the vocal and the visual is elaborated in interpretations more attuned to musical detail than in any of the other chapters. An implicit aim of this part is to show that Verdi's aesthetics—his conceptualization of the relationship of the vocal to the visual in opera—run as deep as Wagner's. Indeed, *Falstaff* is often considered Verdi's response to Wagnerian notions of opera. Thus, I have chosen to interpret Zeffirelli's more traditional production of *Otello* as a cinematic treatment of an opera that represents one of the culminating moments of the tradition of Italian song. Similarly, I have chosen Friedrich's production of *Falstaff* because Friedrich is a director immersed in staged and screened productions of Wagner who can illuminate aspects of Verdi's opera that reveal it as a response to Wagnerian aesthetics.

The sense of the difficulty or ease with which the visual and the vocal come together is not just a feature of these productions but rather the outcome of the inner possibilities of each opera. *Otello* seeks to present a voice beyond any physical embodiment, a voice that no image can match, whereas *Falstaff* plays with the voice's different, often grotesque, embodiments, matching and mismatching them with the image. These different relations between the vocal and the visual determine the tragic outcome of *Otello* and the comic resolution of *Falstaff*. An operatic voice fated to die, as in *Otello*, differs from an operatic voice celebrating life, as in *Falstaff*. *Otello* is the culmination of depictions of the death of voice, and *Falstaff* opens the possibility to address this fate comically. The two operas combined manifest the comic resolution of the tragic fate.

Part 2 further elaborates on both the theme of silence and of the relation of voice and death, which is broached in part 1. In his production of

Otello, Zeffirelli almost seems to fear silence. Even though the opera calls for a crucial moment of silence when it brings its heroine onstage to sing nothing, Zeffirelli abstains from visually representing that staged silence and removes Desdemona altogether from the scene. In *Falstaff*, Friedrich does not alter anything within the body of the opera but, surprisingly, adds to it, inserting silent visual interludes between the opera's scenes. Through these interludes, Friedrich demonstrates that the visual can arise out of the vocal and, even more strikingly, that music can arise out of silent visuality.

The third part of the book, "Remains of the Voice," develops an account of the sense of the immortality of the operatic voice. Cinema, in recalling the operatic, allows its voices to echo; it provides opera with a peculiar afterlife. Chapter 5, "Opera on the Phone: The Call of the Human Voice," interprets Poulenc's opera *La voix humaine* and Rossellini's film *Una voce umane*. The film and the opera were created independently of one another; initially, their only relationship was that they were based on the same play by Jean Cocteau. Rather than examining what the filmic image makes of the operatic voice or how film incorporates an entire opera, I examine how film and opera react differently to an identical text—one that precisely invokes the themes of the vocal, the aural, the visual, and death.

The opera and the film take on the idea of a silent voice, a voice on the other side of a phone line, the source of which is not located in an image. A comparison between the film and the opera reveals complexities in the interrelations and differentiation of notions such as "unheard," "silent," "mute," "voiceless," and "speechless." It is the unheard and invisible voice that becomes the driving force of events. But, at the same time, this nonpresence brings about the power of the voice that we do hear to construct the whole world enacted in the works.

The different conceptions of voice and vision growing out of the same text reveal different sensitivities to death. Despite its modern, technological setting, the opera takes the traditional notion of solitary singing unto death to its extreme and constructs an opera-length death song. Rossellini's *Una voce umane*, which is independent of opera, is not bound to the operatic dependency of voice on death and is free to offer an alternative. In the film, Rossellini does not remain with the deadly invisible voice on the phone but generates an intense expectation for an apparition to be conjured out of that voice. Although Rossellini does not change the deadly outcome in Cocteau's play, he does add a second film, *Il miracolo*, which provides a glimpse of the future in the sound of a baby's newly formed voice.

In the sixth and final chapter, "Fellini's Ashes," I interpret Fellini's *E la nave va* as offering a spectacle of the afterlife of the operatic voice. This possibility of a future after the death of the voice was intimated in Rossellini's film, where it was figured in nonoperatic terms. Fellini's film, by contrast, is all opera. This film incorporates themes discussed in all of the earlier chapters. *E la nave va* includes scenes of vocal acrobatics, pyrotechnics, and vocal contests, as do *The Phantom of the Opera* and *A Night at the Opera*. Operatic excess is carved into the film's very style as in *The Phantom of the Opera*; it captures the ridiculous and absurd side of the operatic voice as in *A Night at the Opera*; it employs technology to sound the voice as in *Una voce umane* and *La voix humaine*; and it evokes fantasies of the perfect operatic voice as in *Otello* and carnavalesque visions of the voice as in *Falstaff*. Fellini's film evokes, more than any of the other films considered in this book, the total phenomenon of opera. I do not interpret the many associations with opera; in its overwhelming references to opera, the film almost calls for an abstention from such an endeavor. In being "too much" it allows us to select moments, like mementos, to stand for the rest. It is in this spirit that I interpret what I identify as its most deep-seated attraction to opera, namely, its attraction to the death of the medium of opera itself.

Fellini's film begins, rather than ends, with the death of the operatic voice when it stages the funeral of the most famous prima donna of all. The film portrays her voice indirectly: not by sounding it, but by staging the cult of that voice. *E la nave va* shares with other films I discuss in the book the attraction to the operatic voice through the filter of silent film. It opens with an imitation of a silent film. The funeral procession of the prima donna is placed in a silent film sequence. A nostalgic return to cinema's silent decades depicts the start of the funeral at sea, where her ashes are spread. Toward the end of the film, the use of the gramophone to sound the voice of the prima donna serves to further relate the reproduction of the operatic voice to the essentially nostalgic nature of the cinematic image. Fellini thus intimates that the birth of film coincides with the death of (at least) the Italian tradition of opera. More important, he understands film to provide opera with an afterlife.

In *E la nave va*, cinema not only does not correct opera's deaths but also uses the occasion of the death of a prima donna to show, beyond any specific opera, that death threatens both the characters of opera and the medium itself. The film allegorizes the death of the singing voice as the end of opera. In so doing, it places, alongside its own anxiety over the death of cinema, that of the death of opera—understanding one by way of the other. If, in 1925, *The Phantom of the Opera* exhibited the fear that opera will haunt it and that cinema will never replace opera, in 1983, at the occasion of cinema's one-hundredth birthday, *E la nave va* exhibits, through its operatic past, the fear of the end of cinema. Through the death of the operatic voice, Fellini envisions the death of the medium of cinema, a death that is, for Fellini, no less than a vision of a world bygone.

＝＝

Introductions are tricky. They call out for manifestos and clear-cut declarations that in my case are at odds with a more cautious, tentative, modest, and interpretative style. No single theoretical framework or opera-and-cinema method could serve as a rubric or road map for the various arguments I present here. My most elaborate theoretical discussion appears in chapter 1, where I rely on a Lacanian notion of voice. The second part of the book, chapters 3 and 4, considers operatic music in great detail, cinematic productions of whole operas, and depends to a great extent on musical analysis. Chapter 6 involves cultural history and uses what might almost be called a montage technique, a thick nexus of texts.

The shifts in techniques, or even in scholarly attitudes, are, in part, the after-echo, reflecting the radical heterogeneity of the phenomena I am trying to bring into view. There is no theoretical framework that I know of that could deal with one phenomenon I am working with, the transitions or passages between one medium and another. There are no established assumptions that make working between opera and cinema easier; the modulations between opera and film require a different starting point every time, require that one start with the specificity of the work.

I find that I cannot even imagine a single, specific cinematic style that would be most suited, or preferable above all the others, for portraying the operatic voice. Rather—as in *E la nave va*, *The Phantom of the Opera*, and *A Night at the* Opera—different cinematic styles invoke different traits of the operatic. One finds expressionism (as in *The Phantom of the Opera*), burlesque (as in *A Night at the Opera*), and the grotesque (*E la nave va*). Even Rossellini's *Una voce umane* brings the style of neorealism to its limit, combining the realistic and the operatic. Any one of these filmic styles (the expressionist, the burlesque, the grotesque, and the neorealist) can come to approximate the condition of opera. These films are not analogous to opera. They become operatic.

Still, there is one theoretical domain that I want to address, and that is the issue of what is sometimes called internal and external criticism. Interpretative positions with respect to opera often adopt two opposed sides. Internal criticism, one might say, is completely engaged in the work, completely absorbed by it, by its magic. In opera, this tends to take the form of elucidating opera's power over the listener and often deals with voice in the abstract or operatic singers specifically. Sometimes the writing itself is carried away in an attempt to recapture the ecstasies of the medium and its powerful attraction through verbal excess or an open confession of the emotions that opera engenders. Hence Wayne Koestenbaum's poetically explosive language: "Opera has the power to warn you that you have wasted your life. You haven't acted on your desires. You've suffered a stunted, vicarious existence. You've silenced your passions. The volume, height, depth, lushness, and excess of operatic utterance reveal, by contrast, how small your gestures have been until now, how impoverished your physicality; you have only used a fraction of your bodily endowment, and your throat is closed."[10] Collaborating on an opera, as Koestenbaum did in *Jackie O.*, does indeed seem the next step after that kind of writing.

The second interpretative position, external criticism, views operatic works as a function, or even symptom, of various social or cultural forces. In this domain, opera's attraction is socially regressive and politically dubious, since opera is invariably ideologically motivated. Implicit in its assumptions is the idea that opera is, properly, a phenomenon of the past, linked to the emergence of a bourgeois world. If opera continues to fascinate, this is cause for alarm. As Theodor Adorno writes: "It would be appropriate to consider opera as the specifically bourgeois genre which, in the midst and with the means of a world bereft of magic, paradoxically endeavors to preserve the magical element of art." This is something that one, at most, clings to nostalgically: "what happens on the operatic stage is usually like a museum of bygone images and gestures, to which a retrospective need clings."[11] Jeremy Tambling, in his writings on opera and the media, is equally suspicious. He calls for us to correct opera, seeking ways to expose its many disguises and wrongdoings. Tambling argues that our experience of opera should be totally altered by the estranging effect that he hopes postmodern cinema will have on it.[12]

Some writers are amphibious, so to speak. Catherine Clément, for instance, feels the force of opera and expresses it in her style of writing about the works, but at the same time she strongly senses the problematic nature of a medium that habitually kills its heroines and aestheticizes their deaths. Even Adorno starts from a position of suspicion but comes to admit that, together with the negative ideological moment of semblance, there is, in opera, at least the promise of another happiness.

Is it possible to find a stance between the inside and the outside, to sense the transformative truth of opera but also the problematic nature of its lure? Can we do this as easily as we acknowledge opera's success and recognize its failure, realize at once its power and weakness? What I propose is that thinking about opera and cinema together can provide a position that assumes neither total immersion in the operatic work nor ideological estrangement from it.

In a sense, such positions are opened by the transformation of the very life, or afterlife, of opera in cinema, the ways in which opera loses itself and finds itself anew in cinema. Cinema can thus speak for opera's truth, give it voice, and at times replace it, criticizing its failures and illusions. A look at films that are driven by opera—drawn to it or haunted by its presence—reveals what might have been hidden if one were totally immersed in opera or if one were too skeptical of its powers. Thus, in the idea of the refraction of one medium in another, we find the possibility of interpretation and criticism that avoids both the wholly internal and the wholly external perspectives.

Given my preference for metamorphic transitions, it is not surprising that I swerve toward a style of writing that holds to the tensions and paradoxes of bringing together film and opera while respecting the independence of each. In this regard, Stanley Cavell as well as Carolyn Abbate have served as models. If I have profited from their insight and perceptiveness on the subject of opera and film, I have also tried to learn from an example they set of writing that is responsive to phenomena, like opera and film, that is always polysemic and never easy to see at first glance. In their work, an attraction to opera is both set at some distance and responded to in full. The fundamental meaning of voice and singing in opera is thus made uncanny or strange and shown to be inherent to the medium as such. Something fundamental about opera is conveyed not by rationalization but by responding with equal verve.

Cavell, for instance, first gave voice to one of the main ideas I have borrowed in this book: the excesses of opera as linked to deep intimations of ephemerality, the constant threat that singing will be terminated. What is nevertheless essential for Cavell is how even such excesses, transgressions, and failures reflect something essentially human—as though the human is essentially beyond itself, bringing out the contours of the human voice. Cavell writes:

> Such a view will take singing, I guess above all the aria, to express the sense of being pressed or stretched between worlds—one in which to be seen, the roughly familiar world of the philosophers, and from which to be heard, one to which one releases or abandons one's spirit (perhaps to call upon it, as Donna Anna and Donna Elvira do; perhaps to forgo it, as the Marschallin and as Violetta do; perhaps to prepare for it, as Desdemona and Brünnhilde do; perhaps to identify it with this one, as Carmen does), and which recedes when the breath of the song ends. This expression of the inexpressible (for there is no standing language of that other world; it requires understanding without meaning) I described as a mad state, as if opera is naturally pitched at this brink.[13]

Abbate expresses a related thought by stressing the presence in opera of unheard song or music that sings itself, thus bringing out the unattainable nature of song, or its inherent "beyondness." Its absent sounds are what make them resonate so powerfully: "One might therefore say that contemplating the ineffability of music entails seeking out places where opera posits inaccessible music beyond what we can hear, as a specific sign for that general elusiveness." That elusiveness demands writing about music that is commensurable with it. It is "choosing to write about music in certain ways: no pins, no jagged edges."[14] We might be made uncomfortable by reminders that experiences of opera remain personal (and are not universal) and that the very language in which we couch our "scholarly" interpretations, in itself, performs the work of interpretation. This discomfort should be momentary. As I have found, and as I hope to convey in this book, accepting the reality of opera's force can make for a scholarly conversation that is full of life.

PART I

SILENT VOICES

❧

CHAPTER 1

The Phantom of the Opera:
The Lost Voice of Opera in Silent Film

Film's ATTRACTION TO opera began not with the technical possibility of synchronizing the operatic voice with the image but earlier, in the silent era. In the *New York Times* of August 27, 1910, Thomas Edison declared: "We'll be ready for the moving picture shows in a couple of months, but I'm not satisfied with that. *I want to give grand opera.*"[1] What did silent film seek in opera? Would a silent film of or about opera have any meaning? What are the possibilities for silent opera? How would an operatic voice make itself manifest in a silent film?

Following Stanley Cavell's perceptive remark that "what happened to opera as an institution is that it transformed itself into film; . . . film is, or was, our opera,"[2] I inquire in this chapter how silent film forms a link in this continuation or reformulation of opera, paying special attention to one peculiarly "operatic" film—*The Phantom of the Opera* (1925). I ask whether film represents a kind of visual takeover of the operatic voice, whether an image can take over a voice or convey longing for that voice, whether silent film can stand for or replace opera, and if so, what we would mean when speaking of opera.[3]

The Silence of Voicelessness

The explanations usually offered for film's attraction to opera focus on films from the thirties on, rather than those of the silent era. These explanations are of various kinds. Some are of a sociological nature in which opera is associated with money and class and film's stars are perceived as creating an aura of status, prestige, and fame while promoting images of taste, luxury, and European culture. Other explanations relate to film's operatic, death-ridden metaplot in which the ideal of love is "operatically" represented and opera's conflicting elements are erased. Other explanations are musical. Jeremy Tambling, for example, notes that "there seems to be an interest in the voice for itself in film's use of opera."[4] Authors who address silent film's attraction to opera also tend to evoke the theatrical, arguing that silent film and opera share an extravagance of gesture and movement (operatic gestures exposing vocal excess are taken as analogous to filmic gestures compensating for the absence of voice).[5] Yet even this explanation for the affinity that existed between opera and silent film does not address *the paradox* inherent in collapsing opera into a silent medium.

Let us begin with the meaning of silence in the silent era since silent films were silent only with regard to the on-screen human voice. Possibilities for musical accompaniment were numerous, varying from screening to screening and depending on local musical abilities and the theater's forces, finances, and willingness to provide more or less elaborate accompaniment. Film directors and producers could recommend or suggest a compilation of music but not guarantee its application.[6] Films were accompanied by piano, orchestra, orchestra with vocal or instrumental soloists in the theater, or a combination of recorded music and live performers. In films relating to opera, highlights from the opera's orchestral music were often used to accompany the image on the screen for additional effect. This also happened with films unrelated to opera, where the accompaniment could be a pastiche of mostly orchestral music drawn from canonic operas. When drawn from an opera that is shown or referred to within the film, operatic music obviously established associations with that opera; operatic music accompanying films unrelated to opera, however, functioned as "unheard" background music.[7]

Operatic voices attached to the visual representation of singing were also heard during the silent era. This would seem to be the obvious meeting place of the two media, where the illusion of synchronization between voice and image could be created by live vocal accompaniment.[8] Here, however, I elaborate on a less obvious intersection of the two—one that takes into account the awkwardness of their juxtaposition given that opera epitomizes voice and vocality and silent film embodies the absence of voice. I account for what occurs when film indirectly points to its relation to the human voice through the voice of opera and to what results when the silence of silent film combined with the voice of opera shows the voice of opera itself relating to muteness and silence.[9]

To elaborate on this idea, it is necessary to stress an important moment in the vicissitudes of voice in opera. As Michel Poizat has emphasized, opera at its peak touches on the edge or extremity of song and points to something beyond song, be it a cry or silence.[10] That is, operatic singing derives its force not simply from the extravagance of the singing voice but rather from its pointing to the limits of vocal expression and to meaninglessness.[11] Peaks of melody disintegrate in the sheer materiality of voice. That which lies at the limit of meaningful vocal expression and constitutes a hidden focus to which voice is drawn can be understood in terms of that which transcends the stylized operatic voice, whether the cry or the silence beyond song. If we focus on this aspect of the voice, then, surprisingly, silent film is uniquely suited to revealing opera's tendency to go beyond song in its fascination with and anxiety about silence. The way voice is "absent" in silent film can be associated with the way opera attempts to "transcend" voice. Introducing the voice of opera into silent film does not change the universe of silence, as voice in opera functions in the condition, or under the constant threat, of the loss of that voice, of disintegration into the cry and into silence. It is this, rather than the forced synchronization of sound and gesture, that demonstrates silent film's fascination with opera. The relation between the two media, then, is based on analogy rather than compensation.

Early film showed various sorts of attraction to opera, the most common being the use of an operatic plot.[12] However, the silent film I have chosen to interpret, *The Phantom of the Opera*, reflects on the *medium*'s very attraction to opera, being a film centrally concerned with the power of and quest for the operatic voice.[13] The setting of the film reinforces the connections with opera: it takes place on, behind, and below the stage of the Paris Grand Opéra. Gounod's *Faust* (1859) is being staged in the course of the film's narrative. The opera's plot complicates that of the film, which deals with the relationship between the Phantom's voice, his deformed appearance, and his obsession with the voice of Christine, the prima donna. The film employs elements of *Faust*, relating them to the theme of ghostly power over a human soul without reenacting the opera's plot. Some arias from Gounod's *Faust* are represented "as sung," providing the possibility of synchronizing the sound of these numbers with their visual counterparts. It is tempting to see these arias as the most obvious way for a silent film truly to have a voice. However, following Adorno and Eisler, I argue that these moments show the difficulty of carrying voice into film.[14]

Synchronization, as Adorno, Eisler, and Arnheim saw it, signifies a loss of intimacy between sound and image. Silent film is a specific construction of images in relation to the absence of speech; it struggles with expression under such a predicament. For silent film, muteness is a formative force. In this sense, it approaches the condition of opera where a vocal medium is constantly impelled toward moments of speechlessness.

The muteness of silent film conveys a loss fundamental to the medium of film as a whole. In recent film theory, cinematic loss is articulated as being founded on the lack of an object or a referent. Desire in film is, according to Kaja Silverman, about "finding a surrogate with which to cover the absent real. . . . Film theory has been haunted since its inception by the spectre of a loss or absence at the centre of cinematic production, a loss which both threatens and secures the viewing subject."[15] "Cinema," Silverman continues, "revives the primordial desire for the object only to disappoint that desire, and to reactivate the original trauma of its disappearance."[16] André Bazin and Christian Metz also consider lack as intrinsic to the cinematic operation.[17] Cavell elaborates on this insight when he writes, "In viewing a movie . . . I am present not at something happening, which I must confirm, but at something that has happened which I absorb (like a memory)."[18] Within this matrix of loss, music's function in film had always, according to Adorno and Eisler, been "to spare the spectators the unpleasantness involved in seeing effigies of living, acting, and even speaking persons, who were at the same time silent. The fact that they are living and nonliving at the same time is what constitutes their ghostly character, and music was introduced not to supply them with the life they lacked . . . but to exorcise fear or help the spectator absorb the shock." That fear is created by the audience's experiencing itself as "being threatened by muteness."[19] Adorno and Eisler argue that silent film conveys the very foreignness of speech to the medium. Picture and speech are intrinsically contradictory: those who seem to speak on the screen are really mute. Sound pictures do not overcome this, for film, like ballet and pantomime, is fundamentally gestural.[20]

In this context, I suggest that sound, music, voice, and speech in later film not only create greater realism and assist narrative continuity but also serve to cover the medium's uneasiness and anxiety. *The Phantom of the Opera*, then, reflects on the affinity between silent film and opera as sought neither in attempts to represent singing nor in the liveliness of the operatic music accompanying what is screened, but rather in moments conveying anxiety about silence.[21] In both silent film and opera, moments of generic anxiety, so to speak, are signified by the gesture of the cry. An operatic death, the genre's high point of vocality, is a moment at the utmost limits of song: the character's own death cry. Film aspires to the condition of opera in the representation of the cry, where the silence of the filmic emission of voice and the vocality of the operatic voice converge. Silent-film cries rely on a visual analogy to the human voice, where visuality in its extreme conveys voice in its extreme.[22] In *The Phantom of the Opera*, then, the cry is at the very edge—not of the possibility of voice in film but rather of voice in opera and visuality in film. The cry merges the unheard and the heard, film's quest for voice and opera's quest to transcend it.[23]

A Notion of Voice

Before considering *The Phantom of the Opera* in some detail, I offer to place the notion of the operatic voice in a psychoanalytic context. In Lacanian psychoanalysis, the voice is seen as the first manifestation of subjectivity, even preceding self-recognition in the mirror. In psychoanalytical accounts as interpreted by Kristeva, Rosolato, Silverman, and Chion, the voice is anterior to the gaze, upon which the mirror stage relies; the voice is nearer to the original state of union, belonging to a state prior to entry into language, a state always retrospectively desired.[24]

Traditionally, voice is conceived as the source of an originary self-presence, as the basic element of language. This is the sense in which the metaphysical tradition is "phonocentric." Voice is seen to have an immediate access to presence, to an origin of the subject. Derridean thought, however, conceives of this premise (voice as constitutive of interiority, the self, and autonomy) as illusory. Derrida's deconstructive turn is to reduce voice to an illusory presence: that is, the sense of immediate auto-affection, of no self-distance, and of self-presence in "hearing oneself speaking" is illusory. Derrida shows that the voice in fact *undermines* self-presence: it is not myself I hear, but a foreign body, a stranger to myself who can appear in different guises as, for instance, the voice of conscience, hypnosis, or the persecutor in paranoia.[25]

Similarly, in Lacanian psychoanalysis, there also exists that which threatens to disrupt pure interiority, since the voice in psychoanalysis is always the voice of the Other imposing itself on the subject: "for psychoanalysis, the auto-affective voice of self-presence and self-mastery [is] constantly opposed by its reverse side, the intractable voice of the Other, the voice that one could not control. But both have to be thought together."[26]

Voice can be further elaborated when thought of in relation to the "partial objects" added by Lacan to those of Freud. In this sense objects are the elusive driving forces of desire. The object voice and the object gaze "give body to what constitutively eludes [the field of the visible and audible] . . . the object gaze is a blind spot within the field of the visible, whereas the object voice par excellence . . . is silence."[27] The object voice refers to a void; in other words, there is a dimension of voice that is against sense and logos. With the entry into language, the object is felt as irretrievably lost, and the trajectory of life is an endless search for the always already lost object. The object voice stands for what, in the object, is more than itself; the unarticulated cry comes close to representing it.

In these terms, opera is essentially about the wish for the autonomization of voice or an attempt to approach voice as detached object. Opera's essence lies in moments of pure voice. Michel Poizat describes these moments as musical eruptions where visual, textual, and musical signification all fail and voice alone exists. In this formulation, the unarticulated cry is opera's goal with respect to voice.[28] Opera is the endless and painful quest for the original Object (Mother, Woman, jouissance). In opera, music "evokes the voice and conceals it, it fetishizes it, but also opens the gap that cannot be filled."[29] Our pleasure in opera, then, is the result of an illusory structure that brings us into the proximity of original jouissance as the voice qua object turns into a cry.[30] Thus, both cinema and opera can be theorized as inevitably doomed attempts to evoke a return or restoration of the original lost object, of the first imaginary state as pleasure and cohesion. In both, the cry is what articulates the edges of vocality and invisibility.

(Notice that in Gaston Leroux's 1911 novel, *The Phantom of the Opera*, which served as the basis of the 1925 film, the Phantom and the prima donna have a problematic relation to lost parents. The wish to recover and re-create an unattainable past, a union with the parent of the opposite sex, is expressed in what the prima donna and the Phantom see in each other, each through the other's voice. The prima donna follows the Phantom's voice since she believes him to be the Angel of Music, the reincarnation of her father. In turn, the Phantom's obsession with the operatic voice of the prima donna is a form of compensation. His relation to his mother was primarily through the voice, as she too could not stand his deformed facial features.[31] The theme of the compensation for the lost relation to the parent of the opposite sex is not represented in the silent movie; thus it raises the question of how this theme of loss in relation to the voice is nevertheless expressed in the film.)[32]

The Voice of Opera in Silent Film: *The Phantom of the Opera*

The Phantom dwells five stories below the Paris opera house and haunts it. Obsessively in love with Christine, the prima donna, the Phantom disables Christine's rival, Carlotta. He speaks to his prima donna through her mirror, and due to his presence, she sings magnificently. Christine, infatuated with the Phantom's voice, agrees to cross over through the mirror to his domain, and for his sake she rejects a suitor's marriage proposal, which would have required her to relinquish singing. The prima donna makes the journey from above to below the opera house twice. On the first journey she turns around to face the horror of the man with the mask; on the second journey she unmasks him and is horrified by his facelessness. She then betrays the Phantom, promising herself to her other suitor. The Phantom abducts her, and all try to rescue her. The film ends when the prima donna and her suitor are happily reunited; the Phantom is chased by a mad crowd to his death. The prima donna enters the film with a voice and leaves it married and silent.

The Phantom of the Opera incorporates elements of Gounod's *Faust* through the use of diegetic performances of the opera *Faust*. These highlight ambivalent issues about the operatic voice, its image, and its relation to death. The sound of Gounod's arias—or rather the vision of this sound—becomes a voice competition between the two prima donnas:

Carlotta and Christine are both identically cast as Marguerite. When performing onstage, they are visually indistinguishable, each identically costumed in distinct long, blond, braided wigs. In other words, the film encourages an "operatic" mode of listening where, because difference is not to be found in appearance, we may obsessively search for and perhaps even "hear" a distinction between the prima donnas' voices. The competition ends at the climax of Carlotta's aria, which turns into a dreadful cry as the chandelier of the Paris opera house falls on the audience, killing a newcomer to opera. Carlotta will sing no longer. This scene in which Carlotta, the wrong voice, is cast out appeals to a myth of the power of the operatic voice—its capacity to shatter crystal. It is as if the chandelier *is* brought down by the wrong singing and not by the Phantom to *stop* that singing; it is as if even a weak operatic voice climaxing into a shrill cry has power over matter and can shatter glass.[33]

In the film's next performance of *Faust*, it is Christine who sings Marguerite. Sitting at the spinning wheel, she sings "Il ne revient pas," an aria of abandonment that for Catherine Clément is the paradigmatic condition for an operatic heroine, for abandonment is a stage on the journey toward the heroine's culmination in singing her death.[34] Here, too, the film reinforces the idea that opera works against the conditions of meaning and leads to a death of language. The Phantom kills the Grand Opéra's prompter, and Christine's song turns into a cry as she is abducted. This scene reinforces connections already brought up in Carlotta's aria between the transformation of the operatic voice into a cry and its relation to death. Here, the murder of the prompter, who serves the memory of the words, stands for the dissolution of meaning, the transformation of opera into a cry.

The Phantom of the Opera is saturated with cries that relate the two prima donnas and the Phantom through the associations they make with opera in general. Carlotta's apparently glass-shattering cry is one such association; Christine's cries on turning around and seeing the Phantom's masked face and, again, when she unmasks him recall the originary operatic myth of Orpheus. (In the myth, Orpheus's turning around is fatal, as it cancels the power of his voice and sends Eurydice back to Hades.) Yet other cries occur when the Phantom realizes that Christine has betrayed him and he will lose her singing voice forever and finally when the Phantom dies. Cries at the edge of operatic singing, cries at horrific sights, cries of proximity to death, and the cry of death: these become the merging of what is visual and what is vocal in *The Phantom of the Opera*.

The film conflates two kinds of obsession with the power of the operatic voice: on one side is the power and attraction of the prima donna's voice. But there is also the reverse power of the Phantom's voice over the prima donna's. He has created the prima donna as the perfected operatic singer; he

Figures 1.1–1.4. *The Phantom of the Opera* (1925) is saturated with cries

Figure 1.1. Carlotta's apparently glass-shattering cry

Figure 1.2. Christine's cry on turning around and seeing the Phantom's masked face

Figures 1.3 and 1.4. Christine's cries when she unmasks the Phantom

is her singing teacher, her master, the Angel of Music. As the all-powerful haunting voice, he is the one who creates both her voice and himself as the object of her voice. He is "the man with the voice," and the reciprocal relations of these obsessions doubles the power of the voice in this work.

The Voice of Distorted Visuality

Distortion in the filmic style of *The Phantom of the Opera*, based as it is on "a quality of expressive emphasis and distortion," is characteristic of expressionist film: strange tormented facial expression and large angular movements.[35] This quality is also seen in the opera house's architecture of torture, in the themes of hauntedness and horror, and in the performance of Lon Chaney, "the man of a thousand faces." *The Phantom of the Opera* continues Chaney's characterization of deformation in *The Hunchback of Notre Dame*, released a year earlier.[36] The son of deaf-mutes, Chaney manifested a unique ability to express himself in a silent medium.[37]

The "quality of expressive emphasis" in *The Phantom of the Opera* is most pronounced in the Phantom's facial features: the visual image stretched out, formless, transgressive, shapeless, emphasizing the hollowness of the skull, the beastliness of the eye, nose, and mouth cavities, and the lack of humanity in the Phantom's face. Described in terms of orifices and cavities—noseless visage, black holes instead of eyes—the Phantom's face is the negative image of a human face. It is a trace of a human body, a phantomlike living corpse.[38] The Phantom is, one might say, not a fixed body image; he leaves no fixed mark but eludes our grasp. People who see the Phantom cannot agree on what they have seen. He is a shadow, a trace or impression, resembling Adorno's on-screen effigies or Lacan's object voice.[39]

Silent film representing the voice of opera wishes to emit a cry, yet the very essence of that cry is that it will not be heard. The cry thus expresses itself as a kind of vocal-visual distortion. The energy pent up in the visuality of the silent cry finds an outlet in the distortion of the open mouth, or the gestures of anxiety at the threat of muteness. Seeing the cry suffices to make us hear it.[40] The film hovers around Christine's (and our) desire to see him and ultimately evokes the failure of his voice in light of his horrific face. I would argue, then, that insofar as silent film as a genre has an operatic "phantom," it exists in the desire of the cinematic picture to express the unbearable search to recover the ever-lost voice.[41]

The Voice in the Mirror

The interchange between what seems on the face of it to be the voice of opera (prima donna) and the voice of film (the Phantom) occurs through a mirror. The prima donna is attracted to the master's voice and crosses through the mirror to his kingdom. The thematics of the mirror and its relation to the thematics of the lost object are seen in the way the film develops the idea of the contest between the two prima donnas. They sing visually identical roles as though the two Marguerites are reflections of one another, yet their voices are not at all identical. The nonidentity is created by the Phantom, and the difference in their voices is what enables only one to pass through the mirror, whereas the other (in the "Jewel Aria") can sing only to her enlarged reflection.

In the "Jewel Aria," Marguerite, sung by Carlotta, finds a casket of jewels and a mirror sent by Mephistopheles.[42] Delighting in her reflection, Marguerite sings to it about her mysterious lover. She wishes Faust to see her as her perfected image reflected in his mirror. The aria is about the mirror's power of transformation. This connects to the film's plot, for it is through the mirror that the voice of the Phantom will overpower the prima donna's voice. The theme of the mirror will recur later on in the film to signify the Phantom's loss of power over the prima donna's voice when Christine crosses through the mirror and sees him: the mirror becomes merely one of the Phantom's fetishized objects underneath the opera house, and at that point it has lost all power.

What is the significance of the mirror in this vocal exchange? How does the mirror function in relation to the object voice? The Lacanian mirror stage invokes a sense of jubilation in anticipation of a unified identity. But the sense of unity is illusory, depending on the earlier stage of blurred boundaries between subject and object.[43] If featurelessness and unrepresentability characterize the lost object, then, for Lacan, what stands in opposition to the self-formation of the subject through the lost object is the unification of the self with and by means of the image in the mirror. That is why monsters are deformed and, like vampires, have no reflection.[44] In Lacanian terms, *The Phantom of the Opera* portrays the impossible quest to account for the difference between the self and its reflection, that is, the distance symbolized by the Lacanian symbols of a-a'.[45] Put differently, that which escapes my mirrored reflection necessarily provokes anxiety. This is why the Phantom has a monstrous and repellent aspect. The prima donna sees her body in the mirror, yet she hears the Phantom's voice issuing from her reflection. Since the prima donna is not fully reflected in the mirror, she passes through it, and what she finds there can be only beyond herself, which is why, ultimately, the film explores the relationship between her operatic voice and the object voice, associated, by means of the Phantom's skull-like face, with death. In the prima donna's response to the Phantom's voice in the mirror, the film portrays the operatic voice as having the ability to pursue an evasive object. In other words, the prima donna's quest for the lost voice expresses her freedom from the fixity of reflection, and, in Lacanian terms, from the illusion of self-cohesion. And that which lies beyond the mirror, beyond her reflection, is within the domain of the Phantom. The object voice, the voice "in the mirror," then, is the gap between the Phantom as voice master and the prima donna's mastered voice.

Orpheus in Silent Film and in Opera: The Power of the Vocal and the Failure of the Visual

When the prima donna unmasks the Phantom, she reveals a monstrous facelessness beneath the mask. He loses the power of his voice, and she breaks away from the source of her singing. Here seeing is death. This aspect of *The Phantom of the Opera* refers back to the myth of Orpheus where, despite the hero's vocal powers, his glance back at Eurydice consigns her to Hades forever.

Opera establishes a relationship between voice and vision.[46] The Orpheus myth describes how Orpheus's grief at Eurydice's death is transformed into enchanting music in his attempt to overcome death. Orpheus's lament gains him access to the other world, and his plea to revive Eurydice is granted. This provides an understanding of the power of operatic song which arises from the suffering attendant upon human separateness, finitude, and mortality but which also manifests itself as the capacity to infuse death with life. The myth is not only about the success of song but just as much about the inability to sustain this success. Singing is essentially ephemeral, and the myth figures the temptation to slip back into conventional ways of experiencing the world, the need for the gaze (Orpheus's turning around). This moment establishes the generically central tension between sound and sight. Eurydice dies ("disappears from sight"), which enables Orpheus's song and her own death cry. It is Orpheus's glance at Eurydice that negates the power of his song. In our film, the prima donna, drawn to the Phantom's voice, is compelled to look at him; she fails to see through his ugliness and hold on to the power of his voice, and she rejects him, losing both her voice and his in the process.[47]

The Phantom of the Opera represents a quest for the source of the operatic voice—that is, for what haunts this voice. The film invokes the operatic founding myth of Orpheus through a visual representation of the power of the operatic voice. The distorted visual images of *The Phantom of the Opera* express the powerlessness of the gaze to sustain its object. They are analogous to the lost voice, to that which can be held on to only as an illusion. Distortion in *The Phantom of the Opera*, then, plays the role that the unattainable perfection of the prima donna's voice plays in opera. In fact, *the reason* for the prima donna's death in tragic opera is precisely this doomed quest. Indeed, one could argue that her death, and thus the death of song, is the necessary goal of tragic opera.

In *The Phantom of the Opera*, however, the Phantom does not accept the destruction of the power of voice by the powers of vision—he rejects the deadly Orphic gesture of the prima donna's turning around and unmasking him. This refusal ultimately leads to his death, and this is where the film renders operatic death in visual terms. It is precisely the Phantom's death that shows him to be the essence of opera, the very source or reason for the film's operatic voice. The Phantom creates music and is the originating force of the singer's voice. Christine can sing only as long as he—the essence of the operatic—haunts her. At the same time, it is he who takes the place of Eurydice: *he* dies and descends to his underworld, and it is the prima donna's relation to him that cannot be sustained through vision. The Phantom, then, points both to the origin of song and to the impossibility of sustaining the world through song.

As the expressionist image of deformity and horror, the Phantom is more profoundly operatic than the prima donna. Without him she faces only a mute, songless existence. Her marriage is fundamentally unoperatic. Heroines epitomizing song in nineteenth-century canonic opera die; they do not marry. The pinnacle of operatic expression in this sort of opera is the prima donna's death song. In *The Phantom of the Opera*, however, both the operatic death and the death cry are embodied in the Phantom himself. The visual excesses in the images of the Phantom—distortion, masking, monstrosity—are analogous to the "meaninglessness" of the voice in its death cry and thus tell us as much about operatic excess as about visuality. At the same time, the film's operatic qualities suggest that film can no more contain its own excesses than can opera.

The Death of the Phantom in Silent Film

There is no simple analogy between the overtaking of opera by film and the overtaking of the voice of the prima donna by the Phantom, as though the Phantom were a Mephistopheles possessing Faust possessing Marguerite. Rather, the question is whether the operatic prima donna's role in the film's happy ending implies that the filmic myth of fantastic happiness has replaced operatic death, or whether the operatic heroine has opened an operatic essence within silent film that is now expressed in the Phantom's death.

The silencing of the heroine at the conclusion of the *Phantom of the Opera* is not a result of the silence of the medium of silent film or a "correction" of death in opera by way of marriage in film. But rather surprisingly, the essence of opera as excessive, fatal, and anxiety-ridden has been carved into the expressive quality of the film itself. The Phantom has not stolen the prima donna's voice; rather, his death marks the end of song.

The happy end of *The Phantom of the Opera*, which demands the silencing of the prima donna's voice, is achieved at the cost of the death of the Phantom. As in opera, where excessive vocality functions under the threat of silence and must end in the death of that voice, the excessive visuality of the Phantom cannot be incorporated, and he must die an operatic death.[48]

CHAPTER 2

༄

Brothers at the Opera

A NIGHT AT THE OPERA (1935) is arguably one of the best Marx Brothers films because within the world of opera they find themselves in their natural element. The absurd medium of opera is not a far cry from the Marx Brothers' ludicrous state of being in the world. As an excessive medium in which words are sung performances, opera can be seen as a parallel to the Marx Brothers' distrust of meaning. Hence the Marx Brothers' reinvention of the world sides with, and not against, opera. In one famous discussion from *A Night at the Opera*, Groucho's, Chico's, and Harpo's "act" piles their insanity on top of opera's own:

Groucho: What's his name?

Chico: What do you care? I can't pronounce it. What do you want with him?

Groucho: I want to sign him up for the New York Opera Company. Do you know that America is waiting to hear him sing?

Chico: Well, he can sing loud, but he can't sing that loud.

Groucho: Well, I think I can get America to meet him halfway. . . . But, anyhow, we're all set now, aren't we? Now, just you put your name right down there and then the deal is—is—uh—legal.

Chico: I forgot to tell you. I can't write.

Groucho: Well, that's all right. There's no ink in the pen, anyhow. But listen, it's a contract, isn't it?

Chico: Oh sure. Hey wait—wait! What does this say here? This thing here?

Groucho: Oh, that? Oh, that's just the usual clause. That's in every contract. That just says—uh—if any of the parties participating in this contract is shown not to be in their right mind, the entire agreement is automatically nullified.

Chico: Well, I don't know.

Groucho: It's all right. That's in every contract. That's what they call a sanity clause.

Chico: Ah, you fool wit' me. There ain't no Sanity Claus!

A Night at the Opera is not the only film in which the Marx Brothers explicitly make reference to the world of opera. In *Cocoanuts* (1929), Harpo destroys a cash register to background music from Verdi's *Trovatore*. In that opera, the Anvil Chorus expresses the Gypsies' joy at their hammering away at work. Harpo takes the chorus's text literally: the Gypsies' hammering music accompanies the hammering of the cash register in the film. In *Animal Crackers* (1930), Chico plays the Anvil Chorus while Harpo accompanies him on horseshoes. In *Monkey Business* (1931), Groucho ridicules an interview with a diva, and Harpo later shuts his ears while accompanying her singing. In the final scene of *Duck Soup* (1933), the Marx Brothers throw apples at Margaret Dumont's operatic rendering of Freedonia's national anthem. In *At the Circus* (1939), when Margaret Dumont enters her gala dinner, a fragment from Verdi's *Aida* is heard. When she attempts to give a speech, the trumpeting sound of an elephant fills the room, overpowering her voice. This circus elephant follows from, and metonymically replaces, the music of *Aida*. Shortly after, an orchestra seated on a floating platform plays Wagner's overture to *The Flying Dutchman* as it drifts out to sea, while the audience is left behind on the shore to enjoy the circus show that replaces the concert. In the Marx Brothers' world, The Flying Dutchman might well be the name of a performer on a flying trapeze in the circus. A trapeze act, in fact, takes place, as the operatic ship sails on.[1]

Glenn Mitchell expresses the view prevalent among scholars: "It is strange to think of the robust Marx Brothers *constantly working in parallel* with that highbrow institution, opera. *A Night at the Opera* deliberately uses it to contrast their wild spirits."[2] I would argue that their involvement with opera is not at all "strange"; rather it is an essential part of their world of associations, one that only superficially competes with their own comic regimes. Moreover, the parody of opera in the Marx Brothers' films functions differently from their parodies of other institutions such as "the university," "democracy," "high society," serious film genres, and so on.[3] The world of opera serves to highlight—not contradict—aspects of their style, and for this reason *A Night at the Opera* is unique. The Marx Brothers' performance style is, in many ways, *analogous* to the relationship between voice and text in opera, as well as to opera's exaggerated and absurd constituents. Thus the Marx Brothers' anarchism is not aimed against opera; it has inherited some of opera's central features.

Silent Opera

I would like to argue for more: the Marx Brothers' film *A Night at the Opera* is an attempt to think through not only the inheritance of opera but the way *silent film* inherited opera, or to rethink the transition from silent film to sound by thematizing the relation between film and opera.

As I argued in chapter 1, early film was marked by a special attraction toward the medium of opera. One way that silent film dealt with the absence of the human voice was through visual appeals to the operatic voice.

Although the appearance of the extravagance of operatic voice within the context of the silent human voice might seem paradoxical, opera proliferated in early film. By virtue of the very choice to show images of voiceless opera, silent films expressed a belief in the power of film to offer new ways of understanding the silence and speechlessness of the human voice.

Early cinema questioned its distance from opera not only in terms of its relation to the voice of opera but also in relation to operatic plots. Chaplin's *Burlesque on Carmen* (1916), for example, parodies the very act of transposing an operatic plot into film. Chaplin's short film refers to Cecil DeMille's silent film *Carmen* (1915), which features the famous prima donna Geraldine Farrar. In Chaplin's film, the murder of Carmen is followed by a scene in which Chaplin—cast in Don José's role—mimics an operatically overdramatic gesture of death. Having killed himself (Chaplin's addition to the opera's plot), Don José arranges and rearranges his collapse over Carmen's body in order to expose the artificiality of both deaths. Carmen and Don José then rise, revived and united in a big smile. Chaplin's film can be seen as dealing with two competing forms of artificiality: that of opera and that of cinema. In parodying the fatal ending of opera, the film reveals cinema's artifice in executing the artificial operatic ending. (In performances of opera, one can identify such a Chaplinesque ending in the singers' "resurrection," designed to elicit the audience's applause.) Chaplin also reveals the illusion behind film's representations of death. He exposes the trick in stabbing someone by showing the fake knife. Chaplin's ending, in which a "dead" actor is revived, raises questions of whether the film has, in fact, ended in death, and whether the very distinction between actor and character is to be reconceived for film.[4]

The attraction of silent film to opera was not just an experimental phase later to be abandoned. There is an affinity between film and the medium of opera which can be detected beyond the silent era, revealing how the ideas or thematics that originally emerged in silent film persist. When film was no longer silent, when it had acquired the capacity to reproduce the sound of the human voice, it inherited silent film's evocation of the voice of opera.

The issue I raise with regard to *A Night at the Opera* is not whether cinema, now possessing a voice, is still attracted to opera, but whether cinema is attracted to opera in the ways in which *silent film* was attracted to it: whether cinema—by way of opera—wishes to remember, is nostalgic for, the absent voice or is at a loss in relation to its new voice, whether, in fact, it wishes to retain a sense of its silent past. I would like, then, to raise the issue of whether the inheritance and memory of cinema's silent past is mediated in fundamental ways by opera.

It is known that Hollywood directors, producers, and actors during the 1930s felt threatened by the ability of film to give voice to its characters.[5]

The Marx Brothers themselves were concerned about the impact of sound on their own art, which owed much to the silent period. As late as 1931, Groucho remarked: "The talkies had just intruded on the movie industry and scared the hell out of most of its members."[6] Many interpreted the advent of the talking film as a passing attraction—one that would eventually disappear in favor of a return to silent film. The loss of a silent medium was felt to be bigger than the gain of speech.[7] I interpret *A Night at the Opera* as a talking film that, indeed, cherishes its silent past, but only indirectly. In other words, it cherishes the past not by actually "resilencing" its voice but in finding "noisy" ways that are analogous to opera's problematizing of vocal emission, expression, and signification.

The Marx Brothers' Phantom of the Opera

In chapter 1 I argued that opera's greatest influence on silent film lay in the attraction to the very idea of the extremity, extravagance, and artificiality of the operatic voice. Opera's unique representation of vocality was inscribed into the very language of cinema: not by creating the illusion of giving voice to the silent humans on-screen or by attempting to substitute verbal for gestural language, but by causing cinematic imagery to "behave" operatically. *The Phantom of the Opera* served as the paradigmatic example of this kind of influence.

In *A Night at the Opera*, silent opera is most poignantly expressed in the striking image of the mute Harpo performing opera in front of a mirror. The idea of silently enacting the voice of opera and, in that very way, remaining loyal to what is essential to the operatic voice—its paradoxical attraction to silence—is precisely what underlies silent film's fascination with opera. The first draft for the script of *A Night at the Opera* featured Harpo, who as the greatest tenor in the world fails, throughout the script, to utter a sound.[8] A trace of this abandoned idea, that is, of the centrality of silent Harpo in invoking opera, found its way into the final version: the film's first scene at the opera house is reserved for Harpo. Enacting the voice of opera, Harpo silently sings to his reflection in the mirror.[9] We are given an image of opera, or opera in a mirror, but without the voice of opera. The gesture of a wide-open mouth is that of an opera singer, but Harpo, as always, is mute. His singing to the mirror enacts the voice of opera as an extension of his overall muteness. The scene separates the image from its sound: with Harpo, there is no need to hear the voice in order to comprehend it as the voice of opera; it is sufficient to see him miming song. The substitution of voiceless sound and gesture for meaningful speech, which constituted Harpo's style and personality throughout his cinematic career, demonstrates, in this scene, that the

Figure 2.1. The Marx Brothers' *Night at the Opera* (1935). Harpo silently sings to his reflection in the mirror.

sense of operatic singing can be signified by silence. The mirror scene asks if opera-within-film is essentially a wish for a visual image of a silent operatic voice.

Harpo's silent song before the mirror also evokes a central theme specific to *The Phantom of the Opera*—enacting the operatic voice in front of a *mirror*. In *The Phantom* the prima donna crosses over to the domain of the Phantom via a mirror. Only the Phantom's chosen prima donna is able to relate to the voice emanating from the mirror, allowing her to go be-yond her reflection and pass through it.

The mirror is not the only element that evokes *The Phantom of the Opera* and its visualization of the voice of opera. During the course of the film, the Marx Brothers act out a variation on the sequence in which the Phan-tom collapses the chandelier, the diva cries, a singer is abducted, and the "wrong" operatic voice is replaced with the "right" voice. The brothers put in motion a plan to enable Ricardo, the tenor of their choice, to be heard at the opera house. During a performance of *Il trovatore*, at the cli-max of the cabaletta "Di quella pira" (sung by the competing tenor, Las-pari), Chico and Harpo darken the auditorium and abduct Laspari. In-stead of the tenor's climactic high note (the high C in "Di quella pira" is one of the most famous high notes in a tenor's repertoire), a shriek is heard and, to everyone's amazement, the tenor disappears. Harpo visually translates Laspari's vocal ascent toward the high note when he, implausi-bly, climbs the stage sets. The duration of Laspari's held note is equivalent to the length of Harpo's leap. This scene thus dramatically positions the Marx Brothers in relation to the visualization and the silencing of the op-eratic voice and its replacement with a "better" one.[10]

Visual Opera

Visualizing the performativity of music is a fundamental theme of the Marx Brothers' performance in films. This theme is played rather loudly in *A Night at the Opera*'s performance of *Il trovatore*. The opera's orchestral prelude, the first music from the opera to feature in the film, metamor-phoses under the brothers' reinterpretation of the role of the instruments. Conventionally, a Verdian orchestral prelude incorporates the opera's mu-sical highlights without the vocal parts. It functions as a summary of the opera heard prior to the curtain's rise. In the orchestral prelude in the film, Harpo and Chico take over the conductor's role and abduct the music, demonstrating how easily operatic music can slide into music for a ball game: the tune for "Take Me Out to the Ball Game" follows smoothly from the prelude. The gap between opera and sports, apparently, is not very wide when it comes to film. (Later the brothers demonstrate an even narrower gap between dying onstage and living on-screen.) In a further dehierarchization, the brothers subvert the conductor's authority and use the conductor's stick itself as a musical instrument within the orchestra. The brothers redivide the orchestra into sections and, as separate conduc-tors, lead each instrumental group. Though absurd (from the point of view of conventional conducting), their conducting "follows the music," and is visually suited to it. Harpo, now joining the instrumentalists in the orchestra, sits in the string section and plays the trombone with a violin bow. The bow is then used to fence the conductor's stick, just as earlier in the scene a violin was used as a baseball bat. We ignore the discrepancy between the music we hear and the instruments we see, as if what the brothers show us is the origin of those sounds. In their act, the Marx Brothers react to the *sight* of the instruments, as it were, overriding the music they produced, as though music were visually rather than acoustically driven.

The idea of visualizing music and emphasizing its performativity is fundamental to the brothers' roots in silent cinema's aesthetic tradition and is reinforced in their customary musical numbers. Harpo's and Chico's musical solos depend on the comic/serious divide between seeing and hearing their playing. On the harp, Harpo's childlike behavior is transformed into angelic virtuoso playing. We are attracted to the new image opened by Harpo's harp and the suddenly solemn expression on his face. He is so transformed that, often, following the movement of his hands is the only comic element left over in the otherwise acoustic pause. Harpo's harp solo is preceded by an introductory piano performance—the "wrong" instrument for Harpo. This serves to delay the onset of the "right" sonority of the harp. We await the "right" instrument, just as we await the "right" tenor's voice. Chico's performance style is also visually determined. His piano playing is better known for its unique image of playing (the shooting finger) and its unschooled technique than for its musicality. Divorced from their image, Chico's numbers are banal or bland; it is the visual component of his playing which incorporates the aural; we depend on seeing Harpo's performance in order to comprehend the musical expression.

The Sanity Clause

The Marx Brothers' relation to language as such reveals the deepest affinity between their world, the world of opera, and silent film. The brothers use the complications that language introduces into film as their main theme.[11] They connect with the tradition of the burlesque silent film but do not dispense with speech. The Marx Brothers' performance does not depend merely on body gestures and the physical. Similarly, opera does not dispense with the libretto and is not composed merely of vocal gestures. In opera and the Marx Brothers' act, words are there to be defeated: both the Marx Brothers and the medium of opera destroy words.

It is important to remember, in this regard, that the Marx Brothers' movies did not evolve solely, or even primarily, from film and its conventions. The brothers were vaudevillians at first. Thus their cinematic performance does not depend solely on the unique possibilities opened by

Figures 2.2–2.4. The Marx Brothers' *Night at the Opera* (1935). A visualization of music, as though music were visually rather than acoustically driven.

Figure 2.2. Harpo sitting in the strings section and playing the trombone with a violin bow

Figure 2.3. The "wrong" instrument for Harpo

Figure 2.4. Chico's piano performance is better known for its unique image of playing (the "shooting finger")

the medium of cinema but is largely based on their lifelong theatrical experience in vaudeville and, later, on Broadway. Their theatrical style, the comic world of chaos and anarchy, is captured, not created, by sound cinema and its camera. In this style, as in vaudeville, and in the silent comedies of, for instance, Chaplin and Keaton, the bodies and the personalities of the characters themselves are comic. As Gerald Mast writes: "the silent clown began with magnificent physical control. Although he usually tried to look funny, it was what he could do with his body that really counted. . . . The 'American Comedy,' the comedy of personality, died [because] as a style of physical comedy its natural medium is silence. The first decade of sound was close enough to the silent era so that the American physical comedy of personality retained much of its vitality."[12] The success of *A Night at the Opera* is, in fact, partly a result of tryouts of comic scenes on tour before a live audience, thus allowing for improvisation, namely changes in accordance with the audience's response, and the timing of laughter without losing the ensuing dialogue. The Marx Brothers' cinematic performance is inflected by the theatrical act and the live and improvisatory setting.

The aim of the Marx Brothers' destruction of language, Mast argues, is annulling conventional modes of communication by revealing individual relationships to talk: from excessive wordiness to speech that is too literal to total muteness. Each brother exemplifies one of these modes of speech. Groucho's speech is illogical; he talks too much and too fast, "swallowing us in a verbal maze, eventually depositing us back at the starting point without knowing where we have been or how we got there. . . . He substitutes the quantity of sound and the illusion of rational connection for the theoretical purpose of talk—logical communication."[13] Chico's comic character toys with the materiality or "grain" of language: his Italian accent turns meanings upside down or distracts us from the sense of what he says. Chico, elaborates Mast, "intrudes on Groucho's verbal spirals by stopping the speed with his erroneous intrusions. He makes different but similar sounds out of the key terms in Groucho's verbal web," interrupting the flow of Groucho's speech with misinterpretations, puns, and so forth. Like Groucho, he ends up "substitut[ing] sound for sense and appearance of meaning for meaning."[14] A third mode is demonstrated by Harpo, who dispenses with words altogether, although his muteness is understood, rendering language altogether superfluous.[15] This teamwork, observes LeJeune, makes it unclear "how much Harpo's dumbness owed to Groucho's gabble, or Groucho's urgency derived from Harpo's pantomime."[16] The brothers' display of the very absurdity, materiality, and sonorous movement of speech or total dispensation with it is on the edge, or on the verge, of communication in speech.

The Marx Brothers' treatment of speech can be compared to the view that the purpose of opera—and here Italian nineteenth-century opera stands for opera as such—is voice. The libretto is seen as negligible. Opera is understood as independent of the need to decipher words, since words in opera are "redundant." They are "unnecessary" for comprehension, as their meaning is supposedly conveyed by other means: an advance knowledge of the opera's synopsis, conventional plot structures, vocal numbers (always standing for dramatic intensity), and the force and beauty of the voice. Exaggeration in opera, then, becomes an example of independence from language. This image of opera is one of vocal acrobatics: vocalization, extreme vocal ranges (high and low), melismas and cadenzas that divide words into unrecognizable syllables, ensemble singing that conflates several texts, and so on.[17] In this respect, the culmination of the operatic voice in song (such as arias or duets) is analogous to the Marx Brothers' comic numbers.

This extreme view (in which opera is "comprehended" without the need, or even the wish, to understand the words sung) is most clearly enacted by Harpo in his mute performance. Once more the paradox: muteness or silence is a figure for opera. Since Harpo is not silent but mute, and his muteness is deciphered and comprehended through surrogate sounds, his is the mode of communication encountered in rendering voiceless opera on silent film. In other words, the enactment of the voice

of opera in silent film does not attempt to compensate for the voicelessness of silent film but acts as an extension, or complication, of the modes
of silent film's communication in silence.[18]

The World of *Il Trovatore*

But why *Il trovatore*? Why this opera, in this film? Verdi's *Trovatore*
(1853) is one of the most popular operas ever: "Few operas have enjoyed
such widespread and immediate popularity, or have so solidly established
themselves in the fabric of social history."[19] It took longer for scholars to
judge its quality. Indeed, over the years, *Il trovatore* has drawn contradictory responses from musicologists, and it is considered both "the defini-
tive melodrama . . . the ultimate challenge of Italian song" and "the most
absurd and far-fetched of all."[20] In the last few decades, however, the
scholarly scene has changed, and the opera has earned a place in the scholars' pantheon of operatic masterworks.[21]

The relationship of *A Night at the Opera* to *Il trovatore* is complex. To
choose an opera such as *Il trovatore* is to choose melodrama at its extreme:
burning babies, a witch hunt, Gypsies at the stake, civil war, amorous rivalry, disguise, confused identities. It is to be attracted to a convoluted, illogical, and at times confused plot. Uncharacteristically for Verdi, the catalyst for the events in the opera does not occur during the opera, but
rather is narrated in the opera as past events. This results in contradictory
narrations, an abundance of misunderstandings and misrecognitions, and,
ultimately, untimely deaths. These mishaps are so extreme that *Il trovatore*
can come to appear as a parody of opera. It is in this sense that the Marx
Brothers' reference to opera is complicated, for the parody that is already
internal to the world of opera is made even more blatant by the opera they
have chosen.

Some of the most hilarious scenes in the Marx Brothers' film parody
opera's physical setting. Harpo, Laspari's dresser, puts on many costumes
at once; each time he takes one off he reveals a costume of yet another
opera. Groucho, in a horse-drawn carriage, circles the opera house; he
plans a late arrival so that he will be sure to miss the entire performance:
"Hey you, I told you to slow that nag down. On account of you I nearly
heard the opera. Now then, once around the park and drive slowly." Later
on, we see Harpo climbing the scenery during the performance, which exposes the backstage. This is followed by abrupt changes of scenery from
different operas that ultimately end with his dropping a backdrop *in front*
of the singer, hiding him from the audience. In his attempt to escape from
his persecutors, Harpo enters a door at midair and falls, ripping the
scenery in two. Then, with the aid of a camera trick, Harpo climbs *up* the

scenery and turns off the electricity, and so on. All this does not constitute just a parody of the external circumstances of an operatic performance. A closer look at these scenes reveals that parody stems from a deep understanding of the medium of opera itself and of *Il trovatore* specifically.

In parodying opera, the Marx Brothers are at the same time parodying the medium of cinema. Take, for instance, the scene where Harpo changes the scenery and climbs the operatic backdrop while the most famous tenor number from *Il trovatore*, "Di quella pira," is being sung. Harpo's changing of the backdrops during this performance points to the insignificance of specificity and detail in an operatic plot. The extravagant and passionate singing continues regardless of the backdrops that have now become those of other operas. (In fact, it continues even when the scenery drops between the characters onstage.) This part of Harpo's act also points to the absurdity of opera's idea of unbroken song. Harpo's interferences are unthinkable, no one in the world of opera would dare to interrupt such singing. This is why the farce goes on for so long. Even in the world of opera enacted in the film, no one would dare interrupt the singer onstage—not even to put a stop to Harpo's shenanigans. Harpo's act is "permitted" to proceed both by opera's catering to song and by a cinematic trick that portrays Harpo's on-screen gravity-defying climb. This scene, like many others in the film, leaves us wondering whether Harpo's ludicrous gravity-defying behavior (swinging on the scenery, climbing up the drops) is not very similar to opera's attempts at transcending the ordinary condition of speech. In other words, one wonders whether the Marx Brothers' act of shattering the world is not similar to opera's attempts to transcend it.

❧

The Marx Brothers' plots, like *Il trovatore*'s libretto, are reputed to have an absurd, illogical, and mischievous progression of events. On the whole, the brothers' earlier films were built around comic scenes with little attempt to develop a progressive sensical narrative that would be resolved at the end of the film. Their films were characterized by irrelevant plot twists, incongruous sight gags, inconclusive conclusions, absurdly contrived human behavior in which mistakes were magnified, and inconsistent and chaotic action. These films were further based on multiplicity and addition rather than unity; their plots were contrived and artificial.[22]

The structural analogy between *A Night at the Opera* and *Il trovatore* is striking. The film shares the structural concern of number opera: how to connect and integrate the solos with the plot. In this sense, *A Night at the Opera* is a "number film." The independent comic numbers and music solos are the improvisational starting points around which a plot is constructed. They are the *raison d'être* of the film. As in opera, the plot of *A*

Night at the Opera is constructed to support the occasions for song, production numbers, comic numbers, and instrumental solos. These all behave like operatic numbers: they expose a new facet of the character (Harpo's change of personality in the harp solos is most pronounced),[23] introduce a halt in plot development, rise into a climax, cadence, and are even followed by audience applause.

Il trovatore's exaggerated, excessive libretto is, in fact, the basis for some of the most famous operatic melodies in the canon. The most popular of these are featured in the film. The operatic numbers drawn from *Il trovatore* can therefore be seen as participating in—rather than creating—the already operatic form of the film. The world of opera, the opera house, and the operatic performance, then, are more than a mere location or institution to be parodied as the film works alongside the duality of plot/music within *Il trovatore*. This, in turn, is paradigmatic of opera as such.

To secure the success of *A Night at the Opera* (the Marx Brothers' first film at Paramount), the director, Irving Thalberg, attempted a more unified and coherently structured narrative. Thalberg's idea was to expand in length and importance the romantic subplot. His goal was to connect the isolated comic acts, construct a clear ending, add integrated production numbers, and better integrate the harp and piano solos of Harpo and Chico.[24] All these changes were intended not in any way to downplay the brothers' fundamental act but rather to construct a clearer narrative around their comic numbers. The modification of the film's plot *increased* its dependence on the operatic plot. The plot conceived by Thalberg and his writers weaves in and out of the operatic plot. The question, of course, is how a clearer narrative would be constructed around an incoherent operatic plot. I interpret the film's dependence on *Il trovatore*'s narrative and music in two ways: through the thematics of the brothers in film and in the opera and through the film's reversal of the troubadour's fate, granting him an illusion of a night of song.

Brothers Singing Opera

Il trovatore revolves around a rivalry between brothers. This paradigmatically absurd opera plot is first and foremost due to the relationship of the two brothers Manrico and di Luna. Throughout the film, the Marx Brothers toy with the theme of fraternity, with the understanding, of course, that everyone knows that *they*, the actors, are indeed brothers. For example, the issue of brotherhood is raised by the Canadian quintuplets, the two tenors whose identities are confused, and the scene in which the Marx Brothers dress up as the three beards (or the three fellows with one beard). This excessive treatment of mistaken identity in relation to brotherhood works toward rescuing the *operatic brothers* from their fate.

It is the Marx Brothers in *A Night at the Opera* who reveal the possibility of avoiding the tragic operatic fate. This act of redemption is made possible through their actions, as if the tragedy of *Il trovatore*—the horror of a fate that repeats itself—could be overcome by comedy that destroys any remnants of meaning.[25]

Ricardo's attempt to sing the role of Manrico, the troubadour, also raises the threat of tragedy inherent to operatic endings as such.[26] The question raised by the film, therefore, is whether the tragic fate of opera can be subverted, whether *A Night at the Opera* can redeem *Il trovatore* and unite Ricardo/Manrico with Rosa/Leonora despite Laspari/di Luna. This question leads us to a deeper level at which the relation of *Il trovatore* and the film must be addressed. The possibility of either a rescue or a substitution that does not repeat the series of tragic substitutions that dominate the plot of *Il trovatore* manifests itself as the possibility of producing the right opera or the opera with the right cast.[27] I suggest interpreting the question of the possibility of rescuing an operatic production as an allegory of film's potential for rescuing the fatality of opera as such. In *Il trovatore*, it is the brothers who bring about the dreadful ending; in *A Night at the Opera*, it is the (Marx) brothers who will redeem opera.

～

The Marx Brothers' film is an interpretation of an ever-deeper facet of the opera. *Il trovatore* positions the quality of being a troubadour—an operatic character who is a singer—at the center of its concerns.[28] As such the opera conveys something about the function of song in opera. It is an opera about the *loss* of the power of singing and how this loss brings about death. The opera is a reflection on Orpheus's incapacity to hold on to the power of song. At the very beginning of the opera, Manrico *is a troubadour*, but, as the opera unfolds, the power of song leaves him. What is at stake is the disappearance of the power of song once obtained. At the outset of the opera all characters allude to the power of the troubadour's song, and it is this quality which wins over Leonora's love: song is emphasized in the rivalry between brothers.

A Night at the Opera positions the rivalry over the soprano who is cast in the role of Leonora in the performance of *Il trovatore* as a rivalry between competing tenor voices (Laspari and Ricardo) for the role of the troubadour. In the film, it is Ricardo who tries to follow his love for Rosa and, as it were, become her Manrico (by singing the role in the performance at the opera house in New York). Yet Rosa is courted by a rival (the famous tenor Laspari) who holds the power granted to him by the world of opera.

In the opera, Leonora is won over by the beauty of the troubadour's voice. Her love depends solely on his voice, and she recognizes him only by that. His song has the capacity to make "earth seem like heaven"; he has the power to transform the world, a hint that the troubadour possesses the Orphic power of song. Leonora has only heard his voice but has never actually seen him. This leads to a famous scene in which Leonora mistakes di Luna for her lover. Crucial to both the opera and to the Marx Brothers' interpretation of it is the fact that the troubadour and di Luna do not know they are long-lost brothers. This unknown kinship may indeed be the reason for Leonora's confusion. Leonora's error is also transported to the film, but unlike in the opera, the film's Leonora corrects her mistake when she hears her true lover's voice. Thus, Ricardo knocks on Rosa's door and hears the tone of voice intended for Laspari. He then retraces his steps and reenters, insisting on hearing a different tone of voice—that which is intended for him, the lover—from behind the door.

A crucial moment for the troubadour in the opera exposes the troubadour's true identity and hints that his rival, di Luna, is his long-lost brother. It occurs in the scene immediately following "stride la vampa" (one of the central arias of the opera) and is featured in the film. "Stride la vampa" is a horrible description by the Gypsy, Azucena, of how she burned her own child to death. This means, of course, that the troubadour *cannot* be her son. Though the troubadour has been raised as her child, as Azucena's aria reveals, her true son is dead. Her story further implies that the troubadour she has raised is, in fact, the child she intended to murder when she mistakenly murdered her own.

Dramatically, this is the climactic moment for the troubadour: his entire existence is shattered. Yet, in response to his mother's narration, he is speechless and songless. His surprise and devastation are expressed in the abrupt ending of the number, and instead of song there is silence, a pause between numbers. There is no dramatic music to express the significance of the moment. The troubadour, who is the "singer" of the opera, has lost his expressive capacities and has failed to make himself heard. In effect, he has relinquished the power of song. The reaction of the troubadour to the revelation of his nonidentity is a momentary surrender of voice. At the moment that he cannot sustain his world, he loses the power of song.

The scene of the revelation of the troubadour's true identity is followed by his description of a "strange feeling" of pity for di Luna. The troubadour tells of a duel between them in which he had the opportunity to kill di Luna yet was prevented from doing so by a strong, mysterious power. The mysterious pity the troubadour felt toward di Luna represents the eruption of the hidden knowledge of his real identity as di Luna's brother. Thus the filmic substitution of tenors (the abduction of Laspari) refers us to the theme of substitution and identity in *Il trovatore* itself with the knowledge that, in opera, such attempted substitutions always end in tragedy.

The filmic abduction at the climax of "Di quella pira" enables the true voice of opera—within the film—to sing the troubadour's role. The abduction thus allows the Marx Brothers—the filmic brothers—to intervene in the progression of fatal events occurring between the operatic brothers.

❧

Toward the end of the film, material from near the end of the opera is performed. The "Miserere" scene is sung by Rosa and Ricardo, the tenor with whom the Marx Brothers replaced Laspari. The two are at last united both on- and offstage. Notice how the film enacts this scene. In the opera, the "Miserere" conveys the troubadour's longing to die. He is accompanied by a chorus of monks singing prayers for the dead. While it is not clear to whom these prayers are addressed, it is clear that they refer to death. And there is so much death around: Leonora has just taken poison, the troubadour and his mother are awaiting execution, and in the background are all the victims of the civil war led by the brothers, who are on opposite sides.[29]

In the "Miserere" scene of *Il trovatore*, the troubadour is unaware of Leonora's presence; his farewell is not intended for her to hear, and he, in turn, does not hear her. The scene in fact creates an unintended duet between two characters physically apart; the troubadour, who is situated offstage (as in the initial scene in which Leonora mistook him for his brother), is thus heard but hidden from view. The troubadour's imprisonment in the tower while Leonora is outside singing for him constitutes a reversal of the customary troubadour role. Here Verdi employs "vocal space" in opera (as well as in the scene of the mistaken brothers) where the voices themselves are theatricalized.

In the film, however, Leonora and the troubadour both see and hear each other, and their singing is conspicuously an "intended" duet. The film uses the "Miserere" scene to unite the lovers in song and subvert the operatic death. In *A Night at the Opera*, the singing of the operatic deaths in *Il trovatore* paradoxically serves as the climax of cinematic happiness, success, love, and marriage.[30]

This gesture of filmic redemption is dissimilar to the idea of a Chaplinesque happy end for opera. There, the happy end fulfills a promise of happiness by parodying opera's fatality. *A Night at the Opera* is only superficially similar to Chaplin's rewriting of an operatic ending. In the Marx Brothers' interpretation of opera, the power of voice is manifested in the very *disregard* for the meaning of the opera's song of death. This is achieved by finally providing Ricardo with the opportunity to sing and thus allowing the operatic plot to converge with the film's plot. The very possibility given to Ricardo to sing not only unites the two lovers in the eyes of all the world but also allows the film to annul the significance of the operatic death song. Put differently, the filmic union does not only redeem the operatic death. The power of the operatic voice—Ricardo's *operatic voice*, which has not been heard until that moment—provides a *filmic* expression for the power of the operatic voice.

Unlike the Phantom, who is swallowed by the fatality of opera—as the vocality of opera is transcribed in his visuality—the vocality of opera in the Marx Brothers is inscribed into a *cinematic opera singer*. In contrast to Chaplin's *Burlesque on Carmen*, the parody of operatic death functions to hide the brothers' *adherence* to the power of the operatic voice. Ricardo is a cinematic character with vocal—not visual—powers. His vocal or operatic power is due not to the fact that we *hear* him sing (it is not the difference between a talking and a silent film) but to the fact that his singing does not signify death in the world of the Marx Brothers. By erasing the meaning of the operatic death scene, the film relies on the visual—on the literal meaning conveyed by lovers singing together. The erasure of the words (those carrying with them the meaning of death) restores the power of operatic voice to the filmic level. Whereas Chaplin's film annuls the deaths of opera by revealing the cinematic possibility to *undo* those deaths, the Marx Brothers take the operatic song of death *itself* to signify the happy end of the cinematic characters. In other words, singing of one's death in opera comes to signify one's happiness when sung in the film. By claiming this as the filmic ending, *A Night at the Opera* retrieves for *Il trovatore* the lost power of the troubadour's song. It is in the film that song simulates a gesture of revival.

❧

But this is *not* the end of the brothers' film. *A Night at the Opera* ends simultaneously (or ends once again) with a display of the brothers' anarchic behavior, with the tearing up of every contract, the breaking apart of every speech situation. During the repetition of the "Miserere" scene in the encore, the Marx Brothers have their final say. Reinterpreting by way of repeating a previous scene in the film, the Marx Brothers (once again) tear up the tenor's contract. This coda—a tail to the closure of the plot—stands for the tearing apart of every structure of tale, turning the tearing up of a contract into the tearing apart of a coattail. Tearing up the contract is a return to ideas about the meaninglessness of words—a return to the contract's sanity clause. Yet it would be too ordered, too symmetrical, to read this as the Marx Brothers' abandonment of words for the sake of the power of voice. *A Night at the Opera* does not wish to "parody opera to silence," but, as encountered in silent film's attraction to opera, it is drawn to the very possibilities opened by the voice of opera in a parody of the visual sphere. The film shows the human voice in another absurd man-ifestation, that is, the human voice as operatic.

But then, what would be the meaning of the "right" tenor's contract being torn up again at this point in the film—after he has made his way into the vocal world of opera with the help of the "happy" brothers of film? Would this represent the tearing up of a contract between singing in opera and singing in film? The tearing up of "singing death" in opera and "silencing death" in film? The tearing apart of brothers in opera and brothers in film? If at first we thought that the end of the film bows to the power of the operatic voice, whether heard or unheard, visual or acousti-cal, then we are confused. This too—in the operatic world created by the Marx Brothers—is absurd.

PART II
VISIONS OF VOICES

~~~

CHAPTER 3

Otello's One Voice

Up TO THIS POINT I have addressed the "tragic fate" of voice in opera, and the transposition of voice in film that attempts to overcome this fate. *The Phantom of the Opera* restaged the failure that occurs whenever the singing voice verges on the cry, and the Marx Brothers' *Night at the Opera* provided for a possibility of dissolving this tragic lapse into comic chaos. But what about tragedy and comedy within opera itself? In histories of opera, it is commonplace to balkanize the two modes as separate genres, even while discussing similarities in musical designs or compositional strategies. This is, for instance, the paradigmatic approach to two paradigmatic texts in the Italian tradition: Verdi's late operas, the "tragedy" of *Otello* (1887) and the "comedy" of *Falstaff* (1893). Verdi's output is overwhelmingly tragic (with the exception of his final opera, *Falstaff*, he composed only one other comic opera, at the beginning of his career). Indeed *Falstaff*, even more than belonging to a comic tradition, reflects on the complementary tragic form of opera. This opera shows that the common ground with tragedy is broader and more fundamental than musical vocabularies or conventional set-piece forms shared with the comic tradition. The approach to *voice* in *Falstaff* is a refashioning or reformulation of voice as conceived in his tragic operas, especially in the opera immediately preceding it, *Otello*. This is exposed in two film versions of Verdi's late works, Franco Zeffirelli's production of *Otello* (1986) and Götz Friedrich's production of *Falstaff* (1979).[1] The two directors stage the operatic voice very differently and, I would argue, not only as a result of their distinct styles, philosophies, or diverse national regions but as a result of the differences between the two operas themselves.

The phenomenon of cinematic productions of opera, "filmed opera," is of course fundamentally different from that of movies like *Phantom of the Opera* or *A Night at the Opera*. In these movies the opera deeply affects the film but is not reproduced in its entirety, and this requires some initial theoretical elaboration, some pressure put on questions that are seldom asked in accounts of opera movies. What kind of meeting place between opera and cinema is a "cinematic production of opera"? Should filmed opera be classified with film music or with cinematic adaptations, on par with more or less straight film adaptations of plays and novels? Is a film of an opera a "quotation" of it? Or is a new genre envisioned in cinematic productions of opera?[2]

Finally, there are serious issues pertaining to the passage between opera as an acoustic phenomenon and cinema as a visual one. Perhaps there is such a thing as the "essentially operatic" that is captured and translated in visual form. But what is it? Vocality can mutate into the visual. But the choices for staging that mutation remain numerous. For instance, exactly *how* a cinematic body-on-screen is seen to produce an operatic voice is only one dilemma: should the body image on-screen downplay the artificiality of singing or overemphasize its strangeness? And what visual transformations should the body undergo (or not) to be understood as adequate or appropriate to containing the operatic voice?

Sometimes film goes a long way toward representing a physical body that might be thought adequate in its own fabulous qualities to the fabulous operatic voice it seems to emit. In Luc Besson's *Fifth Element* (1997), when an opera singer appears, she is a blue, alien, feminine body extended by gel-like tubes. Her vocalizations are electronically manipulated, a computer processing of a real singer that morphs into unreal high-pitched coloratura, indeed no human voice. After singing an operatic aria from *Lucia di Lammermoor*, the diva shifts her performance into rock concert territory. Meanwhile backstage, in the singer's dressing room, a second, more-than-human-woman (Milla Jovovich), dressed in combat boots, is fighting bad guys. Jovovich's heroism thus stands in for the diva's, as the film cuts back and forth between the diva's acrobatic vocal performance and the battle, visually linking the two performances.

Everyone in the battle is after the "four elements," a mystical key to saving the universe, which is supposedly in the diva's possession. All assume that these elements are some precious stones or talismans, and that a diva should have them is a tongue-in-cheek reference to legendary operatic divas of the nineteenth and twentieth centuries and their jewel cases. What neither the viewer nor the cinematic characters know at this point is that the elements are actually hidden inside the diva's body, as part of her organic self, and that retrieving the elements means extracting them from her and in the process killing her, since she would be left as if without a vital organ. Thus a fabulous, blue-tube body sings opera and then dies, just like Violetta in *La traviata*, but unlike Violetta this particular opera-singing body dies because it houses precious stones, which must be delivered up for the universe to continue to exist.

Maybe it is worth pausing here to ask what allegorical meaning is being assigned to the elements, the precious stones. The elements seem to explain the miracle of the operatic voice, implying that ordinary humans or even ordinary space aliens cannot sing like this without some rare secret organ or physical structure. However, the diva's delivery of the aria and "delivery" of the stones, almost as if giving birth to them, are both presented as a *performance*, a quasi-heroic production of presence and mate-

Figure 3.1. Luc Besson's *Fifth Element* (1997). When an opera singer appears, she is a blue, alien, feminine body extended by gel-like tubes.

riality. The film, in other words, perfectly aligns the visual-corporeal with the vocal, making them equivalent, as if what the operatic voice is expressing were an equally precious body. Thus, in science fiction (and with the aid of Bruce Willis) there can be a physical locus that correctly matches the operatic voice.

But this is, of course, an extreme case, a fantasy licensed by science fiction, and although this solution to the problem of a proper visual housing for the operatic voice makes reference to a real opera and real facts of operatic history, its means are not available to more sober cinematic genres. Each filmed production of an opera has to address the problem of embodying operatic voices. My claim is that Verdi's operas in particular force film to confront the question of how the wizardry of operatic singing should be perceived, how bodies viewed on-screen should seem to, and be seen to, produce opera's voices.

Because of this particular focus on the means by which *voice is envisaged*, some curtailing of scope is necessary. To consider filmed opera as a general phenomenon, one could profitably discuss a single director's oeuvre—for instance, Zeffirelli's transformations of opera into film, or his

Verdian films *La traviata* and *Otello*—or contrast cinematic productions of different composers' works by the same director (for instance Götz Friedrich's *Falstaff* set against his *Tannhäuser*), or even compare different filmic productions of the same operatic text. But I want to set opening limits at Verdi's *Otello* (1887) and *Falstaff* (1893) and consider how the operas themselves—not just their cinematic versions—are reflections on visuality in relation to vocality, how the "Orphic strife" between the senses is built into their fabric: fatally in *Otello*, playfully in *Falstaff.* In other words, how in the former the act of "seeing" the singing *voice* determines the deathly outcome, whereas in the latter, "seeing" the singing *body* creates comedy. Historically, a conflict between the optical and the acoustic was already being probed by Italian opera in the late nineteenth century. What one sees in nascent form in *Otello* and *Falstaff* can almost be considered a precinematic intimation, a sense that there was, in opera performed onstage, an unresolved tension between voices and their physical housing, and by extension, between what is given expression by voice and what is symbolized by or conveyed by the body. This tension seems to have engrossed Verdi in his old age, and—beyond Shakespeare and a more "Wagnerian" approach to musical form—it is what is shared by *Otello* and *Falstaff* across the tragedy-farce divide. That tension animates Verdi's two last operas and made them cinematic long before sound cinema came to exist, and long before "lip-synching" in a philosophical sense—as the aesthetics of synchronization and the negotiation between the visual and the acoustic—would haunt the filmed opera of the future.

Images of Opera: Zeffirelli and Friedrich

First, some generalizations are in order. How, in basic terms, do Zeffirelli and Friedrich deal with the visual translation of operatic voice? Very differently, it would seem. Zeffirelli in effect tries to balance and even (quite radically) *replace* the operatic voice with a beautiful excess of things to be seen. His *Otello* is, of course, notorious for leaving out some of Verdi's best vocal moments (like Desdemona's "Willow Song"), as if they have no bearing on the drama. Friedrich's *Falstaff*, as I elaborate in chapter 4, envisions a gargantuan body as the proper extension or optical form for operatic voice. These films in effect stand on two opposite sides of *The Fifth Element*'s apocalyptic joining of operatic voice and cinematic "body," with "body" being understood now not just as the locus for singing, the (apparently) singing human body on-screen, but also as the entire visual landscape in the film. Zeffirelli tilts the weight toward the perfect, visually plausible cinematic body. There are no blue gels or tubes or fantastic organic apparatuses or nonexistent worlds. Rather, everything we see is visually realistic to a fault, as if that hyperrealism were the only proper, possible translation of the singing voice and its beauties. Friedrich, however, both embraces the grotesque and allows the human bodies on-screen and the visual element itself to be submerged by the playfulness of the operatic voices in *Falstaff*. With Friedrich, it is as if—paradoxically—what is seen were nonetheless also disappearing under the sonic roar.

On the face of it, Zeffirelli's production of *Otello* seems the more radical of the two, since it alters the operatic text itself. Zeffirelli relocates and shortens scenes, reorders sections within scenes (cutting and pasting them anew), and even cuts one substantial and long scene altogether (the "Willow Song"). Zeffirelli uses lip-synching actors for minor solo roles (Cassio) and inserts into the chorus actors who "sing," yet their voices are not heard in the final product. His technique of post-synchronized singing is common in cinematic productions of opera, yet, as we will see, his use of dubbing, or rather double-dubbing, is technically radical.

Friedrich's production seems more conservative. *Falstaff* can be mistaken for a relay—that is, for a filming of a staged performance. That is deliberate; Friedrich is scrambling the ontological borders between mechanical reproduction of live performance and mechanical creation of a filmic text. Friedrich never tampers with the operatic text, neither cutting nor shuffling. Nothing is missing from Verdi's score. Something nonmusical, however, is added: mute (or nearly mute) interludes, which are there only as visual material inserted between the opera's scenes.

It might be instructive to place these productions within the context of Zeffirelli's and Friedrich's very different aesthetic stances toward the transformation of opera into film, since the endorsements one might at first attach to them—traditionalist versus radical or conservative mise-en-scène versus *Regietheater*—tend to collapse under interpretive pressure. Zeffirelli, celebrated for staging and filming classics (for example, Shakespeare's plays), has a reputation for "glamorous excess and unbridled romanticism," with sets that are extravagant, "outsized fantasies. . . . The Café Momus in his *Bohème* seems as large as the Colosseum. His *Tosca* is a veritable Perillo tour of Rome, his *Carmen* a Gypsy circus worthy of Cecil DeMille."[3] Zeffirelli's emphasis is on spectacle, beauty, and visual excess. Some would even argue that "Zeffirelli's aesthetic, in fact, seems founded on a principle of excess for its own sake."[4] He is known for his intense sensitivity to visual perfection, so that, for example, when working on the set for *Tea with Mussolini*, a film based on his childhood memories, he scrubs down and refurbishes a street like new: "Suddenly, we saw the city the way it was *intended to be*."[5] Envisioning a lost past becomes, in Zeffirelli's film, an image that is excessive in its Utopian perfection.

Zeffirelli's approach to opera is traditionalist in that he believes he is producing a commodity that is faithful to the original work:

People like my productions because they are what the author wanted the thing to be, plus all the knowledge and the know-how and feeling and taste of others of today. There is a great cultural confusion around the world today. When a piece is faithful to the very essence of what the opera spectacle must be, it can be entertaining, shocking, larger than life! Directors find it is much easier to do their own creation, parallel or discordant to the opera, because it is very difficult to prove what those authors had in mind and put it on correctly. . . . I am a traditionalist, so what?[6]

We should bear in mind this statement when thinking through his provocative "faithfulness" to Verdi.

While Zeffirelli has a clear inclination toward re-creating works of the golden age of Italian opera, Friedrich's range of productions is wide and includes all styles from all periods. He specializes in productions of Wagner and Richard Strauss, yet tackles novelties such as a Bach Passion. Placing less emphasis on immediate visual effect per se, Friedrich is more reflective in his productions. For him, "every opera is actually an opera about opera," and every staging has some say about the medium of opera as such.[7] In contrast to Zeffirelli, Friedrich is interested in new readings of operatic texts that result from the rendition of opera on film. His aim is to open further aesthetic dimensions, and his cinematic treatments of operas have a certain metaoperatic ambition as symbolic representations of the medium's "inexhaustible" potential.[8]

Thus, in outlining a dramaturgy of his music theater, Friedrich states that a work *should be* constantly reinterpreted. A staging should bring the elements of opera into conflict, into a contrapuntal relation to one another. His goal is "to tell scenically and musically what cannot be said and cannot be heard."[9] Unlike Zeffirelli, who desires to pull the musical into the realm of the possibilities of the visual, Friedrich searches for a *musical* structuring enacted through the singer,[10] an interpretation not born of the libretto alone, in which singing determines certain visual effects.[11] Zeffirelli treats singing in films of operas almost as "external": actors do not sing at all, and the singing is recorded after the scenes have been shot, to allow for what he calls "risk-free" singing.[12] Friedrich wants the camera to focus on the images of singing.[13]

Friedrich, further, envisions an alternately cooperative and conflicted relation of the music and the visual components,[14] and he warns against attempts to make things too beautiful and pretty.[15] He positions himself against the visual, as it were, as thinking through "music itself." He is not only sensitive to an opera's historical position—about *Falstaff*, for instance, he gives voice to the familiar critical view that it sums up the style of nineteenth-century Italian opera and points to future twentieth-century opera. He is also aware of specific musical traits; for example, he mentions *Falstaff*'s dissolution of formal prototypes and its relation to Wagner.[16]

Yet, for all that, Zeffirelli's seemingly more naive or regressive approach is not somehow less enlightening of opera's nature. In fact, it is not completely obvious or self-evident what a regressive fascination with visual beauty on the one hand or a deconstructive attunement to opera's divided self on the other might yield when these attitudes actually come to define opera on film. Zeffirelli's and Friedrich's productions each have unexpected aspects, surprising turns. What I want to show is how each Verdian opera's aesthetic means come to affect each film. But more than this, I want to revisit at several points the passage between the acoustic and the optical, and the means by which filmed opera solves a conundrum, inventing the visualized translation or visible substitution that can stand in for what is lost: the sonic excess that is operatic voice.

Perfect Singing

Otello and *Falstaff* are not simply two operas by Verdi. They are always qualified with capital letters: Verdi's Last Operas, his final collaboration with Boito, his operas based on Shakespearean plays.[17] The trajectory they delineate from the tragic to the comic is said to sum up and elaborate Verdi's aesthetics of opera.[18] *Otello* is a metaopera, a manifesto for operatic vocality as such. It reflects on the idea of the perfect voice. Body, physicality, and life itself are abandoned for the sake of pure voice. In *Falstaff*, voice undergoes a carnal metamorphosis. *Falstaff* shows the degeneration of a grotesque body but also offers possibilities for its rejuvenation. It plays with distancing the voice from the specificity of its body. It toys with tragic opera's inability to account for the physicality of the human body.[19] The films of the operas *Otello* and *Falstaff* confront fundamentally different ideas of the operatic voice and radically altered images of the operatic body. They nevertheless allow, in all their differences of style and temperament, for a recognition of Verdi's late vision of opera as bringing together tragedy and comedy, an attitude he embraced toward the end of his life.

Otello is about operatic voice and its capacities, and as such, it gravitates toward self-conscious song.[20] There are so many formal "songs" in *Otello*— a drinking song, a prayer, and a narrative ballad—as I see it, this proliferation reflects certain upheavals in Verdi's compositional attitudes, his drive to refashion an Italian operatic tradition that was outmoded and cast away by the 1880s. Through reconceiving song, Verdi sought the means to participate in a new aesthetics, indirectly. He needed to be indirect in order to swerve around Wagner and operatic Wagnerism, in effect approaching the new Wagnerian "ideal"—unified and continuous musical discourse, realistic time—by reinterpreting an Italian tradition that reified singing and always inclined toward formal melody.

One of the fundamental difficulties in a filmic rendition of *Otello* is coping with Verdi's opera in its aspect as a "narrative of the vocal." This "narrative" plays out in the domain of singing and song, both as they appear in dramatically charged scenes and in their role within the personae of certain characters, and if it has a culminating point, then that point is without doubt Desdemona's "Willow Song." Surprisingly, however, the "Willow Song" is followed immediately by another solo piece for Desdemona, the "Ave Maria" prayer. But in some sense this very excess or redundancy, the presence of two soprano arias in succession, suggests that voice or singing itself is at stake in outlining the "narrative of the vocal" in *Otello*.

What, then, is this "narrative of the vocal"? It is not simply acoustic but is, rather, an allegory about singing, or a representation of what singing "means," which has to exist between the *Otello* drama, the characterizations in Boito's libretto, its representations of singing, and Verdi's music for them. It is a narrative between the lines, as it were. Desdemona's singing is its central red thread. The role of Desdemona has been seen as many things (pure innocence, wronged virtue, and so on), but Desdemona figures the opera's concern with unending, ever-present, and perfected song. Verdi's own description of her is almost musico-morphic, as if she were a continuous sound as well as a coherent character, standing, as it were, for an essence of opera.

> The true Desdemona is yet to be found. . . . Desdemona is a part where the thread, the melodic line, never stops from the first to the last note. Just as Iago must only declaim and snicker. Just as Otello, now warrior, now passionate lover, now cast down into the filth, now as ferocious as a savage, must sing and howl; so Desdemona must always sing. . . . I repeat, Desdemona sings from the first note of the Recitative, which is still a melodic phrase, until the last note, "Otello non uccidermi . . ." which is still a melodic phrase. Therefore the most perfect Desdemona will always be the one who sings the best.[21]

It is significant that Verdi's yearning for opera as song, as endless melody, expresses itself through one particular voice. When Verdi describes Iago or Otello, he speaks in terms of rhetoric, whereas "the most perfect Desdemona" (and this is not equivalent to the singer taking the part) always sings: singing is her *persona*.[22] Verdi's description of the ideal prima donna is indeed a manifesto for the ideal of opera as such: the voice's uninterrupted, ever-present pure and perfect singing. The prima donna truly sings, that is sings alone, only at the very end of the opera in the "Willow Song" and "Ave Maria." The character's singing, however, which culminates in these scenes and which reaches back toward the origins and forward to the limits of singing, shows the near *impossibility* for opera to contain it. The operatic Desdemona stands for what is *beyond* singing, and the paradox resulting from the fact that Desdemona is perfected in song is that she will be, in song, what is beyond the medium of song. But in asking how the opera *Otello* conceptualizes perfect singing, I am always looking at the corollary, asking how that "perfect singing" would be expressed in the same opera on film.

At issue, then, is Zeffirelli's approach to scenes in *Otello* that represent voice: not just where beautiful singing is on display, but where voice itself, even within the operatic text, has become a direct object of symbolic play, a theme even within the plot. The back and forth between the operatic text—as a kind of unrealized, unstaged abstraction—and Zeffirelli's specific realization will, at times, reveal the film version as unable to address the question of voice: visual Utopianism strikes singing mute. At other times, however, the film is faithful in unexpected ways to Verdi's understanding of perfect song, albeit in ways distinct from the artificially staged and recreated "authenticity" Zeffirelli himself so self-consciously embraces.

Deformed Singing

A quest for perfect song is initiated, in the first act of *Otello*, by surrounding Desdemona with deficient forms.[23] The opera opens with negative representation, by taking each of the characters to exemplify a type of deformed song while alluding to Desdemona's perfect singing, which, for the moment, is withheld.

Iago is portrayed as one who *uses* song, manipulates it to his own ends, to mimic, mock, seduce, and deceive. Iago's singing is under control precisely because it has the power not to express true emotion (which is to say that genuine singing always assumes a certain abandon).[24] He easily self-interrupts and self-terminates sung expressions that are always well confined, creating independent, self-sufficient melodious passages. He decides, as it were, on the transformations of his speechlike rhetoric to a songlike rhetoric.[25] This technique represents Iago's cunning in musical-formal terms: he tempts by the melodiousness of his "little songs." The power of these songs is in their unexpected independence from their musical surrounding; they are closed off, self-contained, and swift.

Since film, realistic film especially, would reject the artifice of persuasion by little songs, and since Zeffirelli has no qualms about abbreviating Verdi's score, why not cut them out, invisibly pasting together the surrounding recitatives and extending the idea of cinematic editing to the opera's music? *Otello* as a drama, in fact, does not need Iago's "vocal talents" to illuminate or amplify his dubious character: Boito and Verdi, famously, already provided clear motivation for Iago's evil by adding the "Credo" (which is not in Shakespeare).[26] Zeffirelli, as well as any other director, can rely on the explanatory force of the "Credo" scene. And since virtually every one of Iago's vocal expressions involves the devices mentioned earlier, one can dispense with some of them in the film's editorial process without losing the information they convey.

In a filmic medium, it would seem, Iago's schemes depend far less on his unique *vocality*. For example, in act 1, scene 1, Zeffirelli includes one "little song" and cuts another within a span of a few measures. The little song accompanying the words "and I remain his Moorish lordship's ensign!" survives, but the words just following are cut: "But, as 'tis true that you are Roderigo / so, too, 'tis true that were I the Moor, / I would not wish to see an Iago about me."[27] (This is possible because the little songs—only six measures or so of music—are distinct from and independent of one another in terms of melodic profile, texture, relationship of voice to orchestral accompaniment, tonality, and so on. Thus the first little song does not lead into the second, but the songs are juxtaposed. Facilitating the cut-and-paste operation that Zeffirelli is conducting here is the repetition of the last measure of the first present song and the last measure of the absent second one a tone lower on C.) (See ex. 3.1.)

In the opera, Cassio is identified by incomplete song, song that disintegrates into a blur—into an utter loss of melodiousness. Song's impotence and frustration find their expression in his incapacities. Time and time again, the possibility of expression through song—either in relation to Desdemona or to speak for himself—eludes him. The "Drinking Song" shows Cassio's verbal-vocal failures as a drunken stammer, emerging from someone who is unable even to reproduce a song known to everyone. Here, though the score is highly abbreviated, the film is faithful to the meaning conveyed by the very act of singing for the single reason that in the "Drinking Song" the *only* way to convey the plot—Cassio's drunkenness and loss of control—is *in* song. The "narrative of the vocal" and the plot are one and the same, and the vocal narrative is thus left intact at this juncture. More still: the idea of Cassio's vocal deficiency, present in Verdi's score, is in effect amplified when Zeffirelli uses an actor, not a singer, to lip-synch the role. For Cassio, it is as if the director gives further expression to the character's vocal incapacity through the riveting physical beauty of the nonsinging actor.

Otello's first musical utterance is equally problematic, in the sense of conveying an incapacity to sing. This may seem absurd at first, since his actual vocal entrance, the "Esultate," is one of the famous high-tenor vocal moments in the repertory and is generally assumed to convey the character's power and secular majesty. But doubts can arise: the high notes, the shouts, are also "too much," a quasi cry that may give expression to his

Example 3.1. Otello, act 1, scene 1. Iago's "little songs." Zeffirelli includes one "little song" and cuts another within a span of a few measures.

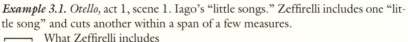 What Zeffirelli includes

hysterical underside or even his non-European Otherness.[28] The burden of the "Esultate" is to provide a musical exclamation point, which resolves the preceding storm music and brings about the first real cadence in the opera, to E major. Otello's entrance clarifies the harmonic uncertainty of the tempest music, just as his emergence from the ship forces the eye to focus on a single character after the chaos of the initial crowd scene. Indeed, his presence is defined as much by his appearance—in the sense of the way in which he becomes visible—as his sound.

But even if Otello's operatic character is thus expressed in sheer strength of voice, in his overcoming all other sound in the opera—as with the "Esultate"—even while he makes manifest the very gesture of singing and the sheer physicality of it, he is not given over to or abandoned to song. And if the aim of such entrances is in part to capture Otello's authority and grandeur in a flash, this gesture is undermined as it is being made. It is not just that these vocal cries may intimate hysteria or Otherness. It is also that his initial singing, being thus limited to shouts, foreshadows his breakdown. And more: in the first entrance, his voice is also an extension of the tempest and the crowd's cheering; in the second, it extends the brawl and noise of the duel.[29] Otello shouts, announcing himself and calling for order. His presence advances the plot (in these scenes he *is* the plot), but he does not "sing." His is an operatic voice without melody, a voice somewhere between melody and noise, an extension or ultimate form of musical representations of noise, which recur in the opera. His capacity to put an end to noise shows his affinity with it.[30] Thus two brief vocal noises, two appearances and disappearances, define his presence in act 1 until, at the end of the act, he finally remains onstage and sings, but even then only in a duet with Desdemona.

To present such a vocal presence in film is no easy task. Otello's problematic expression in song is hinted at in the documentary about the making of the film, where Zeffirelli discusses the difficulty of Otello's entrance as a difficulty in synchronizing Placido Domingo's voice with his image as he emerges from the sea. The difficulty lay in actually "placing" the voice in Domingo's mouth and making sure that such a short and abrupt vocal utterance was coordinated with Domingo's on-screen appearance and his moving lips. The solution for the unanchorable shout was, in fact, to film the scene predominantly from afar so as not to allow the viewer to judge the synchronization.[31]

In his reentrance following the brawl in act 1, Otello overcomes the crowd, emerging against it, not from it. Here the challenge is even greater, as the burden of stopping the action and in effect altering the characters' destinies as quickly as possible is assigned to a musical phenomenon, brief sonorities that pass in series ($f\sharp^1$ as the tonic of $f\sharp$ minor, with the g^1, its local melodic resolution, supported by a passing G major,

Example 3.2. Otello, act 1, scene 2. Otello's second entrance. Voice captures an instantaneous event, the arrest of action.

Très agité

hinting at Iago's reply and leading to g minor; see ex. 3.2). Zeffirelli cannot alter the music of these entrances; they are indispensable for advancing the plot, and their signification does not point beyond their concurrent dramaturgical function. Voice captures an instantaneous event, the arrest of action.

The preparation for Desdemona's entrance involves a mapping out of other characters' allusions to song: mocking song, losing it, being unable to assume it. Significantly, no aria is sung in the first act. Iago's "Credo" in act 2 is the first aria in the opera, thus paradoxically emphasizing the preoccupation of the opera with perfect song.[32] The poisonous plot is set in motion without formal solo singing and is achieved outside traditional vehicles of contemplation and expression in song. The opera hints at the unavailability of melodic means to account for the destruction of Desdemona's perfection in song.

In Verdi and Boito's opera, the prima donna makes her first appearance only after all the other voices have been clearly demarcated.[33] But Desdemona has a unique vocal-visual entrance. She enters the stage momentarily, only to leave it instantaneously, having sung nothing; she is viewed by all yet remains unheard.[34] At the very point where we expect to hear her most conspicuous entrance aria, she withdraws without a sound. She is marked as a prima donna to be looked at and not listened to. As a voice, she is still absent, onstage as a pent voice, a voice in potential. This gesture is unusual, to say the least, in nineteenth-century Italian opera: the prima donna's entrance serves only to impede or put off the sounding of her voice.

Without wanting to overinterpret an idiosyncratic dramaturgical gesture, one must at least pause to allow its idiosyncrasy to breathe. Desdemona's mute appearance seems spectral, as if a premonition that song is unattainable, that the "beautiful moment" of perfect singing cannot endure and ends in silence. There is an elective affinity being staged here for our benefit, a sympathetic resonance between the prima donna, the limits of perfect song, and silence. Indeed, until the "Willow Song" and the "Ave Maria" in act 4, Desdemona's voice is seldom heard at any length for itself; it is heard only in confluence with other voices. Once act 4 has arrived, the connection between her solitary singing and her impending death seems quite clear.

As I argued in chapter 1, the sight of a mute prima donna was familiar in the era of silent film, where the *gesture* of singing sufficed to signify song: in silent film, the gesture of song provides us with its sound. Yet, with Verdi, we are conditioned to hear singing when the lead soprano walks onstage for the first time. Sight makes us expect sound. In this case, the opera uses *mere* sight to create the *fantasy* of a yet unheard sound. The opera stretches hearing to the limit by erasing the voice we expect to hear. This, I believe, is essentially operatic: intense "hearing" when nothing sounds. The transfiguration of the visual in expectation of the aural is opera's fantasized escape from its Orphic fate, the idea of voice beyond any image.

In Zeffirelli's film, however, Desdemona is repeatedly exposed *prior* to the entrance reserved for her by the opera: awaiting Otello's safe landing ashore, greeting him, kissing him, dining with him while entertained by the people, exchanging gazes with Cassio, talking to Emilia and to Otello. This premature exposure is partly a result of Zeffirelli's scene shifting. From the outset, Desdemona's presence plays into the visual festivity Zeffirelli is creating. Placing her onstage for the *opera*'s visual moment of voice would merely extend her other silent appearances (thus making that moment not the least different from the film's initial glimpses of Emilia and Bianca). In fact, the moment of her silent entrance in the opera is disregarded in the film—Zeffirelli refrains from showing her *at all* at this point.[35] Desdemona's silent entrance in the opera is a moment in which the overriding visuality of the film clashes with the opera's comment on the significance of the visual. This operatic moment has been made meaningless: it has been lost to film.[36]

Visual Singing

If, in the first act, Desdemona's vocal presence is an object of desire, in the following act, the opera provides a glimpse of her voice and opens possibilities for her expression in song. In their opera, Verdi and Boito invent a wholly original scene, the "Garden Scene," in which Iago and Otello eavesdrop on the crowd's adoration of Desdemona on the eve of her wedding. The scene identifies the bride, Desdemona, with the holy image of the Madonna.[37] The crowd's song about her is a performance for her, a collective *musica in scena*. Unlike Cassio, Iago, and Otello, who are thus far limited to deformed song, the people are able to sing in a way commensurate with Desdemona's essence.

In the opera, this scene is long—hypnotic in its strophic variations. The verse "Dove guardi splendono" appears twice at the outset and once again at the end. "Dove guardi splendono," in its first appearance in the opera, is accompanied by Iago's recitative; in its final appearance, it is accompanied by both Iago's and Otello's recitatives and by Desdemona's song. Between the repetitions of this verse are three timbral variations on it set to different texts. Zeffirelli's film of *Otello* dispenses with the variations and provides only the initial verse and its repetition. Deleting the middle verses, then, would not seem to alter the scene's narrative, since critical plot information—conveyed by the recitatives rather than the song—is still present in Zeffirelli's shorter version.

Still, we might want to ask what *is* lost when a long strophic piece is cut out: whether meaning is changed when providing for only one repetition and no variations of the verse, or whether film shows us that a scene can be boiled down to one verse—a gist, a minimum of music—which would account for what is seen.

To address these questions, let us consider the scene in some detail. In the opera, Desdemona joins the chorus's song for and about her at the very end of the scene. She sings the main melody as a kind of coda to the chorus's performance. The entire scene prepares us for hearing her voice, for hearing the same music now in the solo voice of the prima donna.

Desdemona joins the singing in her honor and creates the climax of the scene by not merely echoing the chorus. Her alteration is slight; it extends only the range of the chorus's voice. She sings above the others, though their voices are also in a high range and they are singing a nearly identical melody. The scene portrays her voice as an extension of the voice of those who could sing for and about her. And as she is both the object of their song and its very culmination, her singing surfaces as if it were its very result.

The film's editing of this scene changes the balance between Desdemona's singing and the chorus's and flattens out the effect of the mounting expectation of Desdemona's singing. In Zeffirelli's interpretation, a "conversation" between the chorus and Desdemona is created as she becomes merely one of the scene's repetitions. The soprano and the chorus's song is equalized: Desdemona's voice is no longer "the prize" for their song, the unique high solo timbre within the variations and its very goal. The meaning of her song is changed not only by the new balance established but also by a change in placement. Zeffirelli moves the verse "Dove guardi splendono" around. It is now placed *after* Desdemona's singing—the cinematic Desdemona no longer brings the scene to its conclusion. Thus Zeffirelli loses an essential feature: the opera's playing out the impossibility of further song after Desdemona, the fact that *nothing* can come after such singing on her part.

Another change the film introduces relates to the very production of Desdemona's singing. In the "Garden Scene," Desdemona sings her highest note in the opera, b^1, as part of her slight variation on the material of the chorus. The entire scene is directed toward the moment when her voice will be heard through and above all of the other voices. A high note is acoustically privileged in its fragility, parading the risk of its own voicing. Even though in the scene just preceding the "Garden Scene" Otello sings the exact same pitch and it is the highest note in the phrase, the musical context renders them differently. Desdemona's high note completes the chorus's tonic chord, whereas Otello's is foreign, its resolution postponed until Iago's part. Otello's high b^1 is portrayed as an outburst, a convulsive moment, whereas Desdemona's is depicted as a goal or culmination.[38] In his production, however, Zeffirelli *reduces* the volume of Desdemona's high note so that it blends "too well" with the other voices, whereas Otello's high note just preceding the scene is conspicuous. Desdemona's voice—although the acoustic projection of the high range—does not soar above the other voices.[39] Zeffirelli is approximating a cinematic "out of focus," or blurring of *voice*, as he does repeatedly with Desdemona's image in the first act where she is seen veiled by rain, through a haze, surrounded by a halo, and from too far away.

The most dramatic of the film's changes in this scene lies in the placement of Iago's recitatives accompanying the chorus's song for Desdemona. Zeffirelli slices Iago's continuous recitative, delays its appearance, and thus sounds it with the verse's repetition, rather than its initial performance. This makes Desdemona's sung melody a mere variation, symmetrical with Iago's adjoining recitative. It explicitly juxtaposes Iago and Desdemona (something that never occurs in Verdi). In the film then, Desdemona is balanced vis-à-vis other characters—Otello's dissonant high b^1 is comparable to her consonant high b^1; Iago's recitative over the second verse is paired with her joining that verse. Her voice is no longer unique, incomparable.

A further complexity of the "Garden Scene" emerges as one brings in the relation of voice and image. In the opera, the meaning of the "Garden Scene" lies in the way we understand Otello's confusion, which is generated by the tension between what he sees and what he hears in this scene. In Verdi's opera, Otello is not sure whether he sees Cassio just departing from a meeting with Desdemona, while he is clearly moved by the vision of the celebration for and of Desdemona and by the sounds of song. The opera's production book is clear about what Otello is supposed to see. He is to *suspect* that he has seen Cassio leaving Desdemona. (According to the production book, it is Emilia, not Cassio, who accompanies Desdemona *throughout* the scene. Only in the early part of the scene, before Otello's entrance, are Cassio and Desdemona seen from afar. See figure 3.3.)[40] Otello's insecurity about what he has just seen gives Iago's evasiveness the power of voice to explain the image and the authority over Otello's sight.

Zeffirelli disregards the time lapse present in the opera. The filmic Otello does not miss Cassio's approach to Desdemona but rather sees their encounter clearly throughout the film's scene. Zeffirelli *superimposes* the visual narrative (Cassio's request to Desdemona) over the vocal narrative (Desdemona's song). In the film's "Garden Scene," Iago and Otello eavesdrop not only on the wedding celebration of Desdemona in song but also on a superimposed vision of an unheard conversation between Desdemona and Cassio. The film shows Desdemona's singing against an image of an illicit encounter with Cassio by keeping Cassio onstage. Otello cannot doubt what he sees because Zeffirelli provides us with the visual image Iago planted in Otello's mind. Desdemona's voice then must battle with, instead of be supported by, the visual frame: Desdemona's voice must overcome the simultaneity of sight.

The opera presents Otello's confused state as a result of hearing Desdemona's voice.[41] Otello does not know how to interpret the power and beauty of Desdemona's singing in light of his doubts: "that song overcomes me / If she is betraying me, heaven is mocking itself!"[42] In the opera, this is the last expression of Otello's ability to actually *hear* her voice and to be devastated by its beauty rather than to interpret it by way

Figure 3.2. Zeffirelli's film of Verdi's *Otello* (1986). In the film's "Garden Scene," Iago and Otello eavesdrop not only on the wedding celebration of Desdemona in song but also on a superimposed vision of an unheard conversation between Desdemona and Cassio.

of what Iago teaches him to see. Only here will Desdemona's high voice reach beyond the visual frame, only here will voice defeat vision. If only momentarily, her voice triumphs over Otello's uncertain gaze, manipulated by Iago's schemes as it reaches beyond the confines of the plot. In Zeffirelli's rendition of this scene, the film's visual powers compete with the opera's reliance on the capacity of voice: Desdemona's vocal uniqueness must overcome the certainty of sight. The film, by reducing the volume of her voice, tightens the fatality of the visual and shows Otello's confusion as a result of the discrepancy between what he does not hear and what he sees. Zeffirelli's gesture is fatally Orphic: Film shows the vulnerability of the operatic voice when positioned within the visual world.

Dubbing

In the second act, Iago recounts to Otello how he supposedly overheard Cassio talking in his sleep. In the invented fantasy, Cassio expresses his lust

and longing for Desdemona.[43] Iago's delivery of Cassio's supposed unconscious speech to Otello oscillates between imitating Cassio's mur-
mured speech and his own commentary on what he overheard. In this
scene, Iago mimics a voice lodged in another's body, like a sorcerer con-
juring a voice. The scene is a tour de force of Iago's vocal talents.

In the opera, the scene partakes in the overall characterization of both
Cassio and Iago. It is a culmination of Iago's musical portrayal in that it
shows him masterfully sliding in and out of fragments of styles: recitative,
parlando, operatic and real song. But never is Iago portrayed as going so
far as to transform into another. To sound Cassio, Iago reduces his voice's
operatic quality, alters its *material* quality, its color, dynamics, and timbre;
his voice in these moments is performed *ppp, sotto voce*—in a whispered
murmuring parlando. The musical line is flattened into intonation reminiscent of Cassio's disintegration of melody in the drinking song and a
variation on the latter's loss of speech following the staged brawl. Cassio's
supposed murmur in the dream is made to sound similar to Cassio's otherwise vocal drunkenness and speechlessness. For example, Iago's voicing
of Cassio's murmur "My sweetest Desdemona, let us be wary ever, cau-
tiously hiding," is a typical Iagoish intoning on c, gradually ascending to
c♯, then to d; an Iagoish threatening, tuneful chromatic line; a simple
repetitive-patterned accompaniment that gives the impression of songful-
ness; a bare chordal accompaniment in 6/8; and a C major–E major oscil-
lation later clarified into a C major cadence (C major–E major coloring ultimately favoring the C major is typical of Iago).[44] On the one hand, the
representation of the dream requires a double vocal production, an "Iago
voice" and a "Cassio voice," and on the other hand, it intertwines Iago's
and Cassio's musical styles into one (see ex. 3.3).

The opera shows Iago's talents not only to charge his voice with melodiousness, to echo and mime, but to breathe life into a voice: to *conjure* a
voice. In contrast, the film fleshes out Iago's invented dream and demonstrates cinema's powers to anchor Iago's voice in an image of Cassio's
body. Both a voice and an image are conjured. Zeffirelli writes: "I don't
have any qualms about using dubbing; in fact, at one point in the film I
made an absolute virtue of it. At the moment when the lying Iago tells
Otello that he has overheard Cassio talking in his sleep of his love for Desdemona, I showed a naked Cassio on the bed mouthing the words that
Iago is singing—a double dub, as it were."[45] Zeffirelli calls it a double dub
because Cassio is an actor who lip-synchs a singer. The entire film, in fact,
is post-synchronized: the technique employed for filming the entire opera
is a prerecorded soundtrack, later matched to the visuals.[46] What then occurs in the scene of Iago dubbing Cassio is a chain of voices in which Iago
lip-synchs his prerecorded voice and Cassio lip-synchs Iago's voice dubbing him.

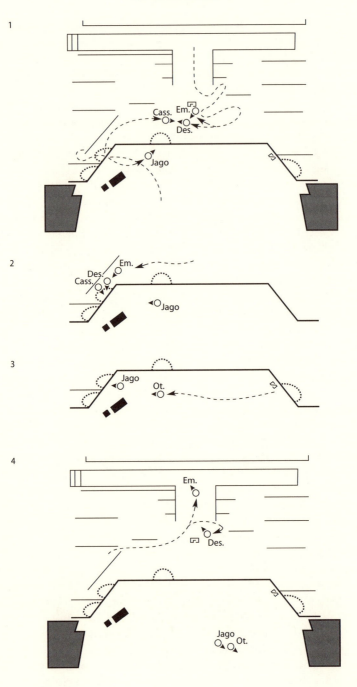

Thus Zeffirelli implants a voice foreign to the body emitting it and further complicates the dubbing effect. The filming of the scene does not hide from our vision the performative aspect of the dubbing as the camera goes back and forth between Cassio and Iago.[47] Iago stages the dream: while speaking in his own voice, the image of Cassio alternates with his own. The film shows Iago lying down, his hand dissolving into Cassio's hand caressing himself in the dream. This is followed by Cassio's "words." A shot/reverse shot sequence introduces Iago's and Otello's reactions. Zeffirelli transforms Iago's operatic acrobatics into an overdetermined moment in which synchronization, post-synchronization, and dubbing coexist.[48] Iago's conjured voice is now further transplanted into the horrified Otello. A dissolve superimposes Otello on the image of Cassio. Otello, convinced by the virtuosity of Iago's voicing, has himself become Iago's-voicing-of-Cassio. *Both* Iago and Otello dissolve into Iago's conjured image of Cassio. The film thus constructs a chimera in place of Iago's vocal sorcery: the voice and hand belong to Iago, the mouth to Otello, the naked body to Cassio.

This is not a simple moment of dubbing—not that dubbing is ever that simple. Since we have *heard* Cassio's "true" voice earlier in the film, whom are we being led to believe we are hearing in this scene? What are we being convinced of? Do we *hear* Cassio as a result of seeing him? If dubbing is a means for cinema to tame Iago's *operatic* monstrosity, then a no less unsettling cinematic beast has surfaced. Otello's reaction to Iago/ Cassio's dream is striking: Otello *sounds* like Cassio's conjured voice. Iago's cinematic Cassio voice gets anchored *in Otello's body*. Zeffirelli's dream scene merging playback, synchronization, and dubbing becomes a series of wandering voices in multiple bodies. It produces a horrific effect.

But the horrific and the monstrous are internal to dubbing itself. Dubbing usually refers to a cinematic technique or aesthetic of implanting a voice foreign to the body emitting it.[49] The voice of the actor is silenced, removed, and replaced by another actor's voice, often in a different language. That voice tries to match the moving lips of its new body image; its original body is unseen. Synchronization, like dubbing, has no soothing effect. On the contrary, by demonstrating that the unity of voice and body is a technological artifact, it draws attention to the meaning of places in which unity is called into question. It is well known that far from seeming

Figure 3.3. According to the opera's production book, Otello is only to *suspect* that he has seen Cassio leaving Desdemona. From *Production Book for the Opera Otello*, compiled and arranged according to the production of the Teatro alla Scala, by Giulio Ricordi, in *Verdi's* Otello *and* Simon Boccanegra *in Letters and Documents*, vol. 2, ed. and trans. Hans Busch (Oxford: Clarendon Press, 1988), 530–35.

Example 3.3. Otello, act 2, scene 5. Iago's invented dream requires a double vocal production, an "Iago voice" and a "Cassio voice"; at the same time, it intertwines Iago's and Cassio's musical styles.

Iago's "Cassio voice"

Figure 3.4. Zeffirelli's film of Verdi's *Otello* (1986). The film constructs a chimera in place of Iago's vocal sorcery: the voice and hand belong to Iago, the mouth to Otello, the naked body to Cassio.

natural, cinema's preference for voice-body unity—for an investment in the synchronization of voice and image—is problematic. As Michel Chion points out:

> The physical nature of film necessarily makes an incision or cut between the body and the voice. Then the cinema does its best to restitch the two to-

gether at the seam. . . . If the talking cinema has shown anything by restoring voices to bodies, it's precisely that it doesn't hang together; it's decidedly not a seamless match. . . . This operation [of grafting the non-localized voice onto a particular body] leaves a scar, and the talking film marks the place of that scar, since by presenting itself as a reconstituted totality, it places all the greater emphasis on the original non-coincidence. Of course, via the operation called synchronization, cinema seeks to unify the body and voice that have been dissociated by their inscription onto separate surfaces (the celluloid image and the soundtrack). But the more you think about synchronization, the more aware you can become . . . of the arbitrariness of this convention, which tries to present as a unity something that from the outset *doesn't stick together*. . . . It is as an inherent consequence of the material organization of cinema that the voice and body are at odds.[50]

The original utterance, as Chion says elsewhere, cannot be forgotten: "Dubbing produces a palimpsest beneath which there runs a ghost-text."[51] Chion seems to be arguing that behind any synchronized utterance lies the ghost of dubbing—itself attempting to mime synchronization.

Similarly, Jorge Luis Borges views dubbing as an "audiovisual anomaly."

Hollywood has just enriched this frivolous, tautological museum [of chimera]: by means of a perverse artifice they call dubbing, they offer monsters that combine the well-known features of Greta Garbo with the voice of Aldonza Lorenzo. How can we fail to proclaim our admiration for this distressing prodigy, for these ingenious audio-visual anomalies.[52]

Mikhail Yampolski further develops Borges's idea and argues that dubbing is a chimera in which "the visible body produces the voice of the body of the invisible," in which there is an illusory division between the visible and the audible. In any sound film, he continues, the source of the voice is outside the body on-screen, it originates in the sound system so that "the body in sound film is always split; it is as if its acoustic substance goes beyond the limits of its shell." In other words, the body as chimera is carved into the nature of sound film as such. "Dubbing," continues Yampolski, "only leads the alienation of the voice from the body to extremely paradoxical and therefore more tangible forms." What occurs, concludes Yampolski, is that "the body is absorbed by voice and becomes voice . . . the voice is transformed into an all-absorbing monster. . . . The body, devouring voice, is in the end absorbed by it."[53]

Yampolski is particularly struck by a tale entitled "Echoes," written by Isak Dinesen, about a prima donna who loses her voice only to rediscover it in a young village choir boy. In the boy's voice she hears an incarnation, a resurrection of her youth's perfect operatic voice. She is determined to give him voice lessons, in the sense of getting a hold on him, possessing

the boy. Horrifically, her voice lessons result in the boy's facial deformation: "She looked up at him to take in his face, and she did not recognize
it or feel sure that it was the face of the child she had taught. This face
seemed to have been all flattened out, the eyes themselves washed away
and half-disappearing in the flatness, pale like the eyes of a blind person
below his twisted brow. It was the face of a little old woman."[54] The boy's
facial features transform into *hers* to "fit" the production of her voice. It is
the operatic voice itself sculpting its face. We can make a leap of the imagination to envision what Iago's voice *would have done* to the opera's faces
if Zeffirelli had chosen to express these vocal powers in visual terms. But
then perhaps not. Perhaps his "operaticness" is not at all translatable into
the medium of cinema.

The Missing Song

The most far-reaching alteration of Verdi's "narrative of the vocal" in Zeffirelli's *Otello* is the treatment of Desdemona's "Willow Song" and "Ave
Maria" in act 4. In the opera, these scenes are crucial, since we finally hear
Desdemona sing: only here does the soprano sing alone and at length.
The scenes have been meticulously prepared for us by Verdi and Boito's
decision to reserve Desdemona's voice for the very end of the opera. The
opera's vocal narrative is marked by an absence of any meaningful song by
the opera's leading role. Desdemona has no entrance aria, nor any aria at
all until act 4. Thus we expect the "Willow Song" and "Ave Maria" to
take the leap toward what we yearn for from the very first moments of the
opera.

Only Desdemona truly sings in the entire last act. Verdi focuses all attention on these moments by returning to, and using to excess, one of the
traditional (and much criticized) functions of the aria—that of stopping
the action altogether and turning on itself, retreating into song as such.
There are many reasons to think of the "Willow Song" and "Ave Maria"
as the opera's ultimate singing. Only here is Desdemona released from all
that surrounded her and is left to sing by herself in solitude. But what
leads me to claim that this is the culmination of the vocal narrative is not
only the beauty and length of that song. More important, it is the fact that
the song takes place in relation to the ultimate fate of Desdemona, in res-
ignation and knowledge of her impending death.

I call this moment the "death song," well aware of the Schopenhauer-
ian resonance such a term must engender. Death songs, which are placed
before the actual death of the heroine, can be found in many of Verdi's
operas, and they are one of their avant-garde aspects, an aspect seldom included in accounts of the composer's innovations. Such songs involve a

situation in which the heroine, aware of her fate, renounces the world and, through that release, achieves in solitude a self-understanding as well as an understanding of the whole chain of events portrayed in the opera. Violetta's "Addio del passato" is a paradigmatic instance. Through this self-understanding, this "being toward death," the heroine escapes the representations imposed on her all through the opera. In a state of perfect self-absorption, she sings, as it were, *for herself*, in her own voice.

The climactic death song in *Otello* is an extraordinarily complicated instance, as it allows Desdemona to think through her identification with perfect singing. In particular, it raises the question of whether Desdemona can achieve this self-closure in song or whether, as I have argued at length in the first chapters, there is an essentially unattainable dimension to song itself. Indeed, the very fact that song is thematized here in relation to impending death shows that it cannot fully incorporate that very limit. It must signify it through failure.

The death song moment in *Otello* is, like Desdemona's silent appearance in act 1, a dramaturgically idiosyncratic instance. Famously, it involves not one scene but two, not one terminal monologue but a pair, and instead of a unified apotheosis, two disjunctive moments—the scene with the "Willow Song" (which is "performed" for Emilia) and the private aria, the "Ave Maria." The two scenes serve a similar dramatic purpose, but through musically contrasting characteristics. They are conspicuous in how radically their pace and style differ from the entire opera. As a pause in the otherwise fast-moving final act, the death song pair in *Otello* significantly slows real time, as if a contemplative being were finally allowed enough leisure to express her true, performative self. This leisure tilts the balance, establishing an unusual proportion between prolonged stillness and rapid acceleration in act 4, a schism between what occurs prior to and what comes after the death song.

The "Willow Song" and the "Ave Maria" emphasize the irretrievable and unattainable. Yet both scenes are also evocations of the basic functions of song. As a folk melody (a song that has been known for a long time) and a prayer, they provide an imagined past—before song turned operatic—surfacing as memory.

The "Willow Song" is a memory of a song once heard. Its form, strophic verses with three repeated refrains, is emphasized to show its gradual disintegration. Desdemona's song is characterized by interruptions, accelerations, interjections of speech, noises, and outbursts.[55] These are built into the very concept of the part and its relation to the accompaniment. Motifs introduced in the scene's orchestral prelude and their reverberation disrupt the structure of the verses and, ultimately, in the final verse, take over altogether and replace the verse itself. The interruptions gain structural importance at the expense of the verses. Desdemona's song becomes its own self-interruption. Song and its disintegration alternate. In turn, the "Ave Maria" is not quite a song in its recitative-like imitation of prayer. Indeed, in these scenes, the soprano sings "too much," in "too simple" a style, and she sings, as it were, twice. The "Willow Song" is far too interrupted and broken up, ending with a remnant of a cabaletta as an outburst; and the "Ave Maria" is reminiscent of a nonoperatic setting.

Surprisingly, then, the death song defies expectations of exemplifying Verdi's image of Desdemona as the embodiment of perfect song. It does not show that "Desdemona must always sing," it is *not* a scene that shows her to have "a part where the thread, the melodic line, never stops from the first to the last note."[56] We must ask, then, why the death song is the goal of a representation of perfected song in *Otello*.

Desdemona's death song is the expression of the very quest for perfect song—the striving for the unattainable, not its fulfillment. It is here that the soprano's song stands for that which is always already irretrievably lost. Thought in terms of the Orphic structure, the loss of the power of song is attributed to the gaze, but the failure of song must nevertheless be understood as internal to the power of music. Music essentially invokes the success and the failure, the power to resurrect through song, but not the power to retain life: Orphic song crosses between worlds and brings back the dead, but its power to resurrect is also its imminent abandonment.

This understanding must lead us to reconsider Zeffirelli's treatment of the scene. Despite Zeffirelli's statement that the "Willow Song" is too slow and uneventful, an uncinematic halt, and despite the fact that he notoriously omits this very important scene, it is not entirely missing.[57] True, the actual verses in the "Willow Song" are absent. But the meaning I find in the scene does not reside in the verses. Zeffirelli cuts, pastes, relocates, and edits, creating a musical montage. He reorganizes the music in the song's orchestral frame—its prelude and postlude—by pasting together isolated measures and phrases. This rearrangement is then followed by a section from Emilia's and Desdemona's *scena* (dialogic recitative preceding the "Willow Song"), followed again by a skip backward to material from the orchestral prelude. Then Zeffirelli skips forward to an interruption within the final verse of the "Willow Song" (Desdemona hears noise) and ends with the scene's very last gesture, the farewell to Emilia, Desdemona's final outburst.[58] Visually, Zeffirelli's camera jump-cuts between Desdemona's and Otello's preparations for death, introducing yet another dimension of interruption.

Zeffirelli does not overcome the slowness and lack of forward movement in the scene. More important, we hear the scene in the fragments Zeffirelli chooses, as he incorporates what touches on, echoes, surrounds, intrudes on, and interrupts her song. The director's repositioning of fragments of the scene adds to the opera's own set of self-interruptions. In this manner, Zeffirelli provides for the essence of the song without sounding it. He not only sustains the dramatic component embedded in it—the murder looming behind the memory of the song—but also, by keeping the promise of song unfulfilled, holds the meaning of Desdemona's song for the opera. Zeffirelli succeeds in pointing to the impossibility of attaining perfection in song, to the notion that song cannot be sustained, song cannot be unbroken, uninterrupted, never ending. What seems to be Zeffirelli's most provocative omission—the "Willow Song"—in fact preserves the meaning of the opera's scene. The vocal narrative is sustained by not sounding the singing voice.[59]

Verdi's opera is a quest for the voice that inevitably brings about the death of the one who sounds it. Otello's doubts, as well as Iago's proofs, emerge as a mere vehicle for the ultimate attempt to reenact the operatic song. The prima donna dies because she embodies this impossible quest for a perfected voice. Her role, repeating opera's quest, reveals the voice's unattainability. And Zeffirelli's film shows this perfectly.

But there is one last twist to Desdemona's perfect singing. In *Otello*, Verdi's last tragic opera, music associated with Desdemona's final song uncannily *continues to sound* beyond that scene, beyond the murder. This is not quite song, for there is no one there to sing, but something resembling Carolyn Abbate's notion of sonorous form. Perhaps these reverberations are a further dimension of Verdi's conception of Desdemona's endlessness in song, which echoes beyond any locality, beyond any embodiment of character, role, or performance. In that sense, Desdemona's death does not entail the end of song but rather intimates song's immortality.

CHAPTER 4

❧

Falstaff's Free Voice

*F*ALSTAFF IS A singular opera. It is as if Verdi and Boito took tragic opera leftovers, all that was not incorporated in tragedy, and created *Falstaff*.[1] The opera replaces Verdi's repeated tales of the solitary voyage of the virtuous heroine to her death with the route taken by two identical love letters to two wedded women, and the events along this route. This doubling—the replacement of the single tragic heroine with a pair of documents—signals the possibility of error, confusion, and chaos, which are essential to the movement from the tragic to the comic. And there are other replacements or substitutions. Falstaff is a hero, not a heroine; he is fat, drunken, penniless, humorous, witty, still believing in his powers of seduction, aging and clumsy, carrying around an enormous abdomen. Falstaff is serving out the sentence of opera's paradigmatic Don Juan, Mozart's Don Giovanni, as if in some alternative form Don Giovanni had been pardoned and grown old.

The opera *Falstaff* is excessively preoccupied with the main character's body, or strictly speaking, one comic part of that body: much is made of Falstaff's abdomen in every scene, the object of exaggerated and hyperbolized speech. As Falstaff's main physical asset, it functions as the pinnacle of his self-image as a seducer. Tremendous effort is invested in cultivating or comforting this part of Falstaff's body while allowing a range of flexible meanings to attach themselves to it. For instance, that Falstaff's sense of his physical self "sits low" demonstrates the human body's affinity with the animal. Finally, Falstaff's grotesque body breaks boundaries and allies itself with external objects. As a body constantly drinking or drowning, it has an affinity to liquids, its size questioned as the body is squeezed into a basket and searched for in the tiniest drawer. Like the Bakhtinian grotesque body, his spills into and out of other bodies, infiltrated, intruded upon, extended, in flux, and preoccupied with what is interior and exterior to it, with what is beyond its confines.

Understanding Falstaff's body as "limitless" is critical to one's sense of the opera that he inhabits. This does not just mean that Falstaff is both the protagonist and in some sense the "creator" of the drama—that all stems from him, all is acted upon and in relation to him. Falstaff's overdetermined, beastly, desiring, suffering body allows for the transcendence of tragedy. Though this may seem counterintuitive, since tragic plots always end with someone's corporeal death, in operatic tragedy the body is paradoxically irrelevant: it is a container for a divine voice that must be destroyed in the quest for the full revelation or the extreme point of voice. In *Falstaff*, the body in the plot parades its unflattering human attributes—degenerate, elderly, ridiculous. It is to this human condition that the operatic voice must adapt itself.

This ridiculous body is thus the catalyst for emancipating opera from the constraints that the Verdian tragic voice imposes. By depicting Falstaff's body as porous, liquid, and carnally present, Boito and Verdi set up the narrative condition to free voices to migrate and reside in other bodies and to conceive of Falstaff's body as assimilating, replacing, and swallowing the voices of others. The opera thus urges us to consider conditions in which the physicality of the operatic *character* reflects on the meaning of operatic voice, to reconsider in turn the tragic opera conventions according to which the protagonist's pure voice is incorporated and allowed a corporeal existence. *Falstaff* forces us to confront opera "carnally." Seeing *Falstaff*, we may remember the enormous Falstaffian body that may be best at producing the ultimate operatic voice, that of the young and tragic heroine. We are reminded that the all-too material body *is* the condition for the voice.

The opera *Falstaff* thus provides a striking contrast to the bodiless perfected voice longed for in *Otello*. *Falstaff* marks a late shift in Verdi's aesthetics of voice. In the operatic transformation from Shakespearean tragedy into comedy, from *Otello* to *Falstaff*, Verdi experiments with the operatic disembodied voice and with the overdetermined operatic body. *Falstaff* the opera detaches voices from their original bodily source. The result is an opera in which, ultimately, bodies can assume different voices, and "vocal gestures" can appear independent of the body altogether.

But here is perhaps my most radical claim. One expects this fundamental shift in the relation of voice and body or image to be thematized in a filmic rendition of *Falstaff*. If Franco Zeffirelli in his *Otello* struggles with the problem of transposing acoustic vocal perfection into visual analogues, then Götz Friedrich, in his *Falstaff*, must address something altogether different. In *Falstaff*, voice is independent and detachable from its original operatic body; it is no longer pure voice but a voice that can migrate grotesquely from one body to another and acquire meaning through its different voicings. Does this not, however, suggest an also proto-cinematic vision on the part of Verdi and Boito? In confronting the sound-versus-body problem head on, in making Falstaff's body a prominent theme in the text itself, and by letting that fictional body's porousness inspire a strange new "transferable" operatic voice, Verdi and Boito seem almost to have foreseen both the aesthetic potential and the problems connected with synchronization. Moving from *Otello* to *Falstaff* brought opera closer to the conditions of cinema. At a historical moment when cinema was not even in its infancy, Verdi and Boito envisaged what something like dubbing might entail.

Visual Opera

Friedrich's approach, in his film of *Falstaff*, is dependent on an important feature in the opera: the proximity of the musical and the visual, the fact that Verdi and Boito have already set the terms for this relationship and brought it to the foreground. This allows a smooth transition to the medium of film. One of the opera's most conspicuous features is the impression it conveys of being visual, driven by appearance, rather than, as in *Otello*, by a quest for pure voice. *Otello* and *Falstaff* thus present different conceptions of voice and body and show alternative relationships between the vocal and the visual in opera.

Zeffirelli attempts to translate the vocal into the visual. The inherent difficulty of this attempt is made manifest in the impossibility of visually translating the perfect voice, thus resulting in heavy editing of the opera. Friedrich, however, allows the images to overflow and follow the opera's immanent logic of vocal flexibility. This leads to the expansion of operatic space into a visual one. Here the film comments on the opera by adding, not subtracting. There is a surplus "space" added in terms of time, sound, and characters. In *Otello*, the film substitutes visual imagery for a quest for the pure voice; in *Falstaff*, the film enjoys opera's indulgence in the creation of voices and joins opera's delight in the migration of voices, in replaying, equalizing, and detaching the voice from its body altogether by generating more visual material. In *Falstaff*, song becomes movement that constantly points to the visual.

Zeffirelli's cinematic production of *Otello* reveals deep tensions between the two mediums. Friedrich's rendition of *Falstaff*, by contrast, allows one to recognize the possibilities of intimacy between opera and film. One might say that with *Falstaff*, opera is giving birth to cinema, and that Friedrich thus realizes a latent cinematic quality in Verdi and Boito's text.

✎

Falstaff's internal "cinematicness" devolves not just on the "dubbing" effect of migrating voices but on the relationship between the musical and the visual in general. As Edward T. Cone points out, Verdi learns "concentration" in *Falstaff*. Verdi's vocal fragments are pregnant with meaning and do not require the obvious development, sequential repetition, and simple modification utilized in his earlier compositions. The opera thus gives the overall effect of being constantly on the verge of becoming. In other words, Verdi does not lose the earlier melodiousness but maintains the melodic essence in this process of crystallization. Yet, if in earlier compositions the voices "become the irregular surface of a basically simple solid," then in *Falstaff* the distinction between surface and substance is erased.[2] This is due to the opera's most remarkable feature—its rapid forward movement, so fast that music only "happens"; there is no time for music to evolve or develop as it does in Verdi's tragedies. In fact, the only moments of stasis in the opera are those with tragic overtones. As a result, what is heard corresponds closely to what is seen, as though music has no claim of its own divorced from the force of the visual, as though there is no melody not derived from the opera's staging. This feature can be interpreted as a shift from an impression of the aural into that of the visual. Verdi's comedy might, at times, remind us of the effects of an animated film, a cartoon.[3]

The forward thrust in *Falstaff* makes it difficult to locate the music. There are very few operatic signposts, few reflective or contemplative moments in the shape of arias. Instead, there are short motifs, which appear as such, without elaboration or reflection. These motifs recur as quotations, as mimed gestures, or as stage effects. Thus the music in *Falstaff* conveys the impression of being contingent on the visual and without independent "deep-seated," metaphysical meaning.

The short motifs in the form of musical quotations and mimed gestures are related to another important feature: textual repetition and duplication. This feature is shared, to different ends, by tragedy where repetition is fatal. In comedy, however, this structure signals that nothing can be final or fixed: two identical letters addressed to two women, two servants, two weddings (one of which is of two men), two scenes of punishment, the duplication of the lovers' duet dispersed throughout the opera, Ford's jealousy aria prefiguring the horns that will adorn Falstaff's head, and the double counterbalancing of the plots (Falstaff's and the women's counterplot, Ford's and the women's counterplot). We further find the repetition of what is staged in the characters' reports of it, as in Quickly's encounter with Falstaff and her later account given to the women in which she literally quotes her previous encounter. The opera abounds with such repetitions and duplications of key words, phrases, and mimed gestures. They are the opera's musical signature. Through them our hearing is oriented, musical associations are made, and recurring motifs are used as if in quotation marks. Such doubling creates a consciously thin surface melodiousness.

Reinforcing this effect of musical ephemerality are constant interferences, interruptions, intrusions, and changes of direction due to events in the plot. What happens and what is seen keep the music in a constant state of upheaval. In this sense, the music seems driven by appearances and presences, by what is materially there. And in this way, the music, without its traditional operatic "gift" of conveying deepened knowledge and awareness, becomes *equivalent to* vision. Music is thus no longer the metaphysical core of the world beyond appearances; rather, it has become a joyful companion of that world. This unusual feature, unusual especially for Verdi, is related to the opera's carnality—a radical attitude toward representations of the body and the musical realization of the voice(s) that body produces.

To come to terms with Friedrich's interpretation, a detailed glance at the opera's musical peculiarities is in order. I begin with an interpretation of the opera's unique treatment of voices, and, scene by scene, I show Friedrich's corresponding interpretations. I then elaborate on the opera's most complex representation of voices (what I call the between-two-and-three gesture) and demonstrate how the most unusual visual feature of Friedrich's production forms his response to the musical gesture.

Swallowed Voices and Voices Set Free

Falstaff initiates the opera's delight in incorporating another's voice. In the first of these instances (act 1, scene 1), Falstaff imagines his seduction of Alice while simultaneously enacting her desire for him. He isolates the phrase he imagines she sings with a register shift to an artificial soprano range, an octave skip above his vocal range. (In so voicing a woman, he might even be referring jokingly to the castrato, famous for his mysterious powers of love and who, in old age, was known to develop a ridiculous, and effeminate, body, not unlike Falstaff's.) In the thin, high range of the falsetto, he declares *himself* while impersonating (the voice of) Alice: "I am Sir John Falstaff's." Singing "in" Alice's voice is fitting for Falstaff's overall description of her in dismembered parts: "Starry eyes! A swan's neck! Her lips? A flower! A laughing flower" (act 1, scene 1). It is as though her voice is one other body fragment that can be detached. Falstaff next performs Meg, the second woman who "desires" him. Falstaff sings at the very top of his range. Though not indicated as falsetto, it is an analogous vocal gesture. Voicing Meg, he reflects on his prime and sings about his glorious past.

These impersonations of women can be understood in various ways. Roger Parker discusses the first as one of "two moments in which one character assumes another's voice" and in which "a narrative culminates in a moment of *mimesis*."[4] For Parker, in such moments, Falstaff does not, as it were, "become" the women but only imitates them.[5] Sander Gilman argues that on the whole Falstaff is masking his true vocal range. In the buffa tradition, such a role would call for a comic basso rather than Falstaff's baritone. The women, Gilman claims, are not fooled by him: "they hear the 'basso' under his baritone voice."[6] Along these lines, Falstaff's falsetto would be an extension of his performance skills that further assist in masking his "true" voice. Elizabeth Wood sees in the unnatural male falsetto a type of transsexualism and a "sonic cross-dressing." Wood calls this phenomenon Sapphonic, indicating a condition in which sex is "not properly housed in the body" and is neither male nor female.[7]

Catherine Clément, arguing along similar lines, explicitly refers to the operatic Falstaff. Clément sees in him a merging of genders, a figure of transgression and marginality that is repeatedly on the verge of becoming. Falstaff is a type of operatic hero who "partake[s] in femininity," as does Rigoletto, the hunchback, or the black-skinned Otello. But, significantly, Falstaff is also "beyond the limits of being merely one of the two sexes." Clément sees such operatic images of men partaking of femininity as tricksters who "divert dogged, straightforward thought and break it into so many splinters that all placid oppositions and shortsighted classifications disappear. In their place appears a jubilant and perverse disorder, the opening up of thought, the impossibility of closing or confining. These beings set free, give birth, and wander. Without them the limits of the world would always be the same."[8] Here I elaborate on an insight by Clément that relates Falstaff's image of blurred gender to images of disorder and freedom. As I show, Falstaff is neither miming nor representing others, but rather, as Clément intimates, he is "repeatedly on the verge" of *becoming* another.

How would a director attuned to what happens musically show these moments of becoming? How would Falstaff's voicing of the women be represented in film? Friedrich shows the two duplicated moments in which Falstaff is voicing women as moments in which he is simultaneously indulging in his *own* image: as Falstaff prepares to voice Alice, he rises from his chair, and a camera shot taken from below enlarges his lower body. A grotesque image of a belly, an exaggerated hand movement, and a tiny head accompany "her" voice. The shot then cuts to his onstage audience's reaction. Pistola punctuates Falstaff's words with an uncontrolled spitting of wine. When Falstaff swallows an imaginary voice, Pistola spits out as if choking on that incorporation. Falstaff's vocal introjection is Pistola's rejection (earlier in the same scene, Pistola's long red nose is praised as being indispensable for Falstaff's spatial orientation, suggesting that Falstaff's senses can reside beyond his bodily confines just as his voice can become a woman's). When Falstaff voices Meg, the film shows him turning around and dancing ballerina-like, fully inspecting his blurred image in a mirror held up by Pistola. It is as if the blurry mirror allows us to imagine the body of Falstaff changing shape as it swallows that other voice. And, in the following act, when Quickly repeats the women's words to Falstaff, the same mirror is used to conflate the bodies of Quickly and Falstaff, thus producing a mirage of very close bodies merging before an attempted kiss by Falstaff causes Quickly's flight "out" of their converged reflection in the mirror.

These filmic images suggest that Falstaff incorporates Alice and Meg within himself, his belly pregnant with the premonition of successful seductions. In Friedrich's film, Falstaff fully enjoys his visual and acoustical extensions. He lovingly watches himself in the mirror as he devours the women's voices. They become part of him as he, and we, inspect the voices' new habitat *in* Falstaff's body.

The film lingers on the operatic moment of voice-body disjunction. It does not attempt to anchor the voice in an "original" body. When a foreign voice (Alice's) emanates from Falstaff's body, the film employs the returned reflection (the mirror) as a doubling of the body that allows the hero to become, for a flash, that juxtaposition of many voices in one body. In that moment, the film emphasizes the opera's loosening of the traditional, or tragic, voice-body union. We are able to "see in the mirror" the body of Falstaff "becoming" Alice, to envision a transformation of the body as a result of the other voice migrating into it. A new operatic voice has been constructed. At that moment the plasticity of the body is most opposed to the rigidity of the laws of tragedy that in the case of Desdemona make every transgression fatal.

There are two other, even more complex, moments in the opera which portray the transfer of voices. The first occurs during Ford/Fontana's visit to Falstaff; the other, during Falstaff's visit to Alice. In both instances, Falstaff is singing a song that belongs to another in the network of floating vocal gestures. In both cases, we can no longer be certain about the significance of the voices hosted as such by other bodies.

In act 2, scene 1, Ford (Alice's husband) disguises himself as Fontana, an unsuccessful suitor of Alice. Fontana, to tempt Falstaff into revealing *his* seduction plans, tells Falstaff of his own unrequited love for Alice. Drawing on the earlier staging, Friedrich has Fontana rise from his chair—as did Falstaff when he "became" a woman—and sing in falsetto. Fontana, however, is not voicing Alice (by now we have heard her; though to complicate things, her voice was predominantly *her voicing* of Falstaff). Rather, Fontana is imitating *Falstaff's voicing of Alice*. This might be what guides Friedrich's interpretation of the scene, as he shows Falstaff distracted and uninterested in Fontana's performance. Fontana cannot be voicing the true Alice since, for Falstaff, she is already *inside his body*.

Fontana continues: "sitting on the stairs [I was] singing my madrigal." To this, Fontana sings a Falstaffian (much too) long trill that causes him to lose his breath. Friedrich shows us a close-up of Fontana out of breath and, at the same time, Falstaff opening his mouth as though robbing the

Figures 4.1–4.2. Friedrich's film of Verdi's *Falstaff* (1979). Filmic images suggest that Falstaff incorporates Alice and Meg within himself.

Figure 4.1. Falstaff's belly pregnant with the premonition of successful seductions

Figure 4.2. Falstaff voicing Meg. The blurry mirror allows us to imagine the body of Falstaff changing shape as it swallows that other voice.

Example 4.1. *Falstaff,* act 2, scene 1. Fontana sings a Falstaffian (much too) long trill. Falstaff, as it were, picks up on the cue—the Falstaffian trill in Fontana's voice—to sing the madrigal in place of Fontana.

song out of Fontana's breathlessness. Falstaff, as it were, picks up on the cue—the Falstaffian trill in Fontana's voice—to sing the madrigal in place of Fontana, to take it out of his mouth (see ex. 4.1).[9]

Fontana's breathlessness leads into Falstaff's song—a song that Falstaff seems to inhale and swallow.[10] It is indeed curious how Falstaff *knows* Fontana's madrigal even before the latter has *begun* singing. But further, the musicality of the madrigal (though not the music itself) spills over beyond the confines of the *musica en scena* to accompany the *conversation* about the effects of the madrigal. In other words, the setting of the spoken exchange is quite surprisingly a musical variation on the madrigal's music instead of a plain recitative. The responsorial style of the madrigal influences even their spoken exchange, which interrupts the song. (As Fontana says, "I've paid a fortune to learn this madrigal," and Falstaff replies, "Such is the poor lover's fatal destiny.") Thus the song that was "bought" by Fontana and "taken over" by Falstaff is finally shared by them, freely floating into the impersonal space of the opera. In this opera, nothing is owned, everything floats from one body to another—even voices and music. Two things, then, are happening in the Falstaff-Fontana encounter: Falstaff is singing Fontana's song, or, put another way, Falstaff becomes Fontana as he sings his song, and the music of the madrigal in the diegesis infuses the nondiegetic space. In other words, the music of the madrigal does not belong either to the body that intended to emit it or to the body who takes it over, or even to a clearly framed aural space in the opera.[11]

Falstaff enables such dislocation of voice again in act 2, scene 2, during his amorous visit to Alice. Led to believe that Alice is reciprocating his love, Falstaff, all dressed up with a flower in hand and high hopes in his heart, pays Alice a visit. In Friedrich's film, Alice faces the audience playing the lute (orchestral music is followed by solo guitar) as Falstaff enters and sings to *her* accompaniment. An editorial cut back to Alice, now turning her back to us, follows the music, which is heard continuously, thus helping to smooth out (or even disregard) this visual editing (common in

Figure 4.3. Friedrich's film of Verdi's *Falstaff* (1979). Friedrich shows us Fontana out of breath and, at the same time, Falstaff opening his mouth as though stealing the song from Fontana's breathlessness.

the employment of music in mainstream film, in which the music grants continuity to the disjointed images projected on-screen). The lute is decorated with ribbons matching Falstaff's, rather than Alice's, costume. Falstaff sings only one line of text before he is interrupted by Alice, who terminates her playing and turns to face him. When she turns around, the film shows a surprised expression on her face. She is clearly surprised by what she *sees*, not by the *voice* she has heard. Alice is astonished by the body *not* fitting, not synchronized with, the singing voice. We, though, are astonished by what we have *heard*: both by the fact that Alice *knows* the accompaniment of an erotic serenade she is *about* to be wooed by, and by the fact that Falstaff once again knows another's song. Or perhaps we are amazed by the revelation that Falstaff is so musical, that he is able to improvise a wooing song from absolutely anything a woman might have chosen to play. Yet, what is most astonishing is that this false encounter is so well synchronized—her music to his text and her orchestral-sounding lute to his voice. We are led to think it is not a false encounter after all—as if the music needed only *them* as an excuse to play itself out.

Thus emphasizing that music seems to seek out its vessels means fundamentally, radically redefining the relation between performers and works, in which a commonsense "reality"—performers are alive and conscious, and works are dead "texts" that they are playing—is imagined in inversion. This was the radical step taken by Carolyn Abbate, who writes, "perhaps musical pieces seek to manifest themselves repeatedly in the world and propel us into motion at their whim, whenever we are required for their purposes."[12] Abbate calls this the "dead-object problem" in music—musical performance involves the seeming reanimation or resurrection, even creation, of human life and human subjectivity, with human bodies appearing lifeless until the moment music gets hold of them.

A parallel to Falstaff's and Alice's astonishing animation by music is found in act 3, scene 1, where Falstaff reads the letter sent by Alice about an old wives' tale. The tale is meant to tempt him into dressing up as a stag for the amorous encounter. Quickly begins to narrate the tale to Falstaff as they leave the stage. When we can no longer hear or see her, the narration is *continued* by Alice, whom we are now able to both hear and see. The tale shifts bodies while the music remains the same with only a difference in vocal timbre. It is as though the voice telling the tale wants to be seen and, to sustain vision, does not mind migrating to another body and being heard mediated by another voice.

Migrating Voices and Voices Set Free

When, in act 1, scene 2, the action is transported to the women's quarters, we encounter Alice and Meg, each reading aloud Falstaff's love letter addressed to the other: Meg reads the letter addressed to Alice, and Alice reads the one addressed to Meg. Apart from the addressees, the letters are identical and are set musically in repeating phrases as one continuous letter delivered in alternating phrases between the women. One person writes two letters, which, by repetition, are now merged into one. Falstaff is present through his words, which are sung in the first person, as well as in the duplicated and combined reading aloud that merges the two back into an original one. The letter reading is musically distinctive from the surrounding vocal style. Tonality, tempo, and orchestration (a move from C major to A major, a slowing down of tempo, a solo English horn) mark it as an enactment. It is a *performance* of "Falstaff": they sing his music and mimic his presence.

The music accompanying the reading of the letters is familiar—a kind of music repeatedly heard in Verdi's death songs, such as Desdemona's "Willow Song" in *Otello*. Typically, this music is a slow, lyrical melody played by a solo English horn (see ex. 4.2). This is not just an ironic stroke. In this (almost sole) instance where Verdi does *not* kill his heroine (but happily marries her), he reminds us of all the deaths in his other works. The musical past of Verdi's tragic operas erupts in a grotesque mismatch between a sound associated with undone women and a conjured image of Falstaff's lust. (This gesture—the eruption of music in the style of Verdi's death scenes—occurs momentarily again as Nannetta sings of her despair at her father's marriage plans. This is indeed the moment in *Falstaff* in which there is a threat that Nannetta *will* suffer those operatic women's destinies.)

As the letter-reading scene progresses, the performance of Falstaff's words increasingly becomes a bodily identification: the trill identifying Falstaff's laughter in *his* description of the women is now internalized by the women when *their* voices sound him. The trill in their voices accompanies the women's fantasy of his body expanding until—when they burst into laughter—his belly explodes (see ex. 4.3).

The trill is Falstaff's musical signature. It is heard repeatedly: at the beginning, just before Falstaff invents a voice for Meg; in the "Honor" scene, when Falstaff sings of his old age (as though the trill were emerging from his cup of wine, invading the world as the wine floating into his body comforts him); in the scene in the forest when Falstaff is dressed as a stag; and so on.[13] A trill is a musical gesture of two notes in the space of one; it brings to the fore musical space itself. It draws attention to the motion occurring between two closely spaced notes and forms a parallel to the way the opera on the whole portrays, as we will see, the tricky space and the passage of time "between two and three."

For the closure of the letter-reading scene, the singing women join the singing men in an octet (expanded further by the punctuation of the

Example 4.2. The sound of women's deaths: a. *Falstaff,* act 1, scene 2, "letter-reading" scene, b. *Otello,* act 4, scene 1, "Willow Song"

lovers' interrupted duet). The women, however, are *again* singing Falstaff's words to the exact same music, as if it has become theirs. They even change the pronouns so that Alice adopts the words in the first person. She sings, "But *my* face shall shine upon *him*,"[14] where Falstaff's letter (also sung by Alice) read, "*Your* face will shine upon *me*."[15]

Why are the women singing Falstaff's letters again? They cannot be *rereading* the letters, nor have they memorized his words. So why is Falstaff's ghost voice still, or again, in theirs? How can the repetition of the letters' words be understood? It cannot be explained by adhering to a compositional technique of closure—ending the scene with repeated material—since the women have already sung a long stretch of another text (they part company, each describing what she will do to Falstaff). Though *Falstaff* is an opera that constantly cadences, the repetition of these lines is not an outcome of formal closure. Thus there is no clear explanation for returning once again to these specific lines at this point. Perhaps what happens is that the voices are "set free," and all of the operatic space is invaded by or comes to sing Falstaff's words. Falstaff, present everywhere and all the time, can sing through anything in the opera.

The diegesis once again has come to include the nondiegetic, or, I would argue, the entire aural/acoustical space of the opera has become diegetic; it has become a space representing a performance of singing. The women—and this is central to my understanding of the opera—are under the influence of the opera's "behavior" as a whole. The women voice Falstaff, fitting his trill into a quartet, squeezing it until it explodes. They mold themselves into the Falstaffian tongue; they are taken over not by Falstaff the fat hero but by *Falstaff* the opera.[16]

Example 4.3. Falstaff, act 1, scene 2. Women voicing Falstaff's trill. The trill in their voices accompanies the women's fantasy of his body expanding in size until—when they burst into laughter—his belly explodes.

Example 4.3. (cont.)

It is difficult for a film of *Falstaff* to *show* this migration of voices. Indeed, this scene in Friedrich's film comes across as an anxious response to setting music free. In the film, the women *destroy* Falstaff's words by setting fire to the letters. It is as if Falstaff's voice—which he inscribed in writing and they sang—can be extinguished. But as we will see, the end of the opera will show the failure of the ultimate attempt of all who surround Falstaff to rid him of his deviant voice. I have suggested how Friedrich enables the illusion born of a voice that is swallowed, a phenomenon in which a character, by imitating another's voice or singing someone else's song, becomes that other character and, as it were, swallows him. But how would Friedrich represent voices that "migrate" from one character to another? I call "migrating voices" those voices or songs that migrate into someone else's body, which might then leave the body and float independently in the opera's aural space as though the entire opera has become the diegetic space.[17] Let me briefly discuss two examples of migrating voices.

The idea of a voice migrating and entering a foreign body is a recurrent theme in cartoons, in films based on cartoon characters, in horror films, and in science fiction movies. Take, for instance, the movie *Scooby Doo* (2002) (the filmed version of the famous cartoon series). At a certain point in the group's adventures, their souls are drained out of them and put in a simmering cauldron with other souls. When these souls are eventually freed, each soul flies in search of its proper body (which behaves like a possessed monster without it). But at first the souls find a dwelling for themselves in the *wrong* bodies. And here lies the importance of the example for thinking about the staging of *Falstaff*'s migrating voices. *Scooby Doo* represents a combination of the soul and the wrong body by having the voice stand for the soul. The voice, like the soul, controls the body. For instance, the voice of Shaggy (who eats his dog's food, is always hungry and scared of everything) residing in the body of Velma (the calculating brain of the group) controls the body it resides in and makes it behave in accordance with Shaggy's *voice* (and in disaccord with what the body actually looks like). The result is an awkward (and funny) disjunction between the dictates of the body and those of the voice, or between what the voice sounds like and what the body looks like. The outcome is that the voice coerces the body into representing it. This is not so far removed from the world of *Falstaff*—which, as I mentioned earlier, shares features with the world of the cartoon. In the opera, voices shift in and out of bodies. Friedrich, however, as we will see, does not choose the *Scooby Doo* option.

Let us turn for a moment to Wagner, since his use of leitmotifs raises issues similar to those raised by Verdi's migrating voices. The question is how a filmic production would *represent* its awareness of this kind of operatic behavior, how a director would visualize (if at all) the web of leitmotifs. The 1987 production of Wagner's *Ring* directed by Nicholas Lehnhoff in Munich provides an extreme example. In this production, the director staged the leitmotifs as independent bodily movements. Often, when leitmotifs were heard, matching movements would be made even though they were (visually) independent from any other representation onstage.[18] Syberberg's film of *Parsifal* is yet another extreme example. This production abounds in visual symbols and imagery that are perhaps inspired by, or analogous to, the technique of leitmotifs, but not in a one-to-one correspondence as in Lehnhoff's staging. Friedrich's solution to the free voices of *Falstaff* is closer to Syberberg's solution than to Lehnhoff's. Friedrich does not employ a one-to-one correspondence to the music but rather shows an awareness of the phenomenon by adding (though much more modestly than Syberberg) visual imagery.

Between Twos and Threes

In *Falstaff* the most far reaching migration of a musical gesture that Friedrich would have to tackle is what I call the between-two-and-three gesture. Before outlining his filmic solution, I interpret in some detail the phenomenon in the opera itself.

Falstaff hands out two letters to Pistola and Bardolfo: "due lettere." These are two identical love letters that Falstaff has written to two wedded women. Of course he does not intend for the women to know of each other's letter. Nevertheless, his hope for an amorous relation between two people is really a threesome, or between two and three. Falstaff thus originates the opera's play on twos and threes; it is he who initiates the fantasies occupying the space between two and three as a time of lust and amorous encounters. The musical gesture "dalle due alle tre" (from two o'clock until three) is implanted by Quickly to seduce Falstaff into a false amorous encounter with both Alice and Meg. The letters' revelation of his appetite for two women, "un paio in tre" (a pair of three lovers), metamorphoses into a distinct musico-textual motif (see ex. 4.4).[19] Falstaff's expectations for a couple composed of three is translated in Quickly's message into the time frame in which the women's scheme for punishing

Example 4.4. The between-two-and-three gesture

Dal - le due al - le   tre.

Falstaff will take place. It is the time of day: Alice is free between two and three, Meg is seldom free, even between two and three. Falstaff both can and cannot visit the two women between two and three. The outcome of "un paio in tre"—the impossible space of two-turned-three—will come to structure the entire opera.

Dramatically, the play on twos and threes begins with Falstaff and the two women, continues with the events between two and three in the afternoon, and ends with two marriages in which not two women and two men, but rather one woman and three men are "married," and with three (rather than two) men ultimately duped.[20] Indeed, the dramatic idea has found a musical image in the gesture between-two-and-three. This gesture floats, surfacing in different voices. It neither gains new meanings nor roots itself but allows the voice greater independence. Not only do voices leave their body of origin, but they also detach from any body altogether and become orchestral. The orchestra now serves as a source for virtual bodies, or, put differently, the opera's space on the whole has become these voices' body. Abbate has written on this phenomenon vis-à-vis Wagner and Richard Strauss, and to identify it in *Falstaff* is not just to reinforce, again, a sense that the opera is an aesthetic "response" to Wagnerian opera. Abbate notes the potential uncanniness of opera's aural space when the orchestra acts neither as commentator on the drama nor as an entity that knows more than the bodies onstage but as one of the protagonists among others. The orchestra reiterates, echoes, and repeats voices back to the characters: "*Das Rheingold*'s motives originate (with rare exceptions) in the singing voices. Repetitions of these voices in the orchestra are not comments on the action but iconic representations of human voice, of *singing per se* . . . collective vocal chords that are set humming to sounds just sung."[21]

If, in *Falstaff*, the opera itself is such a body, tremendous pressure is put on the visual. In other words, if the opera's orchestra can sound like a Quickly, a Quickly can sound like a Falstaff, and a Falstaff can sound like an Alice, how do we interpret the fact that we don't see a Quickly, a Falstaff, or an Alice when we hear one?

This almost seems like a parody of Wagnerian technique. The musical content of the between-two-and-three gesture—short, swift, emphasizing rhythm rather than harmony—is far removed from anything Wagner would employ as leitmotif. The between-two-and-three gesture does not acquire meaning; nor does it deepen our understanding of what happens in the libretto. Rather, it gives the impression of being a mere repetition that in each reiteration carries identical meaning as though it were a quote. Take, for instance, Falstaff's reaction to Quickly's message. It is signaled by his exact repetition of the between-two-and-three gesture. The success of the women's plan depends on the possibility of the between-two-and-three gesture in Quickly's voice to migrate and implant it-self in Falstaff—as his.

What follows in act 2, scene 1, of the opera is more radical, since there the between-two-and-three gesture "refuses" to reside in a body. In this scene, Ford, disguised as Fontana and believing that Falstaff is about to seduce his wife, sings an aria foreign to the comic world of *Falstaff*—one that belongs to the sound world of Verdi's tragic opera.[22] Conventionally, a scene such as this would be musically self-contained and sealed off both from the rest of the opera and from the possibility of motifs migrating from other bodies in the opera. Thus, Ford, a truly jealous husband and, as such, a tragic figure (at least when one is reminded of his predecessor Otello), cannot contain in his song a foreign, free-floating voice. The gesture would be out of place in such a tragic island within the opera. Nevertheless, we can find a hint of it in the reiteration of its rhythm and in traces of its melodic contour in the orchestra.[23] This shows the power of such floating gestures to break into tragic isolation.

In the act 2 finale, Falstaff is duped into believing that the women reciprocate his advances. As the women set the stage for their performance of the amorous encounter, their power over the situation manifests itself through the range, musical flexibility, and theatricalization of the between-two-and-three musical gesture. They reiterate, develop, transpose, vary, and intensify it, until finally it is that time of day: it is between two and three o'clock. The women's performance of false desire ends abruptly when Ford (the jealous husband) breaks in. The women hide Falstaff first behind a screen, then in the laundry basket. Unbeknownst to everyone, the lovers, Fenton and Nannetta, take Falstaff's place behind the screen.[24] Ford conducts a hunt in which Falstaff is called by various animal names. Envisioning him as a wild pig, a dog, and a mouse, the "hunters" are able to detect Falstaff by his trail, his scent. Falstaff is hunted down to be crushed, smashed, smoked out. Hunting this animal known to be of enormous proportions, Ford searches every possible hideout, even the tiniest table drawer. Throughout this scene of riotous noise and chaos, a breathless Falstaff remains hidden, suffocating in the laundry basket. All believe Falstaff is discovered when kisses are heard from behind the screen. The conductor of the hunt exclaims that to reveal Falstaff, silence is required; the lovers, completely oblivious to what is going on around them, sing that their love has no ears for noise. The hunters put their ears to the screen and count: one, two, three. The count from one to three becomes the silent climax of the chaos. Hunting Falstaff culminates in the between-two-and-three gesture stripped of its pitches altogether. The gesture between-two-and-three carves out for itself a silent sphere within the operatic riot (see ex. 4.5).

Falstaff has been seemingly heard (the kisses) but not seen (the kisses

Example 4.5. *Falstaff,* act 2, scene 2. The count from one to three. The gesture between-two-and-three carves out for itself a silent sphere within the operatic riot.

are those of the young lovers).[25] The count from one to three—the *coup de théâtre* exposing not his presence but his absence behind the screen—points to the discrepancy between an acoustical and a visual Falstaff. Falstaff, so to speak, performs a Houdinian disappearance. For a flash, the between-two-and-three musical gesture exhibits its power over the visual, acting as if it magically made Falstaff disappear from behind the screen. As a magician in a magic show, the between-two-and-three gesture announces: "it *is* Falstaff, and yet it is *not*."

〰

"Dalle due alle tre" is overdetermined, excessive—it can voice itself, migrate, implant itself, momentarily transform identities, and be independent of character or body; it can enact silence and mask itself as an image or as a false image. Not only does this gesture shatter our sense of an operatic being in voice, it also shows how the visual can arise out of the vocal. What does Friedrich do in his film of *Falstaff*? He uses neither the *Scooby Doo* solution (the voice coercing the foreign body) nor Lehnhoff's solution (an independent visual account for the musical), and not even Syberberg's solution (an overflow of visual imagery). My interpretative claim is that Friedrich's response to this musical phenomenon in *Falstaff* is radical: he shows that the visual can arise out of the vocal but also the other way around, that music and the vocal can arise out of the visual. His response to the between-two-and-three musical gesture is within the visual domain, but not by way of attempting in any way to visualize the gestures; rather he shows that the visual space that delimits the opera as a whole can also come into play in this movement of the musical.

Visualizing Silent Voices

Friedrich adds visual scenes rather than subtracting musical ones. If Zeffirelli's most provocative change in *Otello* was cutting out nearly all of the "Willow Song," then Friedrich's most provocative move is adding a prelude as well as visual interludes between the scenes of *Falstaff*. These interludes are the most striking feature in Friedrich's film of *Falstaff*. The film inserts silent or nearly silent "visual space" between the opera's "musical space."[26] This in-between nature of the visual interludes mirrors the in-between-two-and-three of the musical gesture. The absence of editing, reordering, or cuts in the operatic scenes renders the acoustical and visual spaces *surrounding* them negotiable.

In Friedrich's production, the camera is in the service of theatricality rather than enhancing cinematic effects. We are not quite certain whether this is a cinematic opera or a technically sophisticated relay of a staged production.[27] Friedrich raises doubts about his film's "cinematicness," and Zeffirelli, as we remember, parades it. With Zeffirelli, we never doubt the medium. But the inserted interludes in Friedrich's production attest to the fact that his *Falstaff* cannot be, in its entirety, a relay. The inserted material could have been filmed only separately.[28] Friedrich's *Falstaff* gives a theatrical impression, but this theatricality is problematized by the essentially cinematic interludes.

The interludes are silent, with occasional noises emanating from the images (objects and actions) on-screen. What is curious about these scenes is that they are not put in for any obvious cinematic reasons and are redundant in terms of the narrative. Take, for instance, the film's visual interlude between the end of act 1 and the beginning of act 2 in which Quickly is seen on her way to Falstaff's lodging to deliver the women's replies. In the opera, the first act ends with the women's planned scheme, and the second act begins with Quickly's visit to Falstaff. There are no gaps in the opera's narrative. In fact, the interludes occur where, in relays, a heading might be inserted such as "act 2, scene 1" before the music of the next scene starts. Why, though, would Friedrich's film, as it were, expand on this in-between space? What are the redundant visual narratives doing to the opera on film?[29] Why insert voiceless and musicless interludes?

The interludes reflect Friedrich's thematization of possible moves from the musical to the visual and from the visual to the musical. In the interludes, Friedrich shows us how the two spheres transform into one another, how they deliver as well as mask one another. Friedrich shows how music can be perceived as a gradation of the visual, how it can make images move, be born from an image, or even assume vision. Images can reveal music's silence, and music, in turn, can make an image disappear. It is in this wealth of phenomena that I locate Friedrich's response to the opera's unique voices and bodies.

Friedrich's film begins with long, silent images: the handwritten inscription "Giuseppe Verdi," then "Falstaff"; a blank background that gives the sense of the materiality of vellum; a pencil sketch of a face. The inscription "G. Verdi" is, in fact, the composer's signature. And yet the same handwriting recurs for the title of the opera. It also, however, looks like Falstaff's signature in the letters he sends to the two women. "G. Verdi," the composer's signature, is, in fact, revealed to be Falstaff's—the character signing his own creation.

The lines drawn within the face outline a beauty mask, the face of the singer/character who will emerge out of this two-dimensional sketch. The drawing is fleshed out in the face of the film's Falstaff. The living face does not match precisely the lines of the drawing from which it emerges. The face stares directly at us. Over the face's close-up the names of the cast are rolled. Falstaff is motionless as long as the credits are rolled over, written onto him. The close-up of Falstaff's face serves as a screen for *all* credits; the names of singers and their corresponding roles are projected on that one image, showing that he can hold them all within himself. No music is heard. The face seems to be a still photo. But really it is a face trying not to move. Suddenly a blink escapes him. Falstaff brings a sealed letter to his mouth, and the camera zooms out. He kisses the sealed envelope. The onset of the music is not synchronized with the image's movement; rather it begins somewhere on the letter's route to Falstaff's kissing mouth. (The emphasis on the mouth partakes in Falstaff's grotesque imagery of incorporation. The mouth, as Bakhtin writes, is where "man tastes the world, introduces it into his body, makes it part of himself.")[30]

Several themes figure in this invented filmic prelude: an inanimate image, a drawing, metamorphoses into the impression of a still photograph that, in turn, moves on to become a cinematic image. In "turning on the music," sound becomes a further gradation in that visual continuum. Later, the image will sing, acquiring a fuller audiovisual depth. Put differently, we first invent the art of painting, then photography, then the moving image known as silent cinema. Finally, the voice is introduced to lend a simile of interiority to the characters on-screen. The visual prelude is a brief genealogy of the art of cinema. The onset of the operatic music marks the move of silent cinema to the possibilities opened by the introduction of the human voice. The images in the prelude suggest a primal narrative. I do not just mean that it *must* be the case that Falstaff had already written the letters before the opera began, since there is no time for him during the opera to actually *compose* them. Rather, we should think of the filmic prelude as one that narrates a genesis. The materiality of the flesh shown in the close-up of the face, ridiculed by the feminine beauty mask as well as the focus on the grotesque mouth, all bear upon the idea of a birth of voice. The prelude is narrating *the origination of voice*.

In the first visual interlude following act 1, scene 1, the image-sound dyad introduced in the visual prelude is reversed. Act 1, scene 1, ends with a gigantic musicalized noise. Falstaff is chasing Pistola and Bardolfo with a broom. The chase continues into the space of the interlude. The acoustical remnant of the chase is the sound of Falstaff's heavy breathing as he collapses, breathless, to the ground. Music and voice are no longer born out of the image of Falstaff, but diegetic sound (breathing) marks the end of operatic music and the onset of the sphere of musicless images, a sphere in which images have sounds, not operatic voices.

The interlude begins, in fact, as a *visual extension* of the sounds of the opera. The sound of music giving the impression of noise becomes the sound of breathing. The interlude will then expand on this sound and include animate and inanimate diegetic sounds (such as footsteps, knocks on doors, water, a rooster calling, and kisses and noises indicating changes

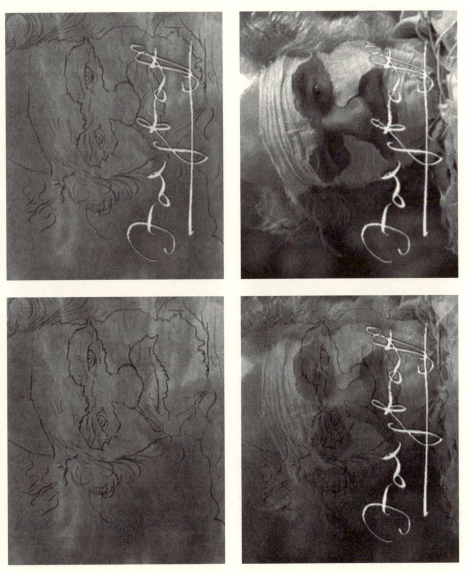

Figure 4.4. Friedrich's film of Verdi's *Falstaff* (1979). The film director adds a filmic prelude narrating the origination of voice.

in location). The characters are constantly moving between locations; their fast pace is achieved without any accompanying music.

The interlude following it introduces yet another possible relationship between operatic music and the image: the music of the opera begins in the midst of the visual interlude. Music is now part of the visual images that were invented in the interlude. Only the vocal parts are still excluded, their reappearance marking the end of each interlude. The interlude to act 2 shows us the way to Falstaff's lodging. We peep into his lodging through a broken window and see him in miniature form. The miniature shot of the fat knight partakes in the film's problematization of the relation of Falstaff's body to visual space: the too-close facial close-up in the visual prelude that is exaggerated by the silent soundtrack, the shot taken from below deforming his body proportions at the moment he is voicing another, and here the caged Falstaff, like an animal sqeezed in an enclosed frame.[31] A cut to the inside of Falstaff's lodging finds Falstaff looking at himself in a small mirror held up for him by an always silent child. Music then cuts into the interlude's narrative, bringing us closer to Falstaff and his care of himself. The music, as it were, enters the house with us and introduces us to the view of Falstaff from within the house. He is making himself pretty, putting on a wig to cover his baldness. He looks ridiculous—the wig is in a color different from the rest of his hair. The child laughs. Falstaff sticks out his tongue at him. We cannot see the reflection in the small mirror; we are not led to see what Falstaff sees in his reflection (in act 1, his reflection carried Alice's voice). We don't know why Falstaff needs music to see himself in the mirror. When we (together with Quickly and the music) enter the house, Falstaff puts down the mirror.

Nearly inaudibly, Friedrich claims more and more *acoustical* space for his visual interludes. More and more, the *visuality* of the interludes is what glues together the endings and the beginnings of the *musical* scenes. The interludes become the continuation of the opera in images. As the music stops and resumes, the images function the way that *music* functions in film or the way that a secondary stratum functions in a compound medium.

The silent interlude that follows introduces the diegetic laughter of the women (a sound belonging to the acoustic sphere of the interludes), yet *together* with the onset of the opera's music. (What is further striking about the film's addition of real laughter, both audible and inaudible, is that it points to the *opera*'s several representations of musicalized laughter.) No longer separate, the diegetic "noise" now spills into the space earlier reserved for music. The visuality of the interludes with its diegetic noise not only prepares for the visuality of the opera but also spills into and mixes with it, as though becoming the opera.

So far I have discussed visual insertions within acts 1 and 2. The interlude preceding act 3 employs images established in previous interludes and is far more extreme in its implications. Falstaff emerges from the water after being thrown into it with the basket of dirty laundry. The interlude shows this emergence. In other words, the interlude's locale is the river we are familiar with from earlier interludes and operatic scenes. We recognize it as the women's quarters. Yet the interlude shows Falstaff calling *his* housekeeper. Warm wine is swiftly brought to him from *his* lodging, that is, from the inn, a place with which we are also familiar. There is no more distance between the women's lodging and Falstaff's lodging. They have now been masterfully converged. But that is not all. The *same* location serves as Cajus's lodging, and, on the second floor, in *her home*, Nannetta is said to be practicing her song of the fairies as Falstaff emerges from the side of the house to collect his wet clothes. They *all* suddenly reside in one and the same place. The different spaces of the opera have been merged into one. In the first two acts, Friedrich has familiarized us with the locations. He has carefully distinguished the two main locations throughout the opera—the women's and Falstaff's—and emphasized the spatial distance between the locations (through the sound of steps and the sight of Quickly, Ford, Pistola, Bardolfo, and Falstaff's feet going from one location to another). The onset of the act 3 prelude thus brings about the surprise of their collapse. It provides a cinematic interpretation of the merging of bodies, or of Falstaff's incorporation of voices.

The spatial collapse, what I call the film's visual delusion, is explained in relation to the music in Friedrich's final interlude. By amplifying the sonic environment, it introduces an acoustical delusion that balances the earlier visual delusion. The interlude shows the preparations for the performance of the fairy tale. We see and hear women, men, and children as they laugh, are merely being noisy, and indistinctly speak. The diegetic soundtrack for the final interlude is composed of human voices and howls of invisible animals. Significantly, these noises in the otherwise silent interlude serve Friedrich: when the same images return (now within the space of the opera), they will delude our senses and lure us into believing in noise's power to represent *operatic silence*. The interlude's conditioning of *noise* assists the opera in imagining *silence* within itself. It is the construction of the visual delusion in the interlude (the collapse of space) that enabled the acoustical delusion (the noisy silence) within the opera itself.[32]

To Exorcise and to Vanish

Let us return for a moment to the opera and show how Friedrich's conception of the visual interludes form his response to the opera's representation of vocal deviance. The end of the opera brings all the voices together and provides an understanding of what all the characters punishing

Falstaff ultimately want of him. At the level of plot, they want to punish him for his attempted seductions. Musically or operatically, however, they all want to coerce sounds out of him in order to return his voices to their origin. They pinch and poke until he howls, they prick and sting until he repents. Falstaff yells and howls; he even says "mi ripento," as if saying it will save his abdomen. In the basket scene, he nearly suffocates, but, ultimately, it is not suffocation they are after. They do not want to silence him but, on the contrary, to firmly place a voice inside him. They want him to have a stable voice. They want to stop his migrating, floating voices.

Only after this performance, when costumes are removed and faces are exposed, is he dumbfounded; only when the musical gestures heard repeatedly throughout the opera are reanchored in their originating bodies does Falstaff find himself out of words.[33] It is as if, by anchoring the musical gestures, their truth value is revealed. And now that these voices have been situated in their originating bodies, it is time for a voice to finally reside in Falstaff. Teaching Falstaff a lesson entails wanting him to say certain words in a certain way.

But all is in vain. The attempt to teach the voice to remain anchored in Falstaff's body fails. Falstaff's final fugue shows that he will not be coerced under the new vocal regimen they all try to enforce on him. For in the fugue, he—and with him all of the characters—resume their vocal deviance. In the fugue, at the end of the opera, when all trickery is exposed, Falstaff has his very final say. He sings the subject of the fugue, which will be repeated in turn by everyone. He sings of himself being both the origin and the outcome of it all.

The fugue is one of the opera's sole reposes in song. The opera is very rarely occupied with song for its own sake rather than for the sake of pace and forward motion. Not only does the final scene indulge in singing as such, but it calls attention to itself in its anachronistic turn of style.[34] Falstaff introduces a fugue made up of an even distribution of all voices on material related to the between-two-and-three musical gesture. The form of a fugue precisely guarantees that all characters evenly toss, spin, and bounce off the same vocal gesture. Thus the fugue subverts the determination of voices by specified bodies. All bodies sing the same music.

But, as is customary, the fugue proceeds with material that varies and develops its original subject. As the vocal material becomes more elaborate and free from its constraints to imitate the subject, it gives the impression of improvisation, of voices liberated from their restraining form. This impression of voices set free in the opera's end is an apostrophe, a final bow to Falstaff's free and freeing voice. And thus, at the end, free voice triumphs.

And as for the film, what is its conclusion? In the fugue's climactic final stretto, "tutti gabbàti!" (we all are fools!), Friedrich stages Falstaff conducting a silent pause by raising his hands, quieting all the singing and synchronizing the cadence. The pause in the music allows the camera to zoom in quickly. As in the prelude that introduced the film (when Falstaff's face was shown covered with a beauty mask), Friedrich points in our direction and stares directly at us. The staging has all of the characters look in our direction, but their gaze is slightly off, as if, being as they are in a theater, they do not know how to stare at a camera lens, or as if they are not certain whether we are staring back at them. "Tutti gabbàti": we are included.

The camera gradually zooms out, distancing itself from the image of Falstaff, and cuts to an overview of the set. We are exposed to the scene: a stage with a tree and a crowd in motion blending into the background. But before the music cadences and comes to its end, the set dissolves into an empty version of what we have just seen: an empty stage with nothing but a tree. Only the props and the fog remain. The humans whose costumes allowed them to blend into the set have dissolved into it as if they have masked emptiness all along, as if they have been part of a dehumanized landscape.

"Tutti gabbàti"? All disappear even before the silence at the end of the opera. Can we still be sure about what we have experienced? Were these really bodies and voices? Did they sing at us? The frozen image outlives the opera's music. The characters resemble the set, the film resembles a theater, and ultimately all vanishes. Nothingness. Perhaps we have not truly *heard* the opera that has just disappeared, perhaps we have not truly *seen* what has just fooled our ears.

Friedrich, by inventing visual narratives, acknowledges the vocal ones. He further destabilizes the origin of utterances, extending the ambiguity onto the very images and spaces of the film. He does not employ cinematic techniques to overcome, as it were, the opera's vocal behavior—its preference for swallowed, migrating, and free-floating voices. Rather, an array of unstable and paradoxical visual representations functions as commentary on the opera's own, the play on visuality a response to the play on vocality. In his attraction to gaps opened between the vocal and the visual representations, the film director exposes the unheard and unseen in a film of opera. This is a radical reinterpretation of the relations between the senses that occur within the opera itself, allowing a new intimacy between the two media: a response in kind to what the world of the opera opened. For through the new operatic voices, Verdi and Boito had already envisioned the possibilities that would materialize with the birth of cinematic bodies and their voices.

PART III

REMAINS OF THE VOICE

≈≥

CHAPTER 5

Opera on the Phone:
The Call of the Human Voice

New Operatic Voices, New Operatic Sights

Opera IN THE twentieth century has largely been characterized by a preoccupation with rethinking the quality and redefining the limits of the operatic: what can be considered opera, what determines it as such, and how does opera relate to other twentieth-century multimedia works?[1] One of the main areas of experimentation concerns the possibilities the medium provides for admitting and containing voices that have not traditionally been considered operatic—voices that challenge opera's vocal artificiality and stylization, its exaggerated range, its strained production, and its bordering on the inhuman in an impossible quest for the divine.

Redrawing the boundaries renegotiates the balance between the vocal and the visual in opera, between what is heard and what is seen. As there are tensions between the vocal and the visual, that is, between what revives and what deadens, new voices introduced into the operatic medium raise the stakes in opera's extraordinary belief in the aural sense.

As I argued in my discussion of Verdi's *Otello* and *Falstaff* in chapters 3 and 4, a fundamental feature shared by the operatic canon (of which the majority of operas are drawn from nineteenth-century Italian opera) is the presentation of a journey depicting the death of the voice of opera. These traditional works portray the vicissitudes of voice, striving toward a goal that is achieved only when voice is extended to its extreme. The operatic voice is driven, as it were, to express its own death. An expansion of range, intensification of the degree of difficulty (or intensification of lyric expression), and overembellishment (or oversimplification) are signs of this extreme condition of the stylized voice of opera. The medium of opera is immersed in a ritualization of voices raised to the occasion of expressing death. The actuality, physicality, or ocular testimony of a dead body is insignificant within this matrix. In opera, death is the expectation not for an unbelievable sight but for an unimaginable sound.

Contemporary opera has reacted to this tradition. I give two examples of attempts to go beyond the traditional fate that opera imposes. An important example from the beginning of the twentieth century is Debussy's *Pelléas et Mélisande* (1902), which undermines any correspondence between what is heard and what is seen. As the opera is based on Maeterlinck's symbolist play, what is referred to in words, voices, music, and gestures is not realized onstage but rather is to be imagined. The constituents of the opera collaborate, as it were, to enforce a novel balance between realistic and fantasized sights. *Pelléas et Mélisande*'s renegotiation of the senses culminates in the opera's take on the deadening of voice. Not only is Mélisande's death at the end of the opera vocally indistinguishable from the rest of the singing, but there are no visual cues besides Mélisande's withering and the comments of others that her death is taking place. It is as though her death is represented by the fading out of voice. She has no death song. The work redefines the inheritance of the ritual of vocality as ritual of death through a final stroke in which we no longer count on either of our senses for the representation of her death.

An extreme example from the end of the twentieth century is Meredith Monk's opera *Atlas* (1991), which allows the voice to regress to prelinguistic or inhuman sounds. The work's expressive powers lie in its expansion of vocal techniques and inclusion of novel sounds produced by dancers who are professionally trained in unique kinds of vocalization—animal imitation, ululation, syllabic chanting, and shrieks. There is very little verbal text; the vocalized lines are predominantly wordless melodies—the vocal equivalent of dance mime.[2] Their bodily movements are extensions of vocality. These new voices redefine the plot: it is cyclic rather than linear. The opera ends not in death but in a return to the conditions at the beginning of the opera in the form of a metaphysical rebirth. The work does not call for the complementarity of the senses; while the dancers-singers may look human and tell a tale of humans, they do not sound human. Though *Atlas* portrays a range of unconventional voices diametrically opposed to the stylized, artificial voices usually associated with the world of opera, it too is attracted to the inhuman capacities of the human voice and exhibits a foundational belief in the fantasies of the sense of hearing and a distrust of the sense of vision.

The Invention of the Voice on the Telephone

> Yes, I have the illusion that I'm right beside you. And all at once,
> the cellars and sewers, a whole city lies between us. . . . I have
> wound the cord around my neck. . . . I can feel your voice
> around my neck. . . . your voice surrounding my neck. . . . They
> could hardly cut us off, except by mistake. . . . Oh chéri!
> —Poulenc, *La voix humaine*

Taking as my starting point the idea that new operas downplay the power of the eye to inform the ear, of sight to explicate voice, I will discuss an opera centering on the technological mediation of the human voice. Poulenc's one-act opera, *La voix humaine* (The human voice, written in 1958), is based on a play of the same title by Jean Cocteau.[3] The same text also served for a film by Rossellini, *Una voce umane*, thus creating a filmic double to the opera. The film and the opera were created independently of one another. Thus, rather than examining what the filmic image takes the operatic voice to be, as in *The Phantom of the Opera* or *Otello*, I examine how a film and an opera react to an identical text, which itself invokes the themes of the vocal, the aural, the visual, and death. I begin by interpreting the opera and consider the film later in this chapter.

Poulenc's *La voix humaine* is situated halfway between Debussy's opera of the first decade of the twentieth century and Monk's avantgarde works of the 1990s. Poulenc does not undermine the notion of the death song as Debussy does, but rather creates an opera-length death song; nor does he strip the operatic voice of its basis in the human voice as Monk does, but rather locates the human dimension within the operatic voice. *La voix humaine* provides a unique conceptualization of the relations between the voice of opera, its dimension of invisibility, and the death of that voice.

In *La voix humaine*, the operatic voice is delivered by an uncanny machine: the telephone. The entire opera consists of one side of a phone conversation.[4] We see and hear a woman whose lover has left her. We, the audience, neither see nor hear him.[5] All that is said and not said on the other side of the line is inferred from her voice, for we are exposed to that voice alone.[6] The conversation is constantly interrupted, cut short, or jammed by the French telephone company. A final farewell is broken up into short "phases"—Poulenc's term, designating units of conversation set to coherent musical units—stretched over forty tortured minutes.[7] The opera ends with the phone cord wound around the woman's neck: the woman's anxiety over being disconnected by and from the machine is realized, and cruelly reversed, when the "voice" of her lover—through the wire of the phone—chokes her, leaving her attached to the machine in a death that epitomizes the end of voice. The phone acquires a truly monstrous, unheard-of dimension, making manifest the power of the invisible and unheard voice to bring about death.

To appreciate Poulenc's transformation of the machine into an operatic constituent that can make manifest the deadly power assigned to the invisible voice of the other (or to the invisible other within the voice), let us turn for a moment to the origins of the machine itself.

An article that appeared in 1887 in *Scientific American* described the anxiety created by the invention of the telephone as arising from the mysteriousness, the sense of material non-existence, of that part of the machine and its belongings that lies beyond one's own instrument. . . . I can imagine my friend at the other end of the line. But between us two there is an airy nowhere, inhabited by voices and nothing else—Helloland, I should call it. The vocal inhabitants of this strange region have an amazing vanishing quality. . . . The consciousness of such an experience produces in sensitive men, I am sure, a sensation of nervous shock, somewhat akin to seasickness. And sometimes . . . you hear the confused murmur of a hundred voices. You catch more expressions from private conversations than your nerves can transmit to the central office of your brain; and if you are imaginative, you may undergo, as I have, a feeling as if you had a hundred astral bodies that were guiltily listening at as many keyholes. . . . The telephone seems to you to have no visible agency. . . . Your applications and complaints go over the wire to that one impersonal, impalpable voice.[8]

In the years leading to the invention of the telephone, even before Edison, human and animal organs were employed for the purpose of recording and transmitting auditory signals. In 1829 a talking machine was invented which employed an elastic tongue modeled on a human one in order to transform frequencies into tones. In 1857, in an invention predating the gramophone needle, coarse, short hog hair was used in place of the elastic tongue. In 1874 Alexander Bell invented the first model of a phone receiver using an ear membrane taken from a human corpse's ear. The first telephone receiver was, in fact, a human ear, a machine that transmitted a living human voice by way of a dead human's ear.[9]

The telephone aroused anxiety in its association with absence and death. It brought forth absent voices while constantly pointing toward the ultimate silence in death. I quote Proust describing the voice of his grandmother on the phone.

A real presence, perhaps, that voice that seemed so near—in actual separation! But a premonition also of an eternal separation! Many were the times, as I listened thus without seeing her who spoke to me from so far away, when it seemed to me that the voice was crying to me from the depths out of which one does not rise again, and I felt the anxiety that was one day to wring my heart when a voice would thus return (alone and attached no longer to a body which I was never to see again), to murmur in my ear words I longed to kiss as they issued from lips for ever turned to dust.[10]

For Proust, the voice on the phone is a premonition of an encounter with the world beyond that of the living. Hearing the bodiless voice on the phone arouses anxiety as though one were encountering the dead returning as voice.

In her work *The Telephone Book*, Avital Ronell describes the telephone as a machine that connects the voices of disconnected beings. The unexpected suddenness of the ring of the telephone is associated with the blind cruelty of fate and the ultimate message of death. Picking up the receiver summons one to an unknown encounter, setting terms of agreement before anything is even said.[11] As such, the phone is not under our control, not determined by our will. The telephone has the technical ability to transport the human voice (it does not reproduce the voice but transmits the original voice), yet it is not human, lying somewhere between an object, a machine, and a work of art. The telephone, continues Ronell, both transmits life and represents its absence, showing the unclear demarcation between the living and the nonliving. The telephone is where the outside world and the voice of the other intrude; the connection of voices erases geographic, and spatial distances between self and other and undermines the relations of subject-thing, self-other.[12]

The anxieties and fantasies underlying the history of the invention of the telephone echo with those underlying the mythical origins of opera as related in the myth of Orpheus. As I claimed in previous chapters, taking the myth of Orpheus as the core of the operatic medium reveals opera's problematization of the relation between voice and gaze. This myth portrays the anxiety inherent in the voice by evoking both its power and its failure in overturning death. The myth elaborates the power of voice as making present that which is absent, by bringing back the dead Eurydice. It also conceives of the gaze as that which deadens by insisting on a full presence. The fantasies associated with the scientific-technological wish to transmit a disembodied voice, to mechanically conjure a ghostly presence, parallel the highest stake that opera places on the presentation of the illusory faculty of voice to resurrect the dead.[13] In Poulenc's *La voix humaine*, opera has found its peculiar kin in the telephone. As this opera shows, the operatic medium is attracted to the very properties of the telephone where the cancellation of the visual and the powers of the vocal are successfully imagined.

Opera on the Phone

The issue I raise with regard to Poulenc's opera touches on the very wish to imagine the voice of opera on the phone, the implications it might have on the delivery of death, and the ways in which Rossellini's *Una voce umane*—by virtue of being a film—differs from its operatic double.

Let us note that Poulenc's choice of the telephone is not intended to distort the singing voice, at least not directly.[14] We do not hear the heroine's voice mechanically reproduced or filtered through the phone, yet the presence of the telephone alters her singing. The presence of the machine provides her with a powerful sense of hearing, as her voice interprets what is acoustically inaccessible to the audience. As such, the technology affects the meaning of the voice.

Let me repeat that there is no action, no plot, and no voice on the other end of the line.[15] The opera's meaning lies in the extreme power lent to the heroine's vocality: the entire operatic space is the one created—heard, performed, voiced, visualized, invented—by the prima donna. All the external world we expect to hear and see is conjured by the Orphic power of her voice. Does this mean that we are totally trapped within the prima donna's voice? Or can we decipher other voices within her voice? And if so, how are we to differentiate between these voices and the prima donna's voice, since we hear only her performance?

I suggest that we hear voices other than the woman's voiced utterances; these "musicalized voices" are delivered by the voiceless music. There are two such categories in Poulenc's opera that are central to my discussion. In the first, musicalized voices are produced, as it were, by the inanimate machine onstage. A distinct instrumental motif renders the diegetic noise of the telephone. In the second category is music that takes the place of the (unheard) voice at the other end of the line and that the woman's responses "literalize" into a specific text. In contrast to the distinct ringing of the phone in the first category, *any* music may stand for the meaning of words and the voice of the lover on the other end. Music as such (not a specific motif or an identifiable tonality) may "speak" the otherwise unheard voice of the lover. We are made to hear that he is speaking, if not what he is saying. Here, orchestral music shows the capacity to signify a voice.

A distinct instrumental motif renders the voice of the inanimate machine. A single pitch is repeated in sixteenth notes on a metallic xylophone, reserving the xylophone's timbre solely for sounding the ringing of the phone. The pitch and duration of the ringing change, but the timbre remains constant and imitates the voice of the phone.[16] It is important to note that the motif of the ringing of the phone does not function as a harmonic arrival. In other words, the reiterated pitch on the xylophone is not an outcome of or resolution to the music preceding it. Rather, it distinctly interrupts the music, punctuating and causing, as it were, the woman's speech. This power granted to the telephone is a result of its unmusical nature. It is a sound that challenges musicality.

The distinct musicalized ringing of the phone is first heard after the opera's brief, eighteen-measure orchestral prelude and develops into the woman's voice as she repeatedly answers the phone. The orchestral prelude foreshadows the technique employed in the opera as a whole. Drawing on the entire chromatic scale, the prelude employs semitones not for the purpose of emphasizing or clarifying a tonal center but to constantly reinterpret structural tones and their relation to passing dissonant tones.

Let me sketch the use of semitones in the prelude. In terms of sheer quantity, nearly ten out of the eighteen measures are accompanied by a trill in the bass that serves as a semitone-motion drone for the initial few measures of the prelude; for the final measures of the prelude, the notes of the trill ascend a third. In terms of the motivic material, all of the motifs introduced in the prelude are composed of semitone motions. For example, the semitone motion of the first motif heard in the first measure is "ironed out" (that is, it appears without its semitone embellishment) when the same motif is repeated a few measures later (at no. 3). The first motif of the opera is indeed presented together with the trill drone in the bass. The prelude's second motif (at no. 1) is composed entirely of semitone motion. The semitones are retained when that motif returns in transposition (at no. 4). Finally, when the motif of the ringing of the phone is heard for the first time at the end of the orchestral prelude, there are no semitones at all, only a bare repetition of one single note (at no. 5) (see ex. 5.1).

Poulenc alludes to tonality without providing for a tonal center. (Only at the end of the opera is there an arrival of a clear cadence in a minor; yet the tonal implications throughout the opera do not prepare for this ultimate closure on a.) The music is motivically, not tonally, driven, yet the motivic material itself is dominated by tonal colorings—half steps or leading notes, or sevenths, or appoggiaturas—which raise expectations for tonal functioning and tonal resolutions. The technique of eschewing any grounding of tonal centers is typical of Poulenc's style, as it is an accumulative, rather than developmental, technique.

My interpretive claim is that in *La voix humaine* this technique is drawn into the representation of the phone. The sound of the phone even further decontextualizes the recurring strategy of the semitone motion and the sense of instability in the piece. The phone's music—the slow tremolo played by the xylophone—is a contraction of the overwhelming semitone motion across the opera into a unison tremolo motion. Poulenc restricts his musical means for the sake of the expression of the inhuman machine. The phone's "voice" is a flattening out of the overwhelming half-note motion across the opera—into recitation.

Poulenc's restriction of musical means also condemns the voice of the operatic woman to recitative-like, fragmented utterances, frequent silences, and the ritual of picking up the phone and voicing telephonic texts such as "*Allò! Allò!*" "*On avait coupé*," and so on. The woman's voice—the voice of opera—is approximated to the voice of the telephone.

A similar relationship occurs on the formal level of the opera. The form

Example 5.1. La voix humaine, orchestral prelude

of the opera is the result of the mechanism of the phone—the connection and disconnection of one or several calls. This form is combined with the distortion of a linear predetermined structure of musical time. The opera is divided into phases emotively distinguished from one another: the woman remembers their first days of love (which began with her phone call), lies about her present situation and about what she has been doing or what she is wearing, describes the reaction of his dog to his departure, cries, is angered, alludes to her suicide attempt, and so on.[17] The phases falsely seem improvisatory, as though the music, bound to her condition, is taken by surprise by each turn of emotion, going nowhere or doomed. The illusion is of music that does not progress anywhere but that remains continual in the present. This corresponds to the sense of endless fragmented phone calls that compose the one and last phone conversation. The structure of the opera thus enhances the impression of being dominated by the phone.

Poulenc has included technology as an operatic constituent: the phone's voice determines the musical vocabulary, the span between the phone's ringings and its disconnections determine the opera's structure, telephonic words and the ringing of the telephone are motivic, and the prima donna's voice approximates the operatic rendering of the noise of ringing. This fatal trajectory of the voice drawn into the sound of ringing is further related to the death of that voice if we consider the second category of musicalized voices—that of the voice at the other end.

What is exceptional about Poulenc's operatic heroine is that she hears the opera's music *throughout*. That is the only way to conceive of her singing. Except for very few instances where the music functions as an accompaniment to her singing, she *converses* with the sounds uttered by the orchestra. It is extremely unusual to have a character hear music nearly all the time. Not a rare auditory moment, in which a character perceives, as Carolyn Abbate puts it, his or her acoustical surrounding, but as though the woman herself were a gigantic hypersensitive ear. Perhaps the woman in the opera hears music—and understands it as specific words—precisely *because* it does not issue from another character onstage, precisely because it is not sung.[18]

The machine, then, situates opera on unfamiliar ground, undermining conventional modes of thinking about its music. A voice entering on the other end of the line would instantly introduce operatic subjectivity; the music would be *that* character's music, reflective of his or her being in the opera. But here, provocatively, music assumes the very role of a voice. Poulenc's setting cannot be interpreted as a reflection of the woman's own subjectivity, as originating in the heroine's interiority. In other words, it is not an echo of her imagination (that is, it is not all in her head, nor is she mad; it is not her interpretation of what he might or might not be saying). Rather, the music she hears has become, for her, *transparently linguistic.*

Though Avital Ronell complicates the notion of what is at stake in the relationship between text and music in opera, she does not allow for the radicality this opera offers. She writes, in relation to *La voix humaine,* that "opera figures the irreducible difference in language and music. Language, for its part, is left a little emptied by the encounter, for it discovers that it can never hear itself unless music plays the other of itself." However, she continues without granting music the power to signify: "this does not mean that music scores a victory over language. Music finds in language that it has been critically denied access to saying what it means. It is like Papageno, gagged."[19] Poulenc's opera, however, shows the possibility for the exact opposite phenomenon: music does not signify when adjoined by words. It is the absence of words that marks *music's transformation into words imaginable.*

The orchestral music is not an unreal surrounding we accept as naturally operatic, but it becomes *real* for the woman as she hears it. It is as if it were the embodiment of an absent other. But more precisely we might say that the music becomes an embodiment of that otherness that the "I" has in itself, neither totally outside nor just inside; it is that which disturbs any closure. *Music* is made to embody the speech of the other, and yet that other is neither present nor the figment of the woman's imagination arising out of her song. It is an otherness moving her voice and made manifest by it.[20]

≈

La voix humaine participates in traditional opera fantasies of death. It partakes of an operatic ritual not fundamentally undermined in this opera. *La voix humaine*'s use of the telephone also preserves the framework, form, and thematics of the traditional operatic death song. As I pointed out in discussing *Otello,* the structure of interruption and musicalized noises is thematic in death songs. Such interruptions emphasize the character's self-absorption and isolation at this moment as well as make manifest the impossibility of fulfillment and closure in song. We can consider Poulenc's opera as an extreme depiction of what canonic opera traditionally reserves for the very end—character isolation and an apotheosis of song expressing the knowledge of death. In Poulenc's opera there is nothing but the death song, nothing but a presence unto death. *La voix humaine* is an opera-length death song.

And yet something is being added to our understanding of the relation of voice and death. Poulenc finds a new way to relate opera's death plots with the idea of the death of the voice. In the first place, the machine as such is about the dissolution of the voice and its tending toward mere ringing sound. But further, the machine shows death to be internal to the voice or the voice to contain the otherness that signifies death and which can never be incorporated. As there is nothing but the woman's voice in *La voix humaine*, the voice acts out its termination from within itself. "The human voice" in the title of the opera thus interprets the humanity of the voice as its essential mortality. The condition of the human voice is that it always includes within itself a supplication to this otherness that signifies death. It is a solitary voice that, by its very nature, always demands a response from the other that will never be accorded.

Film on the Phone

Rossellini's *Una voce umane* was released in 1948, ten years before Poulenc's opera, and is based, as I mentioned earlier, on the play by Cocteau.[21] *Una voce umane* does not stand on its own. It constitutes the first of two short films—the second is named *Il miracolo*—both of which were released under the title *Amore*.[22] The film was released before the opera and thus was obviously not a response to it. And it seems as though Poulenc had not viewed Rossellini's film (though it is unlikely he was unaware of it, if only through Cocteau). In this chapter I am dealing not with a film simply drawn to opera (although I claim that Rossellini's film is operatic), but rather with an opera and a film operating under similar conditions. In each work, the same themes are raised: the sound of the human voice, its matching image, and its relation to its own death.

I interpret Rossellini's *Una voce umane* in relation to the issues raised by the opera, asking what occurs when voices on the phone—the woman's and the lover's—are transposed from the play into film. This comparison entails a consideration of three intertwined themes that relate the film's auditory and visual spaces: First, the work's sphere of silence, that is, how the other on the other end of the line is represented, or how his silence is given weight; second, the woman's own speech and its effects; and third, the work's construction of the woman's sense of hearing. These dimensions of the auditory space are interrelated and affect the visual space through their intensification of the image. In addition, I discuss three kinds of intensification of the image related to the three acoustic themes: overexposure (related to the silence on the other end of the phone); "operaticness," or operatic nature (related to the woman's "filmic vocality"); and apparition (related to the transformation of voice into image). Finally, I also mention the film's music—a crucial, if elusive, component of the film's auditory space and its meaning. A comparison between the opera and the film will reveal essential features that might have escaped a consideration of each work solely in terms of its own medium.

A Sphere of Silence: The Other End of the Line

Let us begin with the other end of the line. In Cocteau's play, neither words nor sounds are assigned to the lover. In *Una voce umane*, we hear murmuring sounds issuing from the phone. Occasionally, Rossellini adds muffled sounds to stand for the absent voice. The man's words are indecipherable, a noise, a mere trace of speech in the materiality of his voice— yet there is, as it were, a filmic presence at the other end of the line.[23] In comparison, remember the opera's representation of the other end of the line, where music stood in place of the voice of the other. Indeed, the film's gesture is diametrically opposed to that of the opera: the film reduces language to barely audible sound, whereas the opera is radical in the "elevation" of music's signifying powers to denote speech.

The film fashions the sounds and silences of the other on the phone as a deformed *acousmêtre*. This term was introduced by Michel Chion to denote in film the presence of a voice that does not issue from a body within the frame of vision.[24] The acousmêtre's properties derive from the anxiety of an encounter with an invisible voice. Its presence in a film often dictates a trajectory of exposure by which the hidden source, its missing body, is sought to anchor the voice.[25]

Una voce umane deforms numerous properties of the acousmêtre. Though, typically, a phone in film renders an acousmêtre, here some of its central features disappear.[26] To start with, its voice, or rather traces of it, are comprehended only as they resonate in the *woman's* voice. In other words, it is an acousmêtre deprived of its own faculties of being meaningfully audible.[27] Moreover, the trajectory of the film *Una voce umane* does not lead to the exposure of the acousmêtre. To underline this, a scene is indeed added to the structure of the play (perhaps initially improvised)[28] in which Rossellini's woman imagines for us a *deacousmatization*, or an anchoring of the voice to its body: the woman approaches the door as she hears voices in the stairwell, hoping for the appearance of her lover, only to realize her mistake. It is not the voice's body; it was a failed deacousmatization.

I use the term *acousmêtre* to emphasize that this muffled voice, although not an omnipotent and omnipresent voice, does contribute to the sense of the woman's entrapment. Though the anxious mood of the film arises from the constant expectation of the voice and from the certainty that even this trace of it will eventually cease, the film's aural space nevertheless has the power to draw us in. It makes us partake in the woman's persecution. Importantly, the trace of the voice on the phone adds to the sense of *our* proximity. Hearing these murmurs makes manifest *our* closeness. It enhances the sense of overexposure that this woman suffers from. As if in reaction to the opera's emphasis on the power of the voice to con-

Figure 5.1. Rossellini's *Una voce umane* (1948), with Anna Magnani on the phone

jure a whole world by itself, the film shows that one cannot avoid the Orphic fate of being persecuted by the gaze.

This effect of persecuting visuality is registered in the understanding of the film's status as an *experiment* departing from the director's earlier films. "Rossellini always spoke of this film as an 'experiment,'" writes Peter Brunette.[29] The nature of this experiment is the total and utter concentration on the one character that the experiment consists in. In other words, Anna Magnani, the actress, is the subject on which the experiment is conducted. This is echoed by the metaphor Rossellini uses to characterize the camera in the experiment: "More than any other subject, *La voix humaine* gave me the chance to use the camera as a microscope, especially since the phenomenon to examine was called Anna Magnani."[30] The outcome of the muffled voice over the phone, of the absent voice or the absence in the voice, is the overpowering effect of the gaze. It generates a visual close-up, an uncalled-upon exposure of the woman to our inquiring gaze.

Rossellini importantly describes his film as the investigation of the *actress*, not as a portrayal of the character. In fact, Cocteau's reaction to Rossellini's film precisely catches this point. Magnani seems to him overexposed: "In twenty-five takes, amounting to a total of 1200 metres of film, he [Rossellini] has shot a cruel documentary on a woman's suffering. In it Anna Magnani reveals a soul and a face without make-up. This documentary might be entitled 'Woman devoured by a girl' or 'The telephone as an instrument of torture.'"[31] In a sense, perhaps, the film does not enable a character to emerge from the actress; it is the real Magnani.[32] The experiment is a crossing from the sphere of representation to the *real* presence of the actress.

This is striking. The situation of the woman in the opera leads me to attribute a peculiar realism to the music she hears, as it takes on both the voice on the phone and the real noise of the telephone ring. Similarly, the film creates its own unexpected form of realism. Beyond any neorealist convention, it is the very presence of the flesh-and-blood Anna Magnani, the actress beyond or above the character she portrays, that makes this film so realistic.

A Vocal Sphere: The Film's "Operaticness"

Rossellini films Anna Magnani in static long shots, replacing montage editing of short takes. He deliberately chooses bad and unbeautifying angles, thus highlighting Magnani's *vocal* persona. Anna Magnani was, in fact, a popular singer.[33] In *Una voce umane*, there is vocality precisely by not relying on a sophisticated text, on narrative interest, or on action. What is created is an intense vocal presence. *Una voce umane* is a film of vocal performativity; it depends predominantly on nuanced inflections in Magnani's voice; its constant "vocal close-up" pits claustrophobic visuals against intense expansions in sound.[34]

Everything hinges on how Magnani uses her voice. The auditory-vocal space is intensified as hearing and speech are strained to the utmost. The voice suffuses the image or the image drowns in voice. This all-encompassing vocality leads to what I think of as the "operaticness" of the film.[35] I emphasize this feature since it is common to contrast realism and the operatic (at least on the whole). Here, due to the peculiar conditions of the film, they come together.

Cocteau's text engenders a double move in which the opera pulls toward the cinematic and the film toward the operatic. Poulenc, by approximating the voice to the ringing of the phone, reduces its extravagant operatic nature; Rossellini, by raising the stakes of voice in his film, treats it as though it were operatic. And yet, at the same time, as each of the works behaves as though it belonged to the other medium, it also exemplifies an aspect of its own medium driven to an extreme.[36] Just as I interpret the excessive and deformed visuality of *The Phantom of the Opera* as operatic, a move into the operatic edge in silence, and just as in *A Night at the Opera* the degeneration of language as communication borders on the operatic, so in *Una voce umane* the stake in the auditory-vocal space leads to the operatic nature of the film.

A Sense of Hearing: Audible Noises, Inaudible Music

The first aspect of the acoustic space of *Una voce umane* is the muffled voice on the phone heightening visual exposure; the second aspect is the filmic voice acting operatically. The third, which I want to elaborate on now, is the way in which the acoustic space conjures an apparition.

The woman hears many sounds: water (she washes her face), the howling dog (she addresses it, gives it a cookie), children's voices next door and a baby crying, the neighbors' music, and their phone ringing (she is disturbed by these). The sounds might initially be explained by referring to the film's overall realism. But these noises are tinted by a profound sense of *un*reality, as they are too present, too obtrusive. They are not background noises, but rather heard in every detail. At times they are so intrusive that the woman must shut her ears to them. They are so present to her, and through her to us, that they come to signify the acute effort of hearing that the woman is constantly making. The sounds are aggrandized because the woman awaits one sound, wishing that every noise would become the ring of the telephone. Such sounds surround the woman with a space of anxiety. They make anxiety palpable. The film constructs realistic diegetic sounds so that they have the potential of transforming into something else—the sound of the phone. These diegetic sounds color the auditory space with the intense expectation of transformation, as if at any moment a miracle might happen and the phone will ring. The ultimate miracle the woman is wishing for is the apparition of the caller in person. That apparition never materializes in and through the human voice, but, in a sense, it occurs at the limit of the voice.

In the opera, even the power of the voice cannot bring about the longed-for apparition of the image; in the film too this attempt at crossover fails. Indeed, as I mentioned earlier, a scene is added emphasizing a failed deacousmatization, or the failure of bringing about the appearance of the voice's body. But the apparition does materialize at the limit of voice in *Una voce umane*'s complementary film, *Il miracolo*. This relation between the two films will be made apparent if we make a short digression and discuss the music in Rossellini's *Amore*.

❧

The woman is well aware of all sounds—including diegetic music over the phone and across the walls of her apartment,[37] but as usual in film, she does not hear the film's music. The unheard nondiegetic music, however, plays a very peculiar role.[38]

The nondiegetic sound world of *Una voce umane* contains one recurring melody that is heard only sporadically throughout the film.[39] The music feels external to the film. This is emphasized not only through its appearance and disappearance in ways that seem unrelated to the emotional tone of the happenings in the film, but by sounding it also for *Il miracolo*, the accompanying film. The same melody accompanies the opening titles and credits of both episodes and reemerges again at a crucial juncture within *Il miracolo* (despite the fact that the film has a distinct music of its own).[40] In other words, the music spills over beyond the confines of *Una voce umane* to link the two films.

Il miracolo is about a shepherdess (played by Anna Magnani) who hears voices (thus making her immediately the double of the woman in the first episode). She believes Saint Joseph is speaking to her (maybe this name links him to Giuseppe from the first episode). Encountering a silent stranger passing by (played by Federico Fellini), she is convinced he is Saint Joseph appearing before her. The woman delivers a long monologue, which seems to echo the monologue on the phone in the first episode. But here, the woman does not demand a response, nor does she *leave* any room for a response, since in the man's silent presence she has found the apparition.

The opening of *Il miracolo*, in which she is duped by the stranger who takes advantage of her delusion, recounts an ironic transformation of the hearing of voices into an apparition, for later in the film the woman will realize that she has been "miraculously" impregnated.[41] Instead of recognizing her predicament, she fantasizes about being a second Maria, chosen to give birth to the Son of God.

Thus, despite the apparent differences between the worlds of the two episodes (the locked city apartment with its telephone and the open fields of the countryside), the expectation for the lover to make an appearance in the first episode seems to be fulfilled by an ambiguous apparition in the second. The lover's absent voice in *Una voce umane* materializes into the "saint's" apparition in *Il miracolo*.[42]

Only the soundtrack, however, suggests another understanding for this ironic correspondence between the phone call and the religious calling.[43] The sole music of *Una voce umane* recurs toward the very end of *Il miracolo*, as the pregnant woman, led by a goat, approaches an isolated monastery where she will deliver her child. She approaches this last station after everyone, including the church, has rejected her. The music of *Una voce umane* sounds in the midst of the continuing music of *Il miracolo*. It reintroduces the previous episode into this one, providing a sign for a different understanding. The only sounds remaining at the outskirts of society are those at the limit of meaning: the noise of an animal (the goat), the woman's moans while giving birth, and then the baby's first cry at birth.

Una voce umane's music reemerges in a scene where what is otherwise heard is at the edge of human language.

Indeed, there is hardly any room for full-fledged meaningful human discourse. The reappearance of the very same "inaudible music" from *Una voce umane* as the woman gives birth marks a moment of recognition beyond the delusional fantasy: "My child. . . . My creature. . . . My blood." The movement determined between *Una voce umane* and *Il miracolo* leads from a universe of sounds pregnant with anxious expectancy of the other's presence to the deliverance of the human voice bordering on the nonhuman to the deliverance of that other within. Rossellini in *Il miracolo*—at the risk of blasphemy—ultimately makes speech expendable and voices the sounds at the limit of the human voice.

Calling Death

Cocteau's play is about death. In the preface to the play, Cocteau describes the scenery (the room with the phone), calling it "the scene of a crime": "When the theatre curtain rises it discloses a room which might be the scene of a crime. On the floor in front of the bed, a woman in a long night-dress lies as if murdered." And for the end of the play, Cocteau "would like the actress to give the impression of a woman who is bleeding, losing her life-blood, like a maimed animal, that she is finishing the Act in a room full of blood."[44] Cocteau's woman *begins* the play and *ends* it in similes of death. Cocteau's violent description might not correspond to death caused by a phone, and yet, as we know, the machine's power is deadly.

I interpret the sharing of the same text of Cocteau by Rossellini's *Una voce umane* and Poulenc's *La voix humaine* as posing the question whether "cinema's telephone" can, in fact, differ from "opera's telephone." In particular, whether the difference figures in relation to the meaning assigned to death in each medium, whether death in the film is other than death in the opera.

In the opera, the woman hears an absent voice by way of understanding music as speech, a fatal trajectory of music to so transform itself into speech: opera has pulled absolute music into its matrix of death by means of a machine, a telephone. The woman in the opera hears everything in the opera. Such an ear and such a voice are fatal. I suggest, then, that Poulenc's use of the telephone in his opera is radical. It reinterprets what is inherent to the aesthetics of the operatic voice—the death it is pregnant with. Only in the opera does the voice act out its termination from within itself, expressing death as an outcome of singing as such.[45] Only in opera is the risk taken of voices so high that inventing new voices for opera—the operatic phone call, the single voice signifying two, the invisible, the voiceless—still results in death.

La voix humaine participates in traditional opera fantasies of death, but it has invented a new meaning for the voice of opera. Without allowing the voice to reign and become a fully operatic one, to signify through or rely on its power of beauty, Poulenc finds the humanity of that voice. Refusing to escape by beautifying and stylizing the voice in this opera is an acknowledgment of the human voice within the operatic one. Exposing this voice as human reveals the vicissitudes of voice, its unpaid debt to death. This is its operatic phone call, its death over the phone.

In Rossellini's film, the telephone kills by finding an ally in another machine—the camera. Their cooperation results in the overexposure of the woman, leaving her fatally visible. In so exposing the woman, film must rely on her voice to provide its dramatic content. It thus becomes indirectly operatic, even though it does not originate in relation to opera. And yet the film's extremity of vision almost requires another ending, or another film, to overcome the fate of the operatic voice it has created. *Il miracolo* shows the possibility of transforming the wish for an apparition into the birth of the *real other* delivered at the edge of the human voice.

CHAPTER 6

∾

Fellini's Ashes

It is unsavory to end this book with death.
And yet opera offers nothing else.
—Wayne Koestenbaum, *The Queen's Throat*

HERE IS Federico Fellini, revealing his fascination with a catastrophe, the "end of cinema."

> In the course of the summer I conducted a direct personal experiment. In company with the producer Renzo Rossellini, I made a tour of eighteen Roman cinemas, first-run and repertory, central and suburban, during the prime-time period, namely, from half past six to half past eight in the evening. I went from one cinema to the next with a kind of increasing inebriation, exaltation. Ruin, catastrophe and apocalypse have always given me a sense of excitement. . . . We pulled apart the curtains, looked at the screen and cast our eyes upon the auditorium: hundreds and hundreds of empty seats, like blind eyes, deserted as the holds of a beached ship. Only in four or five cinemas did the audience exceed the number of staff. It was a sight that has its own kind of fascination, as if wrapped in a science-fiction glow. It gave us the impression that the earth was suddenly depopulated while machines continued to function by means of their own inertia.[1]

This anecdote suggests the degree to which Fellini's late style, one could say his entire oeuvre, is about memories, loss, and an awareness of death. Not only the autobiographical, personal, or national past is in peril but also, importantly, the memory of cinema. The contemporary atmosphere of the cinematic milieu in Italy—which Fellini felt strongly—was one of anxiety over the very survival of cinema, especially in light of the advent of its younger sibling, television.

Indeed, accounts of the history of film attest to the striking phenomenon that "in the late 1960s, cinema was pronounced dead."[2] Marcia Landy, for example, writes that

> certain critics [were led] to "assert that Italian cinema is moribund (if not already dead)." In the work of filmmakers in the 1980s and 1990s, the lamentation of the "death of cinema" in relation to television and other electric media played a role much as the cinema earlier played in accounting for the

morbidity of the live theatre and of opera. The cinema continues to reflect on itself but in ways that indicate uncertainty about its character and status in the future.[3]

But at the same time Fellini distances himself from an unproductive tarrying with the question of the death of cinema:

> It's as if they [who celebrate cinema's ninetieth anniversary] lacked the courage to tell themselves that cinema is already dead . . . what's the purpose of asking oneself if it is still alive? It seems to me that it's always talked of now in funeral terms and so, frankly, I don't wish to participate in this event.[4]

Fellini's film *E la nave va* reflects on this sense of cinema's ending, specifically by invoking the fate of opera.[5] Since *E la nave va* does not stage an opera, borrow a plot from an opera, or use an operatic scene to make a point, the question it raises is *how* Fellini's film is about opera. And *what* is opera taken to be in this film? A glimmer of an answer might be sought in the fact that the film is not about opera's typical voyage of death, as exemplified in *Otello*, where Desdemona's death results from the meaning her voice conveys in the opera. Rather, *E la nave va* depicts a voyage of the *remains* of the most famous diva in the world.[6] Since the diva is dead, the voyage, if it is to count as another of her performances, can be called her afterlife. The diva's audience is the film's protagonists, eccentrics from the world of opera—singers, impresarios, conductors, singing masters, admirers—all infatuated with opera and with her singing.

E la nave va is about the death of the carrier of the operatic voice: the death of a mythical prima donna, "Edmea Tetua," the greatest singer ever. The film allegorizes the death of the singing voice as, in effect, the end of opera. In contemplating the threat of cinema's end, the film shows this terminal point in another medium.[7] As a funeral procession for the voice, the film manages to place the historically prior event, opera's own end, alongside its anxiety over the death of cinema.

Death of Opera

> I am often dead. I've always been grateful to opera for dramatizing
> my periodic movement from life to death, and for making death
> seem the higher ecstasy. . . . I wish to correct a misperception: that
> we can meaningfully define the limits of "opera."
> —Wayne Koestenbaum, *Cleavage*

Since Wagner, opera has been concerned with its own extinction. This foreboding, or sense of an approaching end, was understood since the nineteenth century as a crisis connected to melody and song. Wagnerian opera and its undoing of song threatened the future of opera as such.[8] Philippe Lacoue-Labarthe formulates the fate imposed on opera by Wagner's totalization of art in the following terms:

> No doubt, it is not impossible to say that Wagner fundamentally *saturated* opera. A proof of this, which is nonetheless indirect, is that everything which followed without exempting itself from the exorbitant ambition he had imposed upon the form carries the stigmata of the end. . . . Wagner's work left to its posterity a task every bit as impossible as the one left by German Idealism (Hegel) to its great followers in philosophy: to continue that which is finished . . . one might speak of the Wagnerian closure of opera and even of art itself.[9]

Wagner is not seen as ending opera by bringing to fruition the possibilities inherent in it. Rather his operas shift the ground, blocking or closing the possibility of the old vision of opera. He paves the way for twentieth-century music to be "unkind" to melody. His very attempt at totalization expresses itself as musical saturation, which overwhelms song, drowning it in "too much music." This is the result of Wagner's wish to overcome opera, go beyond art forms, and create Art. Opera after Wagner has never been the same: Strauss's compositions manifest "redundancy"; Puccini's "exhaustion"; Debussy's "destructuration"; Berg's and Schoenberg's "rupture and incompleteness."[10]

Two mythical instances of incompleteness can stand for this uneasy sense of opera's end. The first is the fate of Puccini's incomplete last opera, *Turandot*, about which a tale is repeatedly told: "as he reached the conclusion of Liù's death scene, Toscanini laid down his baton and said, in effect (he has been quoted variously): 'The opera ends here, because at this point the Maestro died. Death was stronger than art.' The opera ends here. Toscanini might have been speaking not just of Puccini's last work but of Italian opera in general."[11] This is the mythical ending of the Great Tradition, the death of its last composer in the process of composing the opera's death scene. (Note that Liù's death scene is, in fact, not the end of the opera but a figure for an interruption rather than a natural ending.) The second instance is Schoenberg's incomplete opera, *Moses und Aaron*. In its subject matter and styles of song and speech as well as in its aesthetic and technique, *Moses und Aaron* represents a blockage and brings the medium of opera face to face with the impossibility of its continuation, the end of its journey before having reached the promised land.

The phenomenon of Wagnerian opera was overwhelming, compensating for the loss of song with impressive permanent gains. Under Wagner's aesthetic revolution, the Italian notion of song was undermined. Opera in the twentieth and twenty-first centuries shows that it has accepted such thinning out of song. And yet, we still detect a glimpse of opera's "beautiful moments" of singing.

If the death of opera is formulated as the crisis of song, the question arises whether song belongs only to opera's past, to opera's memories, or whether it can resurface in the present or in some vision of the future. Tom Sutcliffe argues that it is not opera that is under the threat of extinction but its renewal in song: "to regard opera as a museum art, or even a dead art, is to ignore the changing circumstances of operatic life. Musical invention has not stopped. What has become problematic is song."[12] Works are composed and performances attended, yet a battle is fought over song's renewed existence in opera: "When it can once again [sing], opera will have found a voice for the new millennium."[13] Similarly, Henry Pleasants sees the crisis of opera in composers' being "seduced by the lure of a music that would be more than song."[14] He warns of the threat of believing in a music that can take over and replace song. This "more than song" is dangerously seductive; replacing song with "music" is, in Pleasants's opinion, opera's postmortem. And yet, Jean Starobinski sees a further possibility, which paradoxically, might be called the swan song of opera. Starobinski reformulates the fatal connection between the death of opera and song by writing that only in song will opera have expressed its very own end: "Perhaps one day opera will die, like everything else that has been born over the course of time. Opera has not always existed. . . . Let us recognize, however, that it will have lived to sing its own death superbly in the death that is always begun again, the death of its enchantresses."[15] Starobinski intimates that opera is mortal, awaiting an inescapable death. However, the death of opera will have been recognized in song, as opera will have sung its own death. So the paradoxical implication in Starobinski's formulation is that opera will renew its existence in singing its own death. The death of opera *is* its continuous condition of existence. Catherine Clément takes this intuition even further, seeing the possibility of a "song of the future" after opera as we know it has died. This future will overcome the fatal link between song and the death of opera's heroines. Clément writes:

> Beautiful and alive, the women will continue to sing in a voice that will never again submit to threat. They will say something entirely different than the words breathed in delirium and pain. They will ask no more than that they finally be permitted to die. . . . I do not know what this song will be. I imagine it as a lullaby. Listen to the heights of coloratura, to the highest uplift of a suffering voice, listen. . . . Singing there, scarcely audible, is a voice from beyond opera, a voice of the future.[16]

Clément envisions a fragile, scarcely audible song that will resound beyond opera's songs of death, even beyond the existence of opera. It will be the singing of the death of opera. In Clément's future, opera will have died and song's meanings will have transformed. The song of opera will have transcended opera.

Against these historical, philosophical, critical, and psychoanalytical readings, these repeated takes on opera's terminus as a living art, Fellini's film seems both more contemplative and more devastating. *E la nave va* celebrates operatic voice not directly but as an ideational object, surviving in the memories of assorted eccentric characters. The film records the reactions to the prima donna's lost voice and juxtaposes pieces, gathering relics from the cult of that voice, thus encircling the (dead) prima donna, presenting her from all angles in an attempt to reveal the secret origin of her voice. As in *The Fifth Element*, though in radically different terms, one encounters the sense that an operatic voice is an inexplicable miracle, something whose precise organic cause or explanation is an enduring mystery. Fellini tries out images or visual spectacles that might symbolize the voice: a ridiculous image of a crawling snail or a grotesque scene in which the lowest bass in the world hypnotizes a chicken (as well as the film's narrator, the journalist). The mythical singer's voice evokes admiration, jealousy, competition, and unsuccessful attempts to approximate it. It is pictured, described, mythologized, and, ultimately, mechanically reproduced. Fellini takes what opera gathers around it, what it creates in its surroundings, and what it leaves behind. He is interested in the remains of the show while the voice (like the diva's ashes) is blown away in the wind. The cult of the diva is satirized, made absurd, yet it does not stand out conspicuously in the context of either the eccentricity of Fellini's world or the images associated with the world of opera.

When Fellini sounds the voice of the dead prima donna as an accompaniment to the disappearing pile of her ashes, he provides a striking image of the end of opera as a "thinning out of song." And yet, a voice singing beyond the life of the body that produced it attests to an afterlife of the essentially mortal. This peculiar fate of opera inspires Fellini's thoughts on the death of cinema.

Ashes

[O]ut of death, new life arises. The Orientals have understood this idea; it is perhaps the greatest idea they have ever produced, and it is certainly the most sublime of their metaphysical doctrines. It is implicit, but with individual reference, in their notion of metempsychosis: but an even more celebrated example is the image of the Phoenix, of natural life, which for ever constructs its own funeral pyre and is for ever consumed upon it, only to rise again from the ashes as fresh and rejuvenated life.
—Hegel, *Lectures on the Philosophy of World History*

Fellini uses a striking image to illustrate the resonance of the mythical prima donna's death. The ocean liner has departed on a chartered journey whose goal is a ritual to scatter the diva's ashes—the remains of the body that once produced that wondrous voice. The master of ceremonies aboard the ship recites: "Psalm of David: . . . 'You know Man is only dust and ashes. / Dust to dust, ashes to ashes. / The Lord will protect my exit and my entrance / From now on and for all eternity.'" A whistle is blown, two sailors remove the container, the ashes are spread on a cushion, the needle of a gramophone is placed on a record, and the diva's voice is heard accompanying the diminishing pile of ashes.[17] The opera lovers listen; a whistle signals the end of the ceremony; the goal of the voyage has been reached.

This is the only moment in which we hear Edmea Tetua's voice. The music throughout the film is an impressively rich pastiche of operatic and nonoperatic music (Verdi, Tchaikovsky, Saint-Saëns, Strauss, Mozart, Rossini, Debussy, Puccini, Ponchielli).[18] Some of the music is transformed into an operatic mode (combining voice and text), some vocal music appears with newly composed text, some is background music, and some features as performances within the film. Yet the sole sounding of the diva's own voice is through a gramophone recording. Her voice is not astounding in any sense, nor is the music she sings marked in any way to stand out from other operatic sounds in the film. But what *is* striking is the juxtaposition of the recorded sound with the image of the ashes. In other words, the voice is *made* astonishing through its mise-en-scène: it is as though the ashes bring out something inherent in the voice and stand for something acoustic that the spectator is not able to perceive. The longing aroused by a recording of a past voice is intensified by the image of the ashes being blown away. "Nothing excites memory more strongly than the human voice, maybe because nothing is forgotten as quickly as a voice."[19] This was written about the invention of the phonograph, implying that the recording of a lost voice does not overcome that nostalgic quality but intensifies it. The phonograph enriches the meaning of our dead speaking to us. As Koestenbaum puts it:

> A record can't limit the voice's meaning; a voice, once recorded, doesn't speak the same meanings that it originally intended. Every playing of a record is a liberation of a shut-in meaning—a movement, across the groove's boundary, from silence into sound, from code into clarity. A record carries a secret message, but no one can plan the nature of that secret, and no one can silence the secret once it has been sung.[20]

The voices of the dead—on the gramophone, on records, on the radio— are opera's glorious past, a decaying voice, which in its very decay is a thrill to fans. Because opera lives in a fantasy of reliving and re-creating its

Figure 6.1. Fellini's *E la nave va* (1983). The diva's voice is heard accompanying the scattering of the pile of ashes.

past, of bringing back over and over again the same operas—and, if it could, it would do so with the exact same voices—it offers an unexpected model for the life and death of an art form. Its existence has the very characteristics of death. Perhaps opera is, in effect, dead, or it has already died and is living its death, and we would never know it.

The possibility opened by the peculiar power of the recorded voice leads us to ask whether such enlivening can be achieved in cinema's reproduction of the lost past, in its very collecting and recording of the remains gathered around that recorded lost voice of the diva.

Before relating song to ashes, let us ask what the image of death expressed through this ritual entails, for the ritual of cremation can take on many meanings. Decay is the justification of all funeral rites. Rites either try to tame it, hide it, forbid it, retard it, or accelerate it.[21] For Christians, cremation has been theologically difficult to accept. It is associated with pagan rites, it affronts the doctrine of bodily resurrection, and it is associated with the burning of witches.[22]

The theological difficulty with the disposing of the cremated body can be further explained by the unsettling sense of juxtaposing death with a mechanical process of disposal, replacing the passive burial in the earth with an act of destroying the body by fire. It suggests the thought of a corpse as something to dispose of, and the process itself is taken to be a form of active forgetfulness, of hiding and denying death (though it also could be viewed as the exact opposite: stressing the finality of mortal life).

In the ancient world, cremation was a common practice. The Greeks believed that "fire separated the pure soul from the impure body and freed it to ascend, phoenix-like, from its altar of flames to the heavens."[23] The difference between the Christians and the ancient Greeks can be described as that between a belief in resurrection and a belief in reincarnation and transmigration of the soul. For the Greeks, the immortal soul was freed by death to be reborn. Christians, however, believe a person is made whole only by the miracle of resurrection. There is indeed a temporary disembodiment, but this will be overcome on Judgment Day.[24] If Greek myth considered the moment of cremation a climax of purification, then the Christian narrative places resurrection at the end of times.[25] Greek myth, then, saw in fire

> the promise of regeneration and rebirth. Through fire, a superior level of existence could be attained. For example, Herakles stretched himself out on the pyre of Mount Oeta, while Zeus announced to the other gods that Herakles was about to become their equal: the fire would relieve him of his human part, immortalize him, and make him divine. . . . It is therefore not the impurity of the corpse that is implicated in the cremation ritual, but the impurity of the body and the human condition. Ashes are the proof of that impurity; if the body were perfect, it would burn without ashes . . . the charred and purified remains correspond to the rites of integration of the dead in his status in the beyond.[26]

We should, however, also keep in mind the more antique meaning of *cremation* and its link to the regeneration of life in nature rather than the salvation of the soul. This is the meaning Hegel associates with the image of the phoenix. Rituals would recognize the powers residing *in the ashes themselves* to fertilize and regenerate the cycle of growth in nature.[27] Replacing the belief in the immortality of the soul, such a ritual signifies dying and regeneration in nature.

Different meanings assigned to ashes, therefore, relate to different beliefs in the afterlife. In the Christian tradition, cremation is a threat to the wholeness of the human being and thus a threat to the awaited resurrection. In certain Platonic interpretations of the Greek world, cremation provides the purification of the soul, which is now granted the power to be separated from the body. And finally, pagan ritual demonstrates a belief not only in the human being on a journey of reincarnation and transmigration, but how the soul, now freed from its original bodily constraints, obtains the power to regenerate the cycle of nature.

In the world of opera, there are some particularly famous ashes.

Maria Callas's Ashes

> Maria Callas, immortal, died on September 16, 1977. . . . To
> mourn Callas: there, cult happiness begins. She was Callas long
> before she died, but she would be a little less Callas if she were
> still living.
>
> —Wayne Koestenbaum, *The Queen's Throat*

The following is a pastiche of fabulously contradictory biographical narratives of Maria Callas's death. "[H]er death and the ensuing drama are worthy of a gothic novel, filled with hints of suicide, murder, grave-robbing, even cannibalism. Maria, who was a firm believer in reincarnation, may have been an interested observer of the bizarre misadventures that followed her death, as she predicted. Whether or not she enjoyed the show, it was quite a performance."[28] "The funeral was held in the Orthodox Church on Tuesday September 19, but in the three days between her death and the funeral, nobody, not even friends, was allowed to view her corpse."[29]

Both Franco Zeffirelli and Jackie Callas [Maria's sister] later wrote that the sight of Maria's body immediately made them think of the tragic and ethereal heroine of *La Traviata*, who died so picturesquely of consumption. Zeffirelli's description of Callas in death paints a vivid picture: *The cold body on that bed had been two people: Maria the woman who wanted to be loved and Callas the diva who was a Vestal at the altar of her art. They had seemed to battle it out within her and in the end both lost; all that had been left in those last years was little more than the shell which was laid out in that darkened room. Her maid, Bruna, stood by her body, obsessively fussing over her dead mistress: first she would gently comb her long tresses, then she would smooth her precious lace nightdress or brush away some imagined speck, then she would stop for a while and pray a little, then she would begin again, combing, combing, combing. It was a sublime image of the dead Violetta.* It's a haunting scene that Zeffirelli describes, one worthy of the stage. . . . But Franco Rossellini, the producer of Callas's film *Medea*, later reported that in fact Bruna had refused to let Zeffirelli in when he called.[30]

After the religious ceremony, her coffin was taken to the cemetery and, from there, immediately sent for cremation. The people who organized the funeral said that Callas had written in her will that she wanted to be cremated. But the will was never found.[31] Devetzi [Maria's friend] . . . decreed that according to Maria's wishes (presumably expressed verbally at some time) the body was to be cremated. Using the same argument and without any consultation with Maria's mother or sister, undoubtedly the next of kin, the Greek Archbishop in Paris was persuaded to authorize the cremation.

(The Greek Orthodox religion to which Callas belonged does not allow cremation in Greece, nor does it have the facilities. However, if performed abroad, strictly in compliance with the express wishes of the deceased, the Greek Church accedes, albeit reluctantly.)[32]

It is common practice for cremations to take place the day after the arrival of the deceased; moreover, French law requires that it must be requested by a member of the family. This requirement was not observed in Maria's case. The register of Père Lachaise Cemetery records the request for cremation signed by Jean Roer, who was merely the administrator of Maria's business affairs.[33]

The hurried decision in favor of cremation—based solely on Devetzi's verbal assurance that that had been Maria's declared wish—has since been questioned by a number of people, including close friends of hers who think that the idea of cremation did not accord with her moral or religious beliefs.[34]

This raised the doubt, for some, that cremation was not really the wish of Callas but was performed to hide something about the circumstances of her death.

The immediate cause of Callas's death has never been fully explained. The rumors which circulate, some in the press, included a heart attack, suicide, misadventure and manslaughter. None of these theories, more or less connected to the various pills Callas was taking, will ever be proved; there was no autopsy or inquest. It appears that cremation was the easiest way to achieve a possible cover-up. A body can be exhumed, but it is difficult to obtain and analyze ashes. In this case even the ashes may have been worthless as evidence.[35]

In 1980, again saying that everything was in accordance with Maria's wishes, the ashes were thrown into the Aegean Sea during an evocative but rather rhetorical ceremony. Nothing now remains of Maria Callas. Should anyone ever have wanted to investigate the real causes of her death, it would have been impossible to examine anything, not even the handful of ashes left after cremation.[36]

The doubt that her death was not caused entirely by natural causes emerges from a note Callas wrote, found in a prayer book on her bedside table. It is a strange and mysterious note and, what is more, is addressed to her husband, Meneghini, who she had left in 1959 for Onassis. . . . There are five lines underneath: *In questi fieri momenti, tu sol mi resti, e il cor mi tenti. Ultima voce del mio destino, ultima croce del mio cammin* (In these proud moments, only you are left for me. My heart tempts me. The last voice of my destiny, the last cross of my life). They are verses from Ponchielli's *Gioconda*, which the protagonist sings in Act Three.[37] Maria, in writing them down, missed the single word of the first line: "Suicidio" (Suicide).[38]

The suicide theory is even more difficult to prove, but a contemporary romantic scenario was readily to hand: not only had Maria lost her voice, but the man she loved "desperately" had abandoned her for another woman. After his death, Callas was left with a broken heart and nothing to live for.[39]

[The date and address of the note of "suicide" might have been forged,] and the whole thing might have been another effort on Meneghini's part to convince himself and show the world that Maria's last message was for him. The most probable explanation for the note is that Callas wrote the words of this aria in order to memorize them. She often used to do this when she was giving concerts because her memory, though excellent for music, was less good for words. These verses may well have been written in 1971 when Callas gave two concerts in London with di Stefano and the piece was in her programme.[40]

Jackie Callas, in her memoirs, expresses her horror that Maria was to be cremated. . . . When the doors creaked open they revealed an official coming forward with a plain metal box. It was so small and Maria had been such a tall woman. Whatever that little box contained was all that was left of her. . . . I never had anything to do with a cremation before, and the object in front of me looked like nothing so much as a dull metal cash-box, no handles, no inscription, anonymous.[41]

In a macabre twist, the urn holding Maria's ashes mysteriously vanished from the vaults of Père Lachaise cemetery on the day after Christmas in 1978, leading to Vasso Devetzi's appearance on television to plead for its return. When the urn was found the next day in a random corner of the cemetery, Devetzi decided the ashes would be safer in a bank vault.[42]

One result of the stealing and subsequent recovery was that "Devetzi herself declared that it no longer contained Maria's ashes."[43] "The incident may have been staged and the ashes exchanged with others."[44] The transfer of the ashes, which were not clearly Callas's ashes, wasn't made public: "The ashes of Maria Callas were placed in a small loculus in the basement of the cemetery. The loculus was marked N. 16258. Many people went there to pray and place flowers but after eighteen months it emerged that the loculus was empty: The ashes had been removed and placed in a bank vault."[45]

"On June 3, 1979 . . . Vasso Devetzi removed Callas's ashes from the bank vault and took them in a box to Greece."[46] Devetzi "pretend[ed] to believe that the casket—which she herself had ceremoniously brought from Paris as if it contained a holy relic—really did contain the ashes of Maria Callas."[47] "She [Devetzi] had coaxed permission from the Greek government to conduct a ceremony during which the ashes would be scattered from a naval destroyer into the Aegean Sea under the auspices of the Greek Ministry of Culture."[48]

Vasso revealed that she has resolved the problem of Maria's ashes. The Greek government had agreed that they should be scattered on the Aegean and that the ceremony was to be arranged for the following month. Jackie Callas wasn't at all sure about this; it seemed too far from what Maria would have wanted, just like the cremation itself. . . . Vasso took me to the harbor at Piraeus where a destroyer of the Greek navy was waiting to sail us out into the Aegean to the spot chosen for the scattering. . . . The warship bucked and heaved in a brisk Aegean swell and the wind howled in the turret. It was evident to me that Maria definitely did not approve of this business. . . . Why they had chosen one spot in the sea as opposed to another I could not say— for that matter I am still unclear why they imagined that my sister would wish to be put into the water at all.[49]

It is not impossible to imagine that after Maria's remains were consigned to the sea, the tides of the Aegean carried those ashes in a southerly direction . . . finally coming to rest . . . her ashes might even have washed up . . . where Aristotle Onasis lies. . . . In a land where love is immortal although the body is not, it's even possible to imagine that on this island, completing the journey they began in 1959, they are finally together and at peace.[50]

The minister made a speech. The usual things about Maria's greatness were said, much of them lost in the air, carried off by the wind. Vasso held the casket, that same grim box that had so upset me in that cold vault a year earlier. She handed it to the minister and for a moment they both wrestled with the lid. The priest intoned a prayer and then the minister approached the rail and tipped the contents over the side. Precisely at that moment, the worst gust of wind of the whole day blew in from the sea and just as Maria's fluffy gray ashes left the receptacle they were instantly blown back over us all. Vasso received most of the fine powder full in her face and as she had her mouth wide open in order to catch her breath in the driving spray, a great deal went straight down her throat. She began to splutter and retch. Indeed we all got some in the face and mouth and were forced to spit and cough it up. The wind howled in the turret. The ship's horn was sounded in mournful tribute, though it appeared more like the moan of an anguished spirit. Rubbing my lips with my handkerchief I looked around at the illustrious party and realized that we were all swallowing Maria's remains. We were helplessly eating my sister; the greatest diva of the century was being consumed by those who had thought to placate her spirit.[51]

Jackie Callas continues: "When I got home Mother told me off for having a smudge on my nose. "You should always check your make-up," she said.[52]

Biographical accounts surrounding Callas's death read like a confusion of script fragments and cinematic genres: a cartoon, clear about the good guy (Callas) and the bad guy (Devetzi, the world); or a *Big Lebowski*, where ashes of the dead friend scattered in the wind are blown into the heroes' mouths; *The Bridges of Madison County,* where the lovers reunite in ashes; a *Death on the Nile,* where eccentric characters and a murdered body are aboard a ship; a *Fitzcarraldo,* with its excessive adoration of opera.

Fellini's Callas

> A world complete without me which is present to me is the world
> of my immortality. This is an importance of film—and a danger.
> It takes my life as my haunting of the world, either because I left
> it unloved (the Flying Dutchman) or because I left unfinished
> business (Hamlet). So there is reason for me to want the camera
> to deny the coherence of the world, its coherence as past: to deny
> that the world is complete without me. But there is equal reason
> to want it affirmed that the world is coherent without me. That is
> essential to what I want of immortality: nature's survival of me. It
> will mean that the present judgement upon me is not yet the last.
> —Stanley Cavell, *The World Viewed*

What if Fellini's ashes are Callas's?[53] What if the ashes stand for a *cinematic* essence of the operatic Callas? That association is not at all implausible, especially given Callas's own involvement with cinema, in particular Italian cinema. It is well known that Callas modeled herself on the physiognomy of a movie star. She projected herself onto the figure of Audrey Hepburn, trying to look cinematic while sounding operatic. Some even suggest that this transformation, which also involved a substantial weight loss and bodily changes, cost the diva her voice (a narrative intimating the dangers of such an attraction to cinema). Not only was Callas drawn to the cinematic image of herself, but film directors were fascinated by the possibility of cinematizing her as they intimated a new order of intimacy between opera and cinema.

Callas's first involvement, if not directly with cinema then with an Italian film director, was in Visconti's famous 1955 production of *La traviata* at La Scala.[54] Visconti's *Traviata* is well documented (photos of this production appear in most books on Callas). Visconti transformed the face of directing opera and staging its singers. He paid attention to the details in costume, gesture, acting, scenery, and staging and raised the awareness of their importance for the conception of the performance. In a letter to Meneghini, Callas's husband at the time, Visconti prophetically says: "All the Traviatas of the future, soon, but not immediately . . . will contain something of the Traviata de Maria. In the beginning, only a little . . . and later, everything."[55]

Figure 6.2. Callas in Visconti's *Traviata*. Reproduced from Renzo Allegri and Roberto Allegri, *Callas by Callas: The Secret Writings of "la Maria"* (New York: Universe Publishing, 1998), 90.

Fellini evokes that Visconti *Callas*: among *E la nave va*'s excessive show of Edmea Tetua's memorabilia, it shows short films of Edmea privately screened by her admirer, the Count of Bassano (the one planning to erect a museum in her memory, or to keep all of her remains in his possession, or to become her, as he impersonates the diva in the film's séance).[56] In these short films-within-the-film, Fellini's diva is made to look like Callas in the role of Violetta in that Visconti staging. This is evident if we compare fragments from these films-within-the-film with photos of Visconti's *Traviata*.

The Callas look: young, beautiful, slim, in a white dress, with a wide white hat, holding up a white umbrella. The happy days of Violetta. Fellini's filmic fragments are a generic Lady of the Camellias (including a favorite flower) or, in turn, a generic Callas. These short films are not performances but the aftermath of performances or shots of the leisure time between them: sailing on a boat, sending the audience kisses from afar, receiving flowers, thanking her audience,[57] as if hinting that film can represent those moments belonging to opera, yet not part of an operatic performance, that it can show us *more* than what is shown within the frame of a performance.[58] And that happiness lies outside the victimization brought about onstage, with death being the fate of song. These short films remind us that after every performance in which a Violetta dies onstage, a Callas reemerges to acknowledge the admirers. It is in these moments that, out of the death of a character, a singer emerges phoenixlike. (Remember that in the opera *La traviata*, the very moment of Violetta's death is that moment of resurrection: "I feel so happy, so happy, wonderful. As if I were reborn! Ah, how curious. . . . I feel my life returning").

For her admirer (the Count of Bassano, who projects her images on the wall), these filmic images are her, as he feels only he truly knew her. It is a "happy Callas." And yet in these fragments of a silent film as "Callas" is projected, what is heard are noises of the projector rather than her voice.[59] In the process of transposing the operatic singer onto the screen, she has undergone two changes: she has become happy and she had lost her voice. In the move from stage to screen, the image of happiness has come to depend on leaving the voice behind. These short silent films represent the singer's voicelessness as resulting from cinema's shortcomings, its inability to sound its characters' voices (as at the beginning of *E la nave va*, we are in 1914, cinema's silent era). But at the same time, the films-within-the-film precisely raise the problem of the transformation of the operatic diva, whose existence is her voice, into a cinematic figure.

The ghost of Visconti's Callas resurfaces in Franco Zeffirelli's staging of *La traviata* with Maria Callas in Dallas in 1958, and then again in his 1982 film *La traviata*. Zeffirelli casts Teresa Stratas in the role of Violetta

Figures 6.3–6.5. Fellini's "Visconti-Callas"

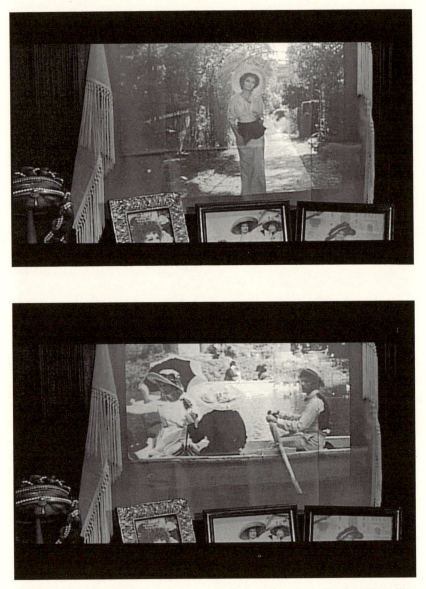

Figures 6.3 and **6.4.** Fellini's filmic fragments are a generic Lady of the Camellias, or, in turn, a generic Callas

Figure 6.5. After every performance in which a Violetta dies onstage, a Callas reemerges to acknowledge the admirers

as a Callas clone.[60] He molds Teresa Stratas's performance into a voice decaying, broken, a nearly lost Callas voice.

In Zeffirelli's film *Callas Forever* (2002), which is indeed about Maria Callas, Teresa Stratas (originally tapped to play the role) was replaced, at her own request, by the actress Fanny Ardant.[61] It may be that the part suits an actress more than it does a singer. But perhaps for Stratas, it was already too much to play not just one of the diva's roles but to impersonate the dead diva herself, miming to the great diva's voice.

In *Callas Forever*, Zeffirelli invents a Callas come back not in opera but in cinema. His film is a fictionalized account of her final months. Instead of retiring, she agrees to film *Carmen*, not using her current voice but miming to her own past recordings. Ultimately Callas renounces the project, and after the film of *Carmen* has been completed, she requests that it never be shown. It seems that what motivated the plot is a story that would *necessitate* the sounding of the voice of the (real) Callas. *Callas Forever* is an attempt to simultaneously "correct" the diva's biography and show the failure of any such attempt. Thus Zeffirelli deals precisely with the question whether Callas on film could have a happier ending than the real Callas or her staged heroines, whether film could offer a form of af-

Figure 6.6. Zeffirelli's "Callas." The ghost of Visconti's Callas resurfaces in Zeffirelli's film of Verdi's *Traviata* (1982).

terlife for the operatic voice, and whether the transposition of the operatic voice into cinema can ever be achieved.[62]

Italian cinema was also deeply drawn to another image of Callas: the primal, archaic Callas. A powerful image, an essence prior to her vocal presence, is captured by Pasolini's casting of Callas in the role of Medea. That casting is based on the knowledge that one of Callas's most famous roles is Cherubini's *Medée*, as well as Norma in Bellini's rewriting of the Medea story. But what is striking in Pasolini's film is the emergence of Callas's intense visual presence. It is not Callas's voice that Pasolini was after but rather something he found Callas to be about that is present without her singing voice. Pasolini commented that Callas "was in truth an ancient woman."[63] It is as if Callas was best fitted for the role of the exiled Medea, most forcefully depicting the foreignness of that Greek figure, precisely by being not just a Greek actress in an Italian rendering of the Greek tragedy but, more important, by not singing in the film. Pasolini's Callas is out of her own operatic element: a diva cast as an outcast. Hence, perhaps, Fellini's choice of Tetua as his Callas-like prima donna's surname, since it evokes Polynesian islands more exotic and alien still, as if European Greece were now too close to home to have any particular symbolic force.

To appreciate the significance of Callas's turn to cinema, we need to recall that Callas was instrumental in reviving the tradition of Italian bel canto opera. She was the singer who brought back into the repertory long-forgotten works, reintroduced bel canto operas, and through them resurrected the intensity of bel canto singing. It was Callas who demonstrated that the intensity of dramatic expression lies within the vocal execution. She, as it were, brought about the return of the reign of the singing voice. The perception of opera—the way we hear opera today—is indebted to Callas's singing. And it is Callas who then chooses, when that voice abandons her, to perform no longer and turn to cinema. Having received many offers, Callas selected *Medea*.[64] She chose to be screened in one of her most famous roles but in a film that does not require her to sing.

The affinity between Pasolini's casting of Callas and *E la nave va* is revealed in one of Pasolini's central and most disturbing scenes in *Medea*: the Dionysian ritual of human sacrifice and fertilization. A young man is sacrificed—his blood and internal organs smeared over the crops in a ritual of regeneration of nature's cycle of growth. The human remains are then burned into ashes. Medea (Maria Callas) is central to the ritual. It is she who operates the wind machine that blows the ashes: human sacrifice, ashes, Callas, paganism, death, regeneration. Clément perceptively relates that scene of the ashes in Pasolini to Callas's own fate—her own ashes. It is Pasolini, Clément claims, who protected Callas from her singing and her fate.

> Let those ashes that she wanted to be ashes have some peace. The only man who hid nothing from himself, loving her enough not to want to make song from her, Pier Paolo Pasolini, is also dead. But the remains of them and their encounter will be the image of a Callas surrounded by brilliant flames, a woman at bay whose face trembled slightly through the flows of expression caused by the burning heat. This blurred face of a Medea, speaking and no longer singing, that was Callas, in flames.[65]

For Clément, Pasolini's casting of a songless Callas is testimony to a certain understanding of the singer, implying that something essential about Callas could not have emerged as long as all "want[ed] to make song from her." This "truth," revealed beyond her singing, Clément associates with the image of Callas in flames. And it is in holding to this fleeting image that one can bring some peace to the ghost of Callas.

Fellini is pointing to the Pasolinian Callas when he names his diva Edmea—an anagram for Medea.[66] But strikingly, in taking the ashes to be Edmea's *own* cremated body, Fellini forgoes not only the voice (since we never hear Edmea Tetua while we are seeing her images projected on-screen) but, ultimately, also the very *visual* presence of the diva that so attracted Pasolini, conveying for him the ancient character he was looking for. For even when Fellini attaches a "face" to his ashes, as in the screened films-within-the-film, it is precisely not the intense face that is so striking in Pasolini's film but the lighthearted, happy Visconti Violetta.

Fellini is known to be absorbed by faces, to choose faces that reveal something of the past, if not of Greek antiquity, then of the Roman world. His characters are not constituted through dialogue or vocal timbre; rather, Fellini's characters *are* their faces: "Fellini's interest in faces is legendary. He is rumored to own file cabinets stuffed with photographs. . . . For Fellini, the human face alone can replace character as a subject. . . . The self/soul [is] pure image."[67] Fellini often placed the following ad in the newspapers: "Federico Fellini is ready to meet all those who wish to see him." Then he would see hundreds of faces: "I look at them all very carefully, and from each visitor steal just a little of his personality. . . . Sometimes I add a new character to the screenplay to accommodate the new face I have discovered. I may see a thousand in order to pick two, but I assimilate them all."[68] Specifically in relation to *E la nave va*, Fellini says:

> Perhaps this time I spent a little more time in choosing faces. I felt that I needed faces that resembled as much as possible those of characters who no longer exist, that time has stolen from us, who nonetheless still touch us, they evoke an interest, we want to know more about them; a certain way of combing their hair, out of style today, their way of laughing, of looking at us, their forlorn glance, want to reveal to us the essence of a story, the unfolding of their existence.[69]

And elsewhere: "the feeling I wanted to create was that of old photographs, the feeling that nothing you see has survived—photographs of unknown people of whom the only thing known is that they are dead."[70] For Edmea Tetua, Fellini records a fleeting recognition of a Callas role, leaving traces not only of Callas the singer but also of her presence in cinema, further linking the fate of cinema with that of opera. In Callas, cinema projects onto opera its own image, as though pointing toward an aspect of opera that always intended to become cinematic; and in Callas cinema also reflects back on itself as though, through her, cinema remembers its own past.

Phoenix

> And then an unearthly and beautiful sound filled the air. . . . It was coming from every thread of the light-spun web vibrating around Harry and Voldemort. It was a sound Harry recognized, though he had heard it only once before in his life: phoenix song.

It was the sound of hope to Harry . . . the most beautiful and
welcome thing he had ever heard in his life. . . . He felt as though
the song were inside him instead of just around him. . . . It was
the sound he connected with Dumbledore, and it was almost as
though a friend were speaking in his ear . . . *Don't break the
connection*. I know, Harry told the music, I know I mustn't.
— J. K. Rowling, *Harry Potter and the Goblet of Fire*

Here are Fellini's words about opera:

Opera has always held a great fascination for me. It is a kind of Italian ritual,
an emblem of Italianness, our most accurate reflection. It has gone on
throughout Italian history: the Wars of Independence, the struggle for Unification, Fascism, the Resistance. It is the form of spectacle that most resembles us, that most directly expresses our psychology, our mentality, our sense
of style. It's as inaccurate, superficial, shoddy, distracting, stupefying—that is
to say, as Italian—as one can imagine. Furious passions, ferocious vendettas,
unimaginably exaggerated affections, unbelievable plots, swashbuckling ex-
ploits, insane libretti, costumes hired from funeral outfitters, nonsensical
lighting, conductors at odds with the orchestra, singers who start running
just when the music reaches its best point. . . . To invite me to direct an opera
is like asking me to direct a solemn mass, a pastoral songfest, a procession, a
military parade or a funeral procession.[71]

Such opinions explain his fascination and also why he resisted opera. If
opera is not identified by way of its contents, of its voice, of its meta-
physics, but rather becomes part of the Italian landscape, then it can figure
in Fellini's film like a funeral procession—or, better even, as the funeral
procession of opera. It is here that Italy, opera, and cinema all come
together.

Can these reflections provide a further insight into my fundamental
question, How is the death of cinema refracted through the death of
opera? Death scenes pose no threat to opera; on the contrary, those deaths
allow its future. As opera's life turns on its deaths, ever anew it awaits the
imminent death that calls for the highest moment of song. The voices of
opera announce their immortality in their death song; their song resounds
precisely in being a death song. And yet, in its attempt to relate to the
voice of opera, Fellini's film is different from films interpreted in previous
chapters.

E la nave va forgoes in advance the attempt to recapture the essence of
the voice revealed in death. The film begins with the journey of the remains. It does not attempt to recapture a lost voice, even though it surrounds it with ridiculous tales of its power; nor does it suggest its intensity
indirectly when the object is already gone. But rather, Fellini's film cap-

tures the burdenless and grotesque side of opera's belief in its quest for the sublime.

Reducing the operatic body to ashes and emitting a technically reproduced voice is the goal of the film insofar as it allows for everything essentially operatic to happen *around it*: this is the way in which Fellini's film takes its power and life from those ashes. A congregation of bizarre characters, in all their diverse physiognomies, nationalities, and eccentricities, are gathered around the bodily remains, as are the various fragments or objects that are the carriers of memory. In the loss of that divine or mythical world the faces of humanity come to gather and provide the spectacle to which Fellini's cinema is attracted. *E la nave va*, says Fellini, "doesn't mean, the moment when the ship leaves, but in colloquial Italian has the symbolic meaning that, despite everything, it sails on—or, life goes on."[72] One can hardly imagine an opera that thematizes what one does with remains. But film, Fellini's film, seems particularly attracted to those traces of a past, as if asserting that the death of film itself would not mean its end, for there can always be a film about these traces of a past. In response to the question of whether the burial of Edmea Tetua represents the funeral of cinema, Fellini answers: "yes, if we accept that this funeral is told by cinema itself; thus at the very moment of this feared end, there is rebirth."[73]

Has cinema, then, died in this film about opera?

The figuring of Callas in a meditation on the death of cinema shows that opera can be reborn *in cinema* without losing what is *operatic* about it. Fellini's opening, mimicking as it does a black-and-white silent film, points to a form of film that has passed away, that has died without any hope of resurrection. But it is not a gesture pointing to the end of cinema. Since the *diva's ashes* magically "enliven" the screen, they introduce coloration and sounds when they are brought up onboard, awakening the film to the enchantment of the world of colors and human voices. The same gesture of voice enlivening the image occurs when, in the film, the princess translates the voices she hears into colors that she is blind to. In *E la nave va*, opera does not appear as such, but its memories and recorded traces are those ashes that can revive film. As a phoenix, a bird miraculously reborn from its own ashes, film, without allowing opera to die in its place, rises from the ashes of opera.

NOTES

INTRODUCTION

1. For a thorough and insightful investigation of filmed operas, see Marcia Citron, *Opera on Screen* (New Haven: Yale University Press, 2000).

2. Catherine Clément, *Opera, or The Undoing of Women*, trans. Betsy Wing (Minneapolis: University of Minnesota Press, 1988).

3. Michel Poizat, *The Angel's Cry: Beyond the Pleasure Principle in Opera*, trans. Arthur Denner (Ithaca: Cornell University Press, 1992), 145.

4. Slavoj Žižek, "I Do Not Order My Dreams," in *Opera's Second Death*, by Slavoj Žižek and Mladen Dolar (New York: Routledge, 2002), 110.

5. Instances of this argument can be found in Carolyn Abbate's latest book: *In Search of Opera* (Princeton: Princeton University Press, 2001).

6. Wayne Koestenbaum, liner notes to *Jackie O*, music by Michael Daugherty, libretto by Wayne Koestenbaum, 1997, Decca Record Company, 455 591–2.

7. See also E. T. Cone's formulation: "[Orpheus's] role as composer-singer symbolizes what it means to be an operatic character." E. T. Cone, "The World of Opera and Its Inhabitants" (1988), in *Music: A View from Delft* (Chicago: University of Chicago Press, 1989), 135. Abbate questions the very meaning of the Orphic power. She writes: "But what voice can recall the dead to life?" See "Orpheus. One Last Performance," in *In Search of Opera*, 1–54; quotation, 53.

8. Stanley Cavell, "Opera and the Lease of Voice," in *A Pitch of Philosophy: Autobiographical Exercises* (Cambridge, Mass.: Harvard University Press, 1994), 140.

9. Franz Kafka, "The Silence of the Sirens," in *The Complete Stories* (New York: Schocken Books, 1971), 430–32.

10. Wayne Koestenbaum, *The Queen's Throat: Opera, Homosexuality, and the Mystery of Desire* (New York: Poseidon Press, 1993), 44.

11. Theodor Adorno, "Bourgeois Opera" (1955), in *Opera Through Other Eyes*, ed. David Levin (Stanford: Stanford University Press, 1994), 29, 41.

12. Jeremy Tambling, *Opera, Ideology and Film* (New York: St. Martin's Press, 1987); and his "Introduction: Opera in the Distraction Culture," in *A Night in at the Opera*, ed. Jeremy Tambling (London: John Libbey, 1994), 1–23.

13. Cavell, "Opera and the Lease of Voice," 144.

14. Abbate, *In Search of Opera*, viii–ix.

CHAPTER 1
THE PHANTOM OF THE OPERA: THE LOST VOICE OF OPERA IN SILENT FILM

This chapter is a slightly revised version of the article "*The Phantom of the Opera*: The Lost Voice of Opera in Silent Film," which originally appeared in *Cambridge Opera Journal* 11, no. 2 (1999): 179–92.

1. Quoted in Tambling, *Opera, Ideology and Film*, 42 (emphasis is mine).

2. Cavell, "Opera and the Lease of Voice," 136.

3. Opera's novel relationship with film occurs concurrently with opera's own requestioning of its relation to traditions and to shifting meanings of the operatic. See the discussion in chapter 5, "Opera on the Phone: The Call of the Human Voice." See also Pierre Boulez, "Opera Houses? Blow Them Up," *Opera* (June 1986): 440–50; Henry Pleasants, *Opera in Crisis: Tradition, Present, Future* (New York: Thames and Hudson, 1989); Tom Sutcliffe, *Believing in Opera* (Princeton: Princeton University Press, 1996); Michal Grover-Friedlander and Eli Friedlander, "Opera," in *Encyclopaedia of Aesthetics*, 4 vols., ed. Michael Kelly (Oxford: Oxford University Press, 1998).

4. Tambling, *Opera, Ideology and Film*, 55.

5. For a discussion devoted to the various explanations of film's attraction to opera, see ibid., chapter 2: "Film aspiring to the condition of opera" (41–67). Here Tambling mentions a few prima donnas who were lent to silent film, but does not account for their silence.

6. Few films in the twenties had musical scores written specifically for them. One example is Satie's musical score for *Entr'acte cinématographique*, directed by René Claire (1924). For a thorough discussion of the music that accompanied silent film, see Martin Marks, *Music and the Silent Film: Contexts and Case Studies, 1895–1924* (Oxford: Oxford University Press, 1997). There is little research on early films of operas. For films of operas through 1906, see ibid., 258 n. 31. For special problems in compiling music for opera films, see Tambling, *Opera, Ideology and Film*, 72–74; for a monograph-length analysis, see David Levin, *Richard Wagner, Fritz Lang, and the Nibelungen: The Dramaturgy of Disavowal* (Princeton: Princeton University Press, 1998). For recent research, see Rose Theresa, "From Méphistophélès to Méliès: Spectacle and Narrative in Opera and Early Film," in *Between Opera and Cinema*, ed. Jeongwon Joe and Rose Theresa (New York: Routledge, 2002), 1–18.

7. For music's functions in film, see Claudia Gorbman, *Unheard Melodies: Narrative Film Music* (Bloomington: Indiana University Press, 1987).

8. Most scholars consider *The Jazz Singer* (1927) to be the first talking film, although the sound was achieved mostly by synchronizing song and a plot about competing styles of song. Even so, the film is, for the most part, still silent. See Martin Marks, "The Sound of Music," especially 248–55, and Geoffrey Nowell-Smith, "Sound Cinema, 1930–1960," 207–19, both in *The Oxford History of World Cinema*, ed. Geoffrey Nowell-Smith (Oxford: Oxford University Press, 1996).

9. See the interpretation of silence and the relation of the operatic voice to speech in *The World Viewed: Reflections on the Ontology of Film*, by Stanley Cavell (Cambridge, Mass.: Harvard University Press, 1979), especially chapter 19, "The Acknowledgement of Silence" (146–60), and *A Pitch of Philosophy*, chapter 3, "Opera and the Lease of Voice," where he writes: "We could almost take the blatant conventionality of opera as meant to call into question the conventions or conditions making civil discourse possible—the pace, the distance, the pitch, the length, at which literal speech is supposed to take place—as though some problem had arisen about *speaking* as such" (136). From the opposite perspective, Cavell

writes that film raises questions fundamental to opera such as "who sings?" "what is singing?" and "what causes it?" (ibid., 135).

10. Poizat, *Angel's Cry*.

11. An interpretation of song as leading to the limit of vocal expression and of signification in language is presented in Søren Kierkegaard's discussion of Mozart's *Don Giovanni* in *Either-Or*, vol. I, trans. Walter Lowrie (1944; reprint, Princeton: Princeton University Press, 1971); as well as in Friedrich Nietzsche's understanding of the essential Dionysian face of opera as an inheritance of Greek tragedy in *The Birth of Tragedy*, trans. Walter Kaufmann (New York: Vintage Books, 1967). I discuss later in the chapter the Lacanian conception of the limit of and the quest for voice, which is the foundation of Poizat's interpretation.

12. For a historical survey of filmed operas, see Marcia Citron, *Opera on Screen* (New Haven: Yale University Press, 2000), especially 20–68. See also Richard Fawkes, *Opera on Film* (London: Duckworth, 2000); Richard Evidon, "Film," in *The New Grove Dictionary of Opera*, vol. 2, ed. Stanley Sadie (1992; reprint, New York: Grove's Dictionaries of Music, 1998), 194–200; and Tambling, *Opera, Ideology and Film*.

13. *The Phantom of the Opera* is based on a novel with the same title by Gaston Leroux (1911). It starred Lon Chaney as the Phantom and Mary Philbin as Christine. *The Phantom of the Opera*, directed by Rupert Julian (Universal Production, 1925).

14. Theodor Adorno and Hanns Eisler, *Composing for the Films* (1947; reprint, London: Athlone Press, 1994). From a psychoanalytic perspective, this impossibility is an immanent outcome of the formation of the subject through its entrance into a prior existing language. The introduction of the subject into language is traumatic. It is along these lines that Žižek renounces the notion of harmonious complementarity between sight and sound. For Žižek, the beginning of sound film does not alter the fundamental relationship between the visual and auditory dimensions, as voice functions as voice object for the visual. The effect of the addition of the soundtrack, then, was not a closer imitation of reality, but rather it made voice autonomous. "The moment we enter the symbolic order [speech], an unbridgeable gap separates forever a human body from 'its' voice. The voice acquires a spectral autonomy, it never quite belongs to the body we see, so that even when we see a living person talking, there is always some degree of ventriloquism at work: it is as if the speaker's own voice hollows him out and in a sense speaks 'by itself,' through him." "'I Hear You with My Eyes'; or The Invisible Master," in *Gaze and Voice as Love Objects*, ed. Renata Salecl and Slavoj Žižek (Durham: Duke University Press, 1996), 92. For other accounts of the loss inflicted on film with the achievement of synchronized speech, see Rudolf Arnheim, *Film as Art* (1957; reprint, Berkeley: University of California Press, 1966); Sergei Eisenstein, *Film Form [and] the Film Sense*, trans. and ed. J. Leyda (New York: Harvest Books, 1969); Amy Lawrence, *Echo and Narcissus: Women's Voices in Classical Hollywood Cinema* (Berkeley: University of California Press, 1991); Rick Altman, "Moving Lips: Cinema as Ventriloquism," *Yale French Studies* 60 (1980): 67–79.

15. Kaja Silverman, "Lost Objects and Mistaken Subjects: A Prologue," in *The Acoustic Mirror: The Female Voice in Psychoanalysis and Cinema* (Bloomington: Indiana University Press, 1988), 5, 2.

16. Ibid., 9.

17. André Bazin, *What Is Cinema?* trans. Hugh Gray (Berkeley: University of California Press, 1967); Christian Metz, *The Imaginary Signifier: Psychoanalysis and the Cinema,* trans. Cecilia Britton, Annwyl Williams, Ben Brewster, and Alfred Guzzetti (Bloomington: Indiana University Press, 1982). See also Jean-Louis Comolli, "Machines of the Visible," in *The Cinematic Apparatus,* ed. Teresa de Lauretis and Stephen Heath (London: Macmillan, 1980).

18. Cavell, *The World Viewed,* 26.

19. Adorno and Eisler, *Composing for the Films,* 75. For related notions, see Cavell, *The World Viewed,* chapter 19: "The Acknowledgement of Silence" (146–61).

20. For the presentation of other positions regarding the advent of speech in film, see Roy Prendergast, *Film Music, a Neglected Art: A Critical Study of Music in Films* (New York: Norton, 1992), chapter 1: "Music in the Silent Film" (3–18).

21. This is why I am concerned solely with the relation of the film to its evocation of opera. The novel on which the film is based indeed raises many issues, but precisely not that of silence for which the medium of film is responsible and evokes in the extreme.

22. Žižek, however, opposes scream and song in *The Phantom of the Opera*: the song's power is in its resonance with the maternal voice, whereas the (vocalized) scream is an entrance into the community, a horrific reaction to the enjoyment. Žižek opposes the silent scream with the scream of "release, of decision, of *choice,* the scream by means of which the unbearable tension finds an outlet: we so to speak, 'spit out the bone' in the relief of vocalization." "Why Does the *Phallus* Appear?" in *Enjoy Your Symptom: Jacques Lacan in Hollywood and Out* (New York: Routledge, 1992), 117. Žižek mentions "the most famous scream in the history of cinema": the scream of the mother in *Battleship Potemkin;* "its entire effect is . . . based on the fact that we do not hear her scream" (ibid.). On the cry in cinema, see also Silverman, *Acoustic Mirror,* especially 77.

23. See also Žižek: "an image can emerge as the placeholder for a sound that doesn't yet resonate but remains stuck in the throat." A scream that is silent marks the moment at which the voice fails, we hear it with our eyes. It is horrifying to hear beyond visual representation, the blind spot, to hear with our eyes, to see the silence: it stands for death. "I Hear You with My Eyes," 93.

24. Julia Kristeva, *Powers of Horror: An Essay on Abjection,* trans. Leon Roudiez (New York: Columbia University Press, 1982); Guy Rosolato, "La voix," in *Essai sur le symbolique* (Paris: Gallimard, 1969), 287–305; Silverman, *Acoustic Mirror;* Michel Chion, *La voix au cinéma* (Paris: Editions de L'Etoile, 1985); Mikhail Yampolsky, "Voice Devoured: Artaud and Borges on Dubbing," trans. Larry Joseph, *October* 64 (Spring 1993): 57–77. See also discussions of the psychoanalytic voice in relation to music in Carolyn Abbate's "Debussy's Phantom Sounds," *Cambridge Opera Journal* 10, no. 1 (1998): 67–96; Tambling, *Opera, Ideology and Film,* 51, and his "Towards a Psychopathology of Opera," *Cambridge Opera Journal* 9, no. 3 (November 1997): 263–80.

25. For accounts of the phonocentric tradition and its undermining, see, for instance, Mladen Dolar, "The Object Voice," in *Gaze and Voice as Love Objects,* ed.

Salecl and Žižek, 7–31; Žižek, "'I Hear You with My Eyes'"; Silverman, *Acoustic Mirror*, Jacques Lacan, "L'angoisse" (unpublished seminar, 1962–63); Giorgio Agamben, *Language and Death: The Place of Negativity* (Minneapolis: University of Minnesota Press, 1991); Gayatri Chakravorty Spivak, translator's preface in *Of Grammatology*, by Jacques Derrida (Baltimore: Johns Hopkins University Press, 1976), ix–lxxxvii; Jonathan Culler, *On Deconstruction: Theory and Criticism after Structuralism* (Ithaca: Cornell University Press, 1982); Carolyn Abbate, *Unsung Voices: Opera and Musical Narrative in the Nineteenth Century* (Princeton: Princeton University Press, 1991); and her "Debussy's Phantom Sounds" and "Opera; or the Envoicing of Women," in *Musicology and Difference: Gender and Sexuality in Music Scholarship*, ed. Ruth Solie (Berkeley: University of California Press, 1993); Kristeva, *Powers of Horror*.

26. Dolar, "Object Voice," 15.

27. Žižek, "I Hear You with My Eyes," 92.

28. Poizat, *Angel's Cry*, and his *La voix du diable: La jouissance lyrique sacrée* (Paris: Métailié, 1991).

29. This is written about music in general, not just opera. See Dolar, "Object Voice," 10.

30. Poizat, *Angel's Cry*, 198.

31. In later versions of *The Phantom of the Opera*, the mother cannot look at him and their relationship is established through her voice; in others, she herself is an opera singer. In the 1943 filmic version of *The Phantom of the Opera*, before his disfiguring accident, the Phantom is a violin player in the opera house orchestra (as is Christine's father in Leroux's novel). In this later version, the Phantom is further associated with the father of the novel both by being elderly and by originating from the same remote village as Christine. In this version, even before his face is deformed, the Phantom secretly pays for Christine's voice lessons. This, however, is the sole remnant of an association between the Phantom and voice in that film. (This version of *The Phantom of the Opera* starred Claude Rains as the Phantom, Susanna Foster as the soprano, and Nelson Eddy as the soprano's lover.) *The Phantom of the Opera*, directed by Arthur Lubin (Universal Pictures, 1943).

32. See Žižek, "Why Does the *Phallus* Appear?" 113–46, for an account of versions of *The Phantom of the Opera* in relation to the quest for the ever-lost maternal voice. For an interpretation of the psychoanalytic account of the maternal voice as enacted in the voice of opera, see Poizat, *Angel's Cry*; Tambling, "Towards a Psychopathology," 263–80; and Heather Hadlock, "Return of the Repressed: The Prima Donna from Hoffmann's *Tales* to Offenbach's *Contes*," *Cambridge Opera Journal* 6, no. 3 (1994): 221–44. Wayne Koestenbaum expands on the theme of the operatic voice and motherhood in another sense when he shows how the prima donna is haunted by her mother and by the voices of other prima donnas. Wayne Koestenbaum, *The Queen's Throat*.

33. In 1896 the chandelier of the Paris opera house did in fact crash and kill someone in the audience. "The horrific accident aroused a sensational reaction in certain newspapers of the day." See the account in George Perry, *The Complete Phantom of the Opera* (New York: Henry Holt, 1988), 18–21.

34. See Clément, *Opera, or The Undoing of Women*.

35. For a discussion of the genre of Expressionism, see, for instance, David Robinson, *Das Cabinet des Dr. Caligari* (London: British Film Institute, 1997), 35; and Lotte Eisner, *The Haunted Screen* (Berkeley: University of California Press, 1973).

36. In 1924 there was no tradition of horror films to build on. See Scott MacQueen, "The 1925 *Phantom of the Opera*," in *American Cinematography* (September and October 1989): 34; Nowell-Smith, *Oxford History of World Cinema*, 198–99; Michael Blake, *Lon Chaney: The Man behind the Thousand Faces* (Maryland: Vestal Press, 1996).

37. Perry, *Complete Phantom of the Opera*, 50. See also the film starring James Cagney as Lon Chaney, about the life of Lon Chaney. *Man of a Thousand Faces*, directed by Joseph Pevney (Universal Pictures, 1957).

38. See Žižek, "Why Does the *Phallus* Appear?" for the threat in the distortion of the amorphic, shapeless flesh hidden by the mask.

39. The Phantom's appearance is altered twice in the course of the film: in the moment of unmasking and in the masked ball. In the latter scene, when everyone puts on a mask, the Phantom changes his to a skull, like a man risen from the dead. (This is the sole colored sequence in the film.) The effect of the unmasked and doubly masked Phantom is horrific, as if the double covering amounts to the same as unmasking. Indeed, in the novel, the Phantom is the only character during the masked ball who is, in fact, *without* a mask, "the skull of this 'Red Death' being his actual face." See the discussion in *The Underground of "The Phantom of the Opera": Sublimation and the Gothic in Leroux's Novel and Its Progeny*, by Jerrold E. Hogle (New York: Palgrave, 2002), 5.

40. For a different context for this idea, see Žižek, "Why Does the *Phallus* Appear?" 116.

41. For a different sense of the impossibility of reconstructing a representation of the lost voice of the operatic castrato, see Katherine Bergeron, "The Castrato as History," *Cambridge Opera Journal* 8, no. 2 (1996): 167–84.

42. The libretto of Gounod's *Faust* reads as follows: "Can it be you, Marguerite? / Answer me, answer me quickly! / No, no, it's no longer you! / It's your face no longer! / It's a king's daughter / . . . Let's complete the transformation! / Now I'm dying to try / the bracelet and the necklace! / Heavens! it's like a hand being laid on my arm!" (trans. Peggy Cochrane). In the novel, the meaning of the aria texts are embedded within the narrative and explicate the main plot. In the film, of course, we only see the operatic voice (silenced or heard); we lack the text.

43. For a discussion of the Lacanian mirror stage in film theory, see Silverman, *Acoustic Mirror*, 7, and her discussion of Jane Gallop's "Where to Begin?" which can be found in *Reading Lacan* (Ithaca: Cornell University Press, 1985), 74–92. See also Lawrence, *Echo and Narcissus*.

44. As Žižek humorously writes, "vampires are invisible in the mirror: because they have read Lacan and, consequently, know how to behave—they materialize *objet a* which, by definition, 'cannot be mirrored.' " Žižek, "Why Does the *Phallus* Appear?" 126. In the 1931 film *Dracula*, the identity of Count Dracula as vampire is exposed when his reflection is missing form the mirror, when he recoils in

horror from looking into a mirror unexpectedly put in front of him. *Dracula*, directed by Carl Laemmle (Universal Studios, 1931).

45. See Joan Copjec, *Read My Desire: Lacan against the Historians* (Cambridge, Mass.: MIT Press, 1994), especially chapter 2, "The Orthopsychic Subject: Film Theory and the Reception of Lacan," 15–38, and chapter 5, "Vampires, Breast-Feeding, and Anxiety," 117–40.

46. For an elaboration of these themes, see the introduction.

47. This is in contrast to the pattern of *Beauty and the Beast*, in which Beauty, overcoming what she sees, has the power to affect the visual so that the beast is transformed into a beauty—a perfected and fitting partner to her beauty. In Leroux's novel *The Phantom of the Opera*, the reaction of the prima donna to the revelation of the Phantom's face is kinder than in the film. It is this empathy, rather than the horror stressed in the film, that structures the novel and its ending in the prima donna's kiss and the Phantom's remorse.

48. It is interesting that there were several versions of the film's ending, specifically with regard to the Phantom's fate. This shows the difficulties in containing the fate of the Phantom even on the level of production and plot. See MacQueen, "The 1925 *Phantom of the Opera*."

CHAPTER 2
BROTHERS AT THE OPERA

This chapter is a slightly revised version of an article published under the title "'There ain't no Sanity Claus!': The Marx Brothers at the Opera," in *Between Opera and Cinema*, ed. Jeongwon Joe and Rose Theresa (New York: Routledge, 2002), 19–37.

1. Yet another reference is found in Groucho's televised version of Gilbert and Sullivan's *Mikado*. See Allen Eyles, "*A Night at the Opera*," *Films and Filming* 11, no. 5 (February 1965): 19.

2. Glenn Mitchell, *The Marx Brothers Encyclopedia* (London: Batsford, 1996), 189 (emphasis added).

3. For a different view that holds that the film retains the social assumptions of earlier films—opera as social snobbery, luxury, money, and entertainment for the rich—see Gerald Mast, *The Comic Mind* (Chicago: University of Chicago Press, 1979), 285.

4. For an account of the complex relationship between actor and character in film, see Cavell, *The World Viewed*, and Leo Braudy, *The World in a Frame: What We See in Films* (Chicago: University of Chicago Press, 1976).

5. Both the director and the producer of *A Night at the Opera* were steeped in images of the silent era. Sam Wood, the director, began his career in filmmaking as an assistant to DeMille, directing his own film in 1920, "thereafter working with Gloria Swanson, Valentino, Jackie Coogan, Norma Shearer and Marion Davies before sound came." See Eyles, "*A Night at the Opera*," 18. The producer, Irving Thalberg, produced several silent films, including *The Hunchback of Notre Dame* (1923), with Lon Chaney—the Phantom in *The Phantom of the Opera*—*He Who*

Gets Slapped (1924), and *Ben Hur* (1925), prior to his collaboration with the Marx Brothers. For an entire list of Thalberg's productions, see Groucho Marx, *Groucho and Me: The Autobiography of Groucho Marx* (New York: B. Geis Associates, distributed by Random House, 1959), 178.

6. Marx, *Groucho and Me*, 166.

7. Chaplin's refusal to use synchronized dialogue in his first sound films attests to a fundamental sense of loss that accompanies the advent of sound: "[Chaplin] realiz[ed] . . . the antithesis of the comedy of physical personality and the structural demands of comedy that uses words to communicate the character's feelings and thoughts." See Mast, *Comic Mind*, 25–26. For theoretical discussions regarding synchronization as the loss of intimacy between sound and image, see chapter 3 of this book.

8. Script by Kevin McGuinness. See Joe Adamson, *Groucho, Harpo, Chico and Sometimes Zeppo* (New York: Simon and Schuster, 1973), 251–300.

9. A similar idea linking Harpo and the operatic voice is voiced by Kramer: "Harpo supplies his own version of the operatic voice whose absence marks his entry into the movie. . . . Garbo may talk all she likes. Harpo whistles." Lawrence Kramer, "The Singing Salami: Unsystematic Reflections on the Marx Brothers' *A Night at the Opera*," in *A Night in at the Opera*, ed. Tambling, 265.

10. For the thematics of silence and the visualization of music with film, see Fred Camper, "Sound and Silence in Narrative and Nonnarrative Cinema," in *Film Sound: Theory and Practice* (New York: Columbia University Press, 1985), 369–81.

11. For the importance of language in the Marx Brothers' performance, see Robert Benayoun, *Les Marx Brothers ont la parole* (Paris: Editions du Seuil, 1991).

12. Mast, *Comic Mind*, 24–25.

13. Ibid., 282.

14. Ibid.

15. For a discussion of Harpo in relation to other mute characters on film, see Michel Chion, "Le dernier mot du muet," *Cahiers du Cinéma* 330 (December 1981): 4–15, and 331 (January 1982): 30–37.

16. C. A. LeJeune in *The Observer*, November 19, 1944, on the occasion of one of the film's reissues; quoted in Eyles, "*A Night at the Opera*," 18.

17. For differing accounts of operatic libretti, see *Reading Opera*, ed. Arthur Groos and Roger Parker (Princeton: Princeton University Press, 1988). For an extreme opinion that totally disregards the libretto, see Paul Robinson, "A Deconstructive Postscript: Reading Libretti and Misreading Opera," in ibid., 328–46. An opposite view, one in which the libretto is crucial, is voiced by Catherine Clément in her *Opera, or The Undoing of Women*.

18. Harpo's early performances were not mute; he sang with the other brothers as one of the three, then four, Nightingales. It was on Broadway that he first transformed his act to a mute one—that is, before the Marx Brothers' move to the film industry in the late 1920s. In this context, the fact that Harpo participated in a silent film from 1925 (*Too Many Kisses*)—the only Marx brother to do so—is more than a mere anecdote, as his acting style did not change after the silent era.

19. Marcello Conati, "Higher than the Highest, the Music Better than the

Best," in *Il Trovatore*, ed. Nicholas John (London: English National Opera Guide 20, 1983), 14.

20. Bruno Barilli, *Il paese del melodramma e altri scritti musicale*, ed. Enrico Falqui (Florence: Vellechi, 1963); and Massimo Mila, *La giovinezza di Verdi* (Torino: ERI, 1978), both quoted by Conati in "Higher than the Highest," 7.

21. For scholarship about the opera, see, for instance, Pierluigi Petrobelli, "Towards an Explanation of the Dramatic Structure of *Il trovatore*," in *Music Analysis* 1, no. 2 (1980): 129–41; William Drabkin, "Character, Key Relations and Tonal Structure in *Il trovatore*," ibid., 143–53; Roger Parker, "The Dramatic Structure of *Il trovatore*," ibid. 155–67; Martin Chusid and Thomas Kaufman, "The First Three Years of *Trovatore*," *Verdi Newsletter* 15 (1987): 30–49; Elizabeth Hudson, "Performing the Past: Narrative Convention as Dramatic Content in *Il trovatore*," in "Narrative in Verdi: Perspectives on His Musical Dramaturgy" (Ph.D. diss., Cornell University, 1993), 192–254; Scott Balthazar, "Plot and Tonal Design as Compositional Constraints in *Il trovatore*," *Current Musicology* 60 (1996): 51–78; James Hepokoski, "*Ottocento* Opera as Cultural Drama: Generic Mixtures in *Il trovatore*," and Martin Chusid, "A New Source for *El trovador* and Its Implications for the Tonal Organization of *Il trovatore*," both in *Verdi's Middle Period: Source Studies, Analysis, and Performance Practice*, ed. Martin Chusid (Chicago: University of Chicago Press, 1997), 147–96 and 207–26; Roger Parker, "Leonora's Last Act: *Il trovatore*," in *Leonora's Last Act: Essays in Verdian Discourse* (Princeton: Princeton Universtiy Press, 1997), 168–87; Michal Grover, "To Die Songless: An Interpretation of a Troubadour's Death," in "Voicing Death in Verdi's Operas" (Ph.D. diss., Brandeis University, 1997), 324–83.

22. Mast, *Comic Mind*, 282–85.

23. For this insight, see Stanley Cavell, "The Acknowledgment of Silence," in *The World Viewed*, 159.

24. The intention was to draw in a female audience, which, according to Thalberg, was interested in films with romantic themes.

25. It is this relation between the tragic and the comic that Nietzsche discovers at the heart of ancient tragedy and that forms the basis of the possibility of an affirmation of life in the tragic. Nietzsche identifies the chorus of satyrs and its anarchic power as the remedy for the melancholy of the one who understands fate. For an elaboration of the tragic in relation to the comic within the world of opera, see part 2 (chapters 3 and 4). For an insight into "the power of film to achieve the happy ending," see Stanley Cavell, "Nothing Goes without Saying," *London Review of Books* 16, no. 1 (January 6, 1994): 3; and Theodor Adorno, "Bourgeois Opera," in *Opera through Other Eyes*, ed. Levin, 32.

26. On this issue, see chapter 3.

27. It is unusual for the Marx Brothers to be involved in their plots to the extent that they attempt to rescue or save the situation. This change in emphasis might be the result of the theme of rescue within the operatic plot of *Il trovatore*.

28. For an elaboration of these ideas, see Grover, "To Die Songless," 324–83.

29. We also hear the bell tolling and an accompaniment of the death topos. On the death topos, see Frits Noske, *The Signifier and the Signified: Studies in the Operas of Mozart and Verdi* (Oxford: Clarendon Press, 1990).

30. The opera has an attempted wedding between Leonora and the trouba-dour. In the opera, however, the wedding is interrupted. The unconsummated wedding is symbolized by an extremely short love duet granted to the couple.

CHAPTER 3
OTELLO'S ONE VOICE

1. I have discussed these works in my "Verdi's Shakespearean Operas: Voice and Body in *Otello* and *Falstaff*" (paper presented at Shakespeare on Screen: The Centenary Conference, Spain, September 1999). For an interpretation of Zef-firelli's *Otello*, see Marcia Citron, "Matter of Belief: *Otello* on Film and Televi-sion," in *Opera on Screen*, 69–111; and her "Night at the Cinema: Zeffirelli's Otello and the Genre of Film-Opera," in *The Musical Quarterly* 78, no. 4 (Winter 1994): 700–741. For a discussion of Zeffirelli's *La traviata*, see Jeremy Tambling, "Between the Spectacle and the Specular: *La traviata*," in *Opera, Ideology and Film*, 176–93.

2. Jeremy Tambling and Marcia Citron have opposite views on the notion of filmed operas as a distinct genre: Tambling does not think a genre is being estab-lished, and Citron argues filmed operas are an independent genre with their own properties. Tambling, *Opera, Ideology and Film*, especially 3; and Citron, *Opera on Screen*, especially 6–10.

3. Brooks Peters, "Classic Vision," *Opera News*, 66, no. 10 (April 2002): 18–28; quotation, 21. For a list of operas directed by Zeffirelli, consult Citron, "Matter of Belief," 71–72; and Gianfranco Casadio, *Opera e cinema: La musica lirica nel cinema italiano dall'avvanto del sonore ad oggi* (Ravenna: Longo Edi-tore, 1995).

4. Martin Dworkin, "'Stay Illusion!' Having Words about Shakespeare on Screen," *The Journal of Aesthetic Education* 11 (January 1977): 59, quoted in *Shakespeare on Screen: A Century of Film and Television*, by Kenneth Rothwell (Cambridge: Cambridge University Press, 1999), 133. For similar accounts, see also Casadio, *Opera e cinema*, 21–22.

5. Dan Lybarger, "Spreading the Wrong Gospel: An Interview with Franco Zeffirelli," *Pitch Weekly*, March 13, 1999. Reproduced on http://www.tipjar .com/dan/zeffirelli.htm, 2–3 (emphasis added).

6. Peters, "Classic Vision," 23.

7. Götz Friedrich, "Zur Musiktheater—Regie heute," in *Die Deutsche Oper Berlin*, ed. Gisela Huwe (Berlin: Quadriga Verlag J. Severin, 1984), 222.

8. "Die Oper zeigt sich in den Medien von einer neuen Seite" (1985), inter-view with Imre Fabian, in *Musiktheater: Ansichten, Einsichten*, by Götz Friedrich (Frankfurt am Main: Propyläen, 1986), 354–55.

9. Friedrich, "Zur Musiktheater," 221–28; quotation, 228.

10. Ibid., 227.

11. Friedrich, "Die Oper zeigt sich," 355.

12. See "Entretien avec Franco Zeffirelli," *L'Avant Scéne Opéra: Verdi Don Carlos* 90–91 (September–October 1986): 200–211.

13. Friedrich, "Die Oper zeigt sich," 356.

14. Friedrich, "Zur Musiktheater," 226.

15. Friedrich, "Die Oper zeigt sich," 356.

16. Götz Friedrich, "*Falstaff* von Giuseppe Verdi: Die Fugue und der Narr" (1985), in *Musiktheater*, by Friedrich, 225.

17. Verdi also composed an opera based on Shakespeare's *Macbeth* (1847) and sketched initial ideas for a *King Lear*.

18. In *Otello*, Verdi and Boito condense the Shakespearean play, reduce the number of characters, and compose new scenes. Their *Falstaff* is based on comic scenes from *The Merry Wives of Windsor* and, to a lesser degree, from *Henry IV*, parts 1 and 2, that portray the character of Falstaff.

19. There has been an abundance of recent scholarship on "the culture of the body." For a recent theoretical discourse on the culture of the body in relation to opera, see Linda Hutcheon and Michael Hutcheon, *Bodily Charm: Living Opera* (Lincoln: University of Nebraska Press, 2000). On Falstaff's excessive and consumptive body, see 190–94. Also see Peter Brooks, "Body and Voice in Melodrama and Opera," in *Siren Songs: Representations of Gender and Sexuality in Opera*, ed. Mary Ann Smart (Princeton: Princeton University Press, 2000), 118–34.

20. For Verdi's own accounts on the matter, see his letter to Giulio Ricordi dated April 20, 1878, and his address to La Scala Orchestral Society on April 4, 1879. Both can be found in *Verdi: The Man in His Letters*, ed. Franz Werfel and Paul Stefan (New York: Fischer, 1942), 343–45. For a more detailed interpretation of Verdi's *Otello*, see Michal Grover, "Desdemona's Death Soliloquy and Opera's Perfect Singing," in "Voicing Death in Verdi's Opera," 69–181.

21. Verdi to Ricordi, May 11, 1887, found in "Verdi's Own Words: His Thoughts on Performance, with Special Reference to *Don Carlos, Otello*, and *Falstaff*," by Martin Chusid, in *The Verdi Companion*, ed. William Weaver and Martin Chusid (New York: Norton, 1979), 161–62. For a comparison, see Verdi's description of Lady Macbeth's singing role: "I would like the Lady not to sing. . . . I would like the Lady to have a harsh, stifled, and hollow voice." Verdi to Salvatore Cammarano, November 23, 1848, in *Verdi's* Macbeth: *A Sourcebook*, ed. David Rosen and Andrew Porter (New York: Norton, 1984), 66–67. See also Roger Parker's cautioning against using Verdi's own words as evidence: "But the distinction between, say, a composer's score and a letter about that score will remain, and we should be wary of automatically assuming a simple connection between the evidence such modes of communication may furnish." See his "*Falstaff* and Verdi's Final Narratives," in *Leonora's Last Act*, 112. See also James Hepokoski, *Giuseppe Verdi:* Otello, Cambridge Opera Handbooks (Cambridge: Cambridge University Press, 1987), 49.

22. The idea of Desdemona's perfection is inspired by Stanley Cavell's interpretation of the Shakespearean play. Cavell conceives of the play as partaking in the problematics of skepticism. He shows how a certain philosophical frame of mind depends on having proof of the existence of a perfect being who has created humanity in his own image. He thinks of *Othello* as the elaboration of this craving for perfection in a domestic setting. See his "Othello and the Stake of the Other,"

in *Disowning Knowledge in Six Plays of Shakespeare* (Cambridge: Cambridge University Press, 1987), 125–42.

23. In the opera, Desdemona's voice is the only female voice.

24. For a different view, one in which Iago is viewed as *unable* to exist in music, as "he has nothing to sing about," see Peter Conrad, *Romantic Opera and Literary Form* (Berkeley: University of California Press, 1977), 66.

25. For other reflections on the opera's styles of song (especially in the form of explanation for the technique of parlando) see Joseph Kerman, *Opera as Drama* (1956; reprint, Berkeley: University of California Press, 1988), 110–15; Noske, *Signifier and Signified*, 135; Poizat, *Angel's Cry*, 79–80. For a detailed discussion, see Grover, "Voicing Death in Verdi's Opera," especially 71–75.

26. On the "problem of believing" Iago, as expressed in his "Credo," see Katherine Bergeron, "How to Avoid Believing (While Reading Iago's 'Credo')," in *Reading Opera*, ed. Groos and Parker, 184–99.

27. "Ed io rimango di sua moresca signoria l'alfiere" and "Ma, com'è ver che tu Roderigo sei, / così è pur vero che se il Moro io fossi, / vedermi non vorrei d'attorno un Jago."

28. For a discussion of the Other in opera, see Ralph Locke, "Constructing the Oriental 'Other': Saint-Saëns's *Samson et Dalila*," *Cambridge Opera Journal* 3, no. 3 (November 1991): 261–302.

29. Gilles de Van sees in Otello's first entrance ("Esultate") a frozen moment that replaces the closed number. He calls it a "miniaturization." Gilles de Van, *Verdi's Theater: Creating Drama Through Music*, trans. Gilda Roberts (Chicago: University of Chicago Press, 1998), 281.

30. Peter Conrad interprets the tempest as receiving *human* form through Otello's emergence from the sea. See his *Romantic Opera*, 57.

31. See BBC/Arts & Entertainment documentary on the making of the film *Zeffirelli's Otello: From Stage to Screen* (1986). This view is different from Citron's, who finds the scene weak since Otello is hardly visible and his voice too loud for the conveyed distance. Citron, *Opera on Screen*, 259 n. 26.

32. I am working with traditional notions of singing (such as aria), since the narrative of the vocal is an allegory about singing, a narrative between the lines that shows itself in the meeting points of traditional and innovative forms of song.

33. This might be the result of, or the motivation for, Verdi's and Boito's dispensing with the play's first act and its introduction of Desdemona in the senate scene.

34. Cassio's punishment can be seen to result from the very meaning of Desdemona's sudden appearance. She emerges from her wedding bed raising the suspicion that the marriage has not been consummated. For the interpretation, see Cavell, *Disowning Knowledge*, 125–42.

35. Notice that this is an outcome of the cinematics of the production. In his *staged* version of *Otello*, Zeffirelli *does* bring Desdemona onstage at this moment. See the video release *La Scala's Bicentennial, December 7, 1976*, director/costume and set designer Franco Zeffirelli, Bel Canto Society. Placido Domingo stars as Otello, Mirella Freni as Desdemona.

36. Not bringing Desdemona onstage at this moment has another conse-

quence: it forces Zeffirelli to cut Otello's words accompanying her visual entrance: "What? . . . My sweet Desdemona also roused / From her dreams on your account! Cassio, / You are no longer captain." And with this cut is gone the opera's reason for Cassio's dismissal. This might explain Zeffirelli's addition of narrative strains (the religious-ritual, the homosexual) to explicate or to replace the vicissitudes of the vocal in the opera. For alternative narratives in *Otello* and *La traviata*, see Citron, "Night at the Cinema," and Tambling, "Between the Spectacle and the Specular."

37. The image of the Madonna shows the complexity of the quest for the perfected image. For an elaboration of the image of the Madonna in relation to Desdemona, see Grover, "Voicing Death," 108–81.

38. For the quest for the high note in opera, see Poizat, *Angel's Cry*.

39. It would be a mistake to suppose that her voice is drowned out by the high voices of the children or by the distance between her and Otello and Iago. For the operatic affects of distance, see Theodor Adorno, "Phantasmagoria," in *In Search of Wagner*, trans. Rodney Livingstone (Norfolk: Verso, 1985), 85–96.

40. See Giulio Ricordi, "Production Book for the Opera *Otello*," in *Verdi's Otello and Simon Boccanegra in Letters and Documents*, vol. 2, *Documents*, ed. and trans. Hans Busch (Oxford: Clarendon Press, 1988), 526–40.

41. This acoustical confusion, or "vulnerable ear," might remind one of the film *The Conversation*, where the main character (played by Gene Hackman) tunes into a conversation in an attempt to isolate it from the surrounding noise. It is the *intonation*—the "music"—of the conversation that he gets wrong, mistaking the murderers with the one to be murdered. His expertise at listening is achieved with sophisticated techniques that eventually lead to the realization of his mistaken interpretation of the materiality of the voice (the same words are differently emphasized within the sentence, differently intoned). The result of his untuned listening is that the murder does take place. Geoffrey Hartman writes that the "vulnerability of the ear" "is linked . . . to real or fantasized words, to an ear-fear connected with overhearing, or to the word as inherently untrustworthy, equivocal, betraying its promise of immediacy or intimacy." Geoffrey Hartman, *Saving the Text* (Baltimore: Johns Hopkins University Press, 1981), 57; quoted in *Between the Sign and the Gaze*, by Herman Rapaport (Ithaca: Cornell University Press, 1994), 227.

42. Iago's musical metaphor of destruction, heard together with Otello's devastated reaction to Desdemona's song—"Beauty and love united in sweet song! / I will interrupt your tender chords"—is hardly audible in the film. Iago's lips are barely moving, and no subtitles are provided. For the effect of unmoving lips in a filmic production of Mozart, see Marcia Citron, "The Elusive Voice: Absence and Presence in Jean-Pierre Ponelle's Film *Le Nozze di Figaro*," in *Between Opera and Cinema*, ed. Theresa and Joe, 133–53.

43. Several scholars have discussed this scene. On the homoerotic overtones of the scene, see William Van Watson, "Shakespeare, Zeffirelli, and the Homosexual Gaze," *Literature/Film Quarterly* 20, no. 4 (1992): 308–25. On "Othello's scopic drive," Cassio as "the elusive object of desire for both men," jealousy as constructed in relation to "possession not being possible," and desire as "circulating endlessly," see Jeremy Tambling, *Opera and the Culture of Fascism* (Oxford:

Clarendon Press, 1996), 86–87. For this image as Cassio masturbating, see Citron, "Night at the Cinema," 723.

44. For tonality in *Otello*, see David Lawton, "On the 'bacio' Theme in Otello," in *19ᵗʰ Century Music* 1 (1977/78): 211–20; Roger Parker and Mathew Brown, "Ancora un bacio: Three scenes from Verdi's *Otello*," *19ᵗʰ Century Music* 9 (1985/86): 50–62; Hepokoski, *Giuseppe Verdi*.

45. Franco Zeffirelli, "Otello," in *Zeffirelli: An Autobiography* (New York: Weidenfeld and Nicolson, 1986), 335.

46. Ibid., 327–39.

47. Chion discusses Syberberg's *Parsifal* as a unique example of a "redemption of playback" because "here playback flaunts itself as such, by emphasizing the alterity of the body from the voice it tries to be attributed to. What is shown is the yearning for unity." Michel Chion, *The Voice in Cinema*, trans. Claudia Gorbman (New York: Columbia University Press, 1999), 156. Syberberg's film of *Parsifal* becomes the paradigmatic example of operatic dubbing in cinema. See discussions of this production in Marcia Citron, "Cinema and the Power of Fantasy: Powell and Pressburger's *Tales of Hoffmann* and Syberberg's *Parsifal*," in *Opera on Screen*, 112–60; Carolyn Abbate, "Metempsychotic Wagner," in *In Search of Opera*, 107–44; and Jeongwon Joe, "Hans-Jürgen Syberberg's *Parsifal*: The Staging of Dissonance in the Fusion of Opera and Film," *The Music Research Forum* 13 (July 1998): 1–21.

48. On post-synchronization in screened operas, see Citron, *Opera on Screen*, 8.

49. The term also refers to dubbing one's own lips as in post-synchronization. See Chion, *Voice in Cinema*, 153.

50. Ibid., 125–27.

51. Ibid., 153.

52. Jorge Luis Borges, "On Dubbing," in *Borges in/and/on Film*, ed. Edgardo Cozarinsky, trans. Gloria Waldman and Ronald Christ (New York: Lumen Books, 1988), 62; quoted in "Voice Devoured," by Yampolski, 66–67.

53. Yampolski, "Voice Devoured," 71–77.

54. Isak Dinesen, "Echoes," in *Last Tales* (New York: Random House, 1957), 153–90, quotation, 184–85.

55. For the idea of more than one voice (in the sense of persona) in the "Willow Song," see Elizabeth Hudson, "Narrative in Verdi"; and Brooks Toliver, "Grieving in the Mirrors of Verdi's Willow Song: Desdemona, Barbara, and a 'Feeble, Strange Voice,'" *Cambridge Opera Journal* 10 (1998): 289–306.

56. See n. 21.

57. See the interview with Zeffirelli "Entretien avec Franco Zeffirelli," 204.

58. Zeffirelli's "Willow Song" is composed of the following measures (and in the following order) taken from Verdi's scene: 324/3/1; 337/2/2 – 5/1; 325/5/1 – 327/3/2; 324/3/4 – 325/3/1; 334/4/2 – 335/2/5; and 336/1/5 – into "Ave Maria" (Schirmer's piano vocal score).

59. Citron has a different view on the score's ability to incorporate Zeffirelli's cuts. She argues that "Verdi's continuous score does not lend itself to fragmentation." *Opera on Screen*, 79.

CHAPTER 4
FALSTAFF'S FREE VOICE

1. For an insightful (and very different) interpretation of *Falstaff*'s singularity, see Emanuele Senici, "Verdi's *Falstaff* at Italy's *Fin de Siècle*," *The Musical Quarterly* 85, no. 2 (2001): 274–310.

2. Edward T. Cone, "The Old Man's Toys," in *Music, a View from Delft: Selected Essays*, ed. Robert Morgan (Chicago: University of Chicago Press, 1989), 164.

3. For a surface or cartoon effect, see Steven Shaviro, "The Cinematic Body," in *Theory Out of Bounds*, vol. 2, ed. Sandra Buckley, Brian Massumi, and Michael Hardt (Minneapolis: University of Minnesota Press, 1993), especially 203–4. For the opposite direction, namely how opera can learn from the cartoon and obtain "a cinematic form of *opéra bouffe* [where] the visual and rhythmic stylization might be adapted to living characters to create an effectively artificial comic opera," see the entry "Film Opera and Film Cartoon," in *Grove Dictionary of Music and Musicians*, 5th ed., ed. Eric Blom (New York: Macmillan, 1954), 109.

4. Parker is referring to two instances in which a character voices Alice (Falstaff and Fontana). He also discusses how Quickly reenacts her encounter with Falstaff by impersonating him.

5. Parker, "*Falstaff* and Verdi's Final Narratives," 100–125.

6. Sander Gilman, "Falstaff's Fat" (paper delivered at the Music and Language Association Conference, San Francisco, 1998).

7. Elizabeth Wood, "On the Sapphonic Voice" (1994), in *Music, Culture, and Society: A Reader*, ed. Derek Scott (Oxford: Oxford University Press, 2000), 83–87. For Falstaff in Shakespeare as "the 'joint' or point of articulation between male and female," see Marjorie Garber, "Out of Joint," in *The Body in Parts: Fantasies of Corporeality in Early Modern Europe,* ed. David Hillman and Carla Mazzio (New York: Routledge, 1997), 27.

8. Clément, *Opera, or The Undoing of Women*, 120.

9. After hearing the madrigal, we retrospectively conceive of Falstaff's earlier "O amor!" inserted between the voicings of Alice and Meg (act 1, scene 1), as a fragment of what will become the singing of Fontana's madrigal.

10. Here Friedrich also toys with the genre of the madrigal as it evokes courtly love. Friedrich turns it into a love duet between the two men, culminating in Falstaff's kissing Fontana.

11. As Herman Rapaport writes, there is a sense in which "voice [is] not located in the subject but *around* the subject." Herman Rapaport, *Between the Sign and the Gaze*, 211.

12. Abbate, *In Search of Opera*, xiv.

13. The trill as Falstaff's signature overturns its origination in the voice of Iago. For an account of Iago's trill, see Noske, *Signifier and Signified*, 149.

14. "Ma il viso *mio* su *lui* risplenderà."

15. "E il viso *tuo* su *me* risplenderà."

16. For the idea of an opera possessing its characters, see Michal Grover, "A Bewitched Voice: Lady Macbeth's Sleepwalking Scene," in "Voicing Death," 182–323.

17. In my argument, the terms "swallowed" and "migrating voices" differ from "recurring themes." The last term describes themes or melodies assigned to characters or dramatic ideas on a one-to-one correspondence. The terms I employ describe a different phenomenon and one that is specific to *Falstaff.* For scholarship on recurring themes in Verdi, see Joseph Kerman, "Verdi's Use of Recurring Themes," in *Studies in Music History: Essays for Oliver Strunk,* ed. Harold Powers (Princeton: Princeton University Press, 1968), 495–510; Carolyn Abbate and Roger Parker, "Introduction: On Analyzing Opera," in *Analyzing Opera: Verdi and Wagner,* ed. Carolyn Abbate and Roger Parker (Berkeley: University of California Press, 1989), 1–24; and Mary Ann Smart, "Ulterior Motives: Verdi's Recurring Themes Revisited," in *Siren Songs,* ed. Smart, 135–59.

18. I would like to thank Carolyn Abbate for mentioning this production.

19. For an account of the between-two-an-three motif in relation to *parola scenica,* see Gilles de Van, who describes what he calls the "transfiguration of the phrase" in Verdi, in which "a phrase of text transform[s] . . . into a musical gesture clear enough that it will appear as a 'natural' musical equivalent. . . . *parola scenica* [is] already a rough sketch of that gesture." *Verdi's Theatre,* 297–98.

20. On weddings composed entirely of males and on the "carnival grotesque exaggeration of the wedding," see Susan Stewart, *On Longing: Narratives of the Miniature, the Gigantic, the Souvenir, the Collection* (Durham: Duke University Press, 1993), 117–25.

21. Carolyn Abbate, "Immortal Voices, Mortal Forms," in *Analytical Strategies and Musical Interpretation: Essays on Nineteenth and Twentieth-century Music,* ed. Craig Ayrey and Mark Everist (Cambridge: Cambridge University Press, 1996), 294–95.

22. For a detailed account of the scene, see James Hepokoski, *Giuseppe Verdi: Falstaff,* Cambridge Opera Handbooks (Cambridge: Cambridge University Press, 1983), especially 98–109.

23. See, for example, the fagott and cello parts in 193/1/3 – 2/4 (Dover, full score).

24. In another context, I have developed the idea that Falstaff's body takes the form of pregnancy not only in that he incorporates women's voices but in that he "delivers" the love of the opera's couple, Fenton and Nannetta. The conflation of Falstaff's fate with the lovers is seen in both punishments (the basket/screen and the staging of the fairy tale in the woods). For instance, Falstaff is dressed as a sacrificial animal, the lovers are disguised for the ritual of the wedding; Falstaff is transformed into a beast, the lovers into fairies. It is as though the exorcising ritual performed on Falstaff's body enables their performance of love, or their fate is delivered by him. See Michal Grover-Friedlander, "Opera's Blind Spot," *Motar,* Journal of the Faculty of Arts, Tel Aviv University (1998): 141–46 (in Hebrew). For a different interpretation of the lovers, see Thomas Bauman, "The Young Lovers in *Falstaff,*" *19ᵗʰ Century Music* 9, no. 1 (1985) and Cone, "Old Man's Toys," 159–78. For the Shakespearean Falstaff as pregnant, see Valerie Traub, "Prince Hal's Falstaff: Positioning Psychoanalysis and the Female Reproductive Body," *Shakespeare Quarterly* 40 (1989): 456–74; Coppélia Kahn, *Men's Estate* (Berkeley: University of California Press, 1981), 72–73; and Patricia Parker, *Literary Fat Ladies and the Generation of the Text* (London: Methuen, 1987), 21–22.

25. *Otello* and *Falstaff* partake in what seems to be a discourse of the kiss. The meaning of the recurrence of the kiss is very different in the two operas, but in both works it is structural. In the tragic world of *Otello* the kiss is open to inter-pretation. Its recurrence may signify Otello's reminiscence of love or the opera's reminiscence pointing to the disturbance in Otello's memory; it may also signify Otello and Desdemona's lost love or persistent love. In the comic world of *Fal-staff*, the opera's couple (of which the woman is indeed a reincarnation of *Otello*'s Desdemona) are identified by recurring kisses. These are dispersed throughout the opera and constantly interrupted and sung about in repeated refrains. (Here Boito quotes from *Decameron*: "a kissed mouth doesn't lose its freshness, for like the mouth it renews itself.")

26. Fred Camper suggests that "a silence 'filled' with film images is different from any other type of silence" and that "the absence of sound gives the images . . . a new priority . . . and allows them to speak with their own unique, music-like rhythms." Fred Camper, "Sound and Silence in Narrative and Non-narrative Cin-ema," in *Film Sound*, ed. Weis and Belton, 369–81; quotation, 372, 378.

27. For characteristics of the relay, see Citron, *Opera on Screen*, especially 85 and 97–99.

28. This must be the case even though Friedrich's obituary in *The Daily Tele-graph* (December 15, 2000) reports that "With Solti as conductor, he [Friedrich] directed on film a live production of Verdi's *Falstaff* (1988)."

29. It seems to me that by repeating narratives Friedrich is not "Wagneriz-ing" *Falstaff* but responding to the unique characteristics of the opera. On rep-etition of narratives in Wagner, see Abbate, *Unsung Voices*, and Levin, *Richard Wagner*.

30. Bakhtin tells the story of a stutterer who enacts a scene of childbirth, the drama of a body bearing the word and finally giving birth to it. *The Bakhtin Reader: Selected Writings of Bakhtin, Medvedev and Voloshinov*, ed. Pam Morris (London: Arnold, 1994), 228. On the image of the mouth in opera, see Abbate, "Orpheus. One Last Performance," 1–54.

31. For the miniature in relation to the grotesque, see Stewart, *On Longing*, 111.

32. The operatic silence is alluded to in the libretto. Fenton sings about the silent night: "From the lover's lips, the love song flies / far off in the silence of the night, until it finds an answering voice." Later in the scene Falstaff hears it: "One, two, three, four, five, six, seven strokes—eight, nine, ten, eleven, twelve. Mid-night! . . . (listening) I hear a gentle step."

33. I am referring to the following musical gestures: Ford's "Caro Segnior Fontana!" Quickly's "Cavaliero," and Falstaff's "Reverenza." I have not elabo-rated on them in my discussion, as I chose the more radical employment of the be-tween-two-and-three gesture.

34. For an analysis of the fugue, see Danniel Sabbeth, "Dramatic and Musical Organization in *Falstaff*," *Atti del III Congresso Internazionale di Studi Verdiani*, Milano, Piccola Scala, June 12–17, 1972 (Parma: Istituto di Studi Verdiani, 1974), 429–33. For relating the fugue to the beginning of the opera—in sonata form, according to the author—see David Linthicum, "Verdi's *Falstaff* and Classi-cal Sonata Form," *The Music Review* 39 (1978): 39–53.

CHAPTER 5
OPERA ON THE PHONE: THE CALL OF THE HUMAN VOICE

A shorter version of this chapter was read at the Opera Analysis conference at Trinity College, Cambridge, 2000, and at a colloquium at Princeton University, 2001. Sections of this chapter, "The Call of the Human Voice in Poulenc's *La voix humaine*," appear in *Music, Sensation and Sensuality*, ed. Linda Austern (New York: Routledge, 2002), 199–210. I thank Carolyn Abbate and the members of the NEH seminar "Opera: Interpretation between Disciplines" (Princeton, Summer 2000) for their insightful comments on an earlier version of this chapter.

1. For scholarship on the relationship between opera and other multimedia works, see Nicholas Cook, *Analysing Musical Multimedia* (Oxford: Clarendon Press, 1998), especially chapter 6, "Reading Film and Rereading Opera from *Armide* to 'Aria,'" 215–60.

2. For discussions of the opera, see Max Loppert, "An introduction to *Atlas*," and Meredith Monk, "Process Notes," in *Atlas* (ECM Records, 1993); and Deborah Jowitt, ed., *Meredith Monk* (Baltimore: Johns Hopkins University Press, 1997).

3. Poulenc composed three operas, all of which reinterpret death's complex dependence on the aural and the visual. *Les mamelles de Tirésias* (1947), a comic opera based on a text by Apollinaire, toys with the metamorphosis of death into a male reproduction of invisible bass-voiced babies. *Les dialogues des Carmélites* (1958) multiplies operatic death: it portrays an ugly and sacrilegious death and a metaphysical, sacrificial, beautiful death in the same opera.

4. There is, to my knowledge, one opera besides *La voix humaine* that consists nearly in its entirety of a phone conversation: Menotti's *Telephone* (1947). Several recent operas contain a scene or several scenes of talking on the phone; for example, *Jackie O.* (1997), by Michael Daugherty and Wayne Koestenbaum, and *Don Giovanni Revisited* (1997), by Mozart and Amnon Wolman.

5. In another of his plays, *Le bel indifférent* (1940), Cocteau has a man remain stubbornly silent throughout the play—even when the woman threatens to kill herself—yet he is *present* onstage.

6. In the preface to the play, Cocteau writes that he sees the actress as playing two roles: "one when she speaks, the other when she is listening and delineating the character of the invisible person who expresses himself by silences." Cocteau's preface to *La voix humaine* (Paris: Editions Stock, 1983), 9.

7. For the use of the term "phase," see the letter to Bernac reproduced in *Poulenc:* Dialogues des Carmelites, La voix humaine, *L'Avant Scène Opéra* 52 (May 1983): 136.

8. Quoted in "Adorno and the Sirens: Tele-phono-graphic bodies," Barbara Engh, in *Embodied Voices: Representing Female Vocality in Western Culture*, ed. Leslie Dunn and Nancy Jones (Cambridge: Cambridge University Press, 1994), 122. See also Friedrich Kittler, who discusses Cocteau and his attraction to other technologies and machines in *Gramophone, Film, Typewriter*, trans. Geoffrey Winthrop-Young and Michael Wutz (Stanford: Stanford University Press, 1999), 191–92.

9. Edison uncannily attempted to contact the dead through thought transfer-

ence. See Melba Cuddy-Keane, "Virginia Woolf, Sound Technologies, and the New Aurality," in *Virginia Woolf in the Age of Mechanical Reproduction*, ed. Pamela Caughie (New York: Garland, 2000), 83.

10. Marcel Proust, "The Guermantes Way," in *Remembrance of Things Past*, vol. 2, trans. C. K. Scott Moncrieff and Terence Kilmartin (New York: Vintage/Random House, 1982), 135.

11. For an elaboration of the notion of an advance agreement (*"Oui Oui*, you are receiving me, these are French words"), see Jacques Derrida, "Ulysses Gramophone Hear Say Yes in Joyce," in *James Joyce: The Augmented Ninth*, Proceedings of the Ninth International James Joyce Symposium, Frankfurt, 1984, ed. Bernard Benstock (Syracuse: Syracuse University Press, 1988), 27–75; quotation, 27.

12. Conceived in terms of Lacanian psychoanalysis, the initial stages of the development of the self are located in an impossible relation with the Other. The relation to the Other is understood as prior to selfhood. The path to the self is necessarily a detour through the Other; "I" is a deposit with the Other. This Other, which is constitutive of the self, emerges in psychoanalytic treatment, which privileges the voice: the analysand does not see the analyst but only hears a voice as the voice of the master, the voice of God. Freud sees in the long-distance phone call a model for the indirect path and inferred access to the unconscious. See Avital Ronell, *The Telephone Book: Technology, Schizophrenia, Electric Speech* (Lincoln: University of Nebraska Press, 1989), 423–24. For Lacanian psychoanalytical interpretations of the operatic voice, see chapter 1 of this book.

13. For a different interpretation of the myth of Orpheus in relation to technology, see Klaus Theweleit, "Monteverdi's *l'Orfeo*: The Technology of Reconstruction," in *Opera Through Other Eyes*, ed. Levin, 147–76.

14. In this context it is interesting to note Poulenc's objection to casting Maria Callas in the role of the woman. He preferred his collaborator in his two previous operas, Denise Duval, creating in *La voix humaine* an operatic role for an unconventional operatic singer. See Henri Hell, *Francis Poulenc: Musicien français* (Paris: Librairie Arthéme Fayard, 1978), 277.

15. These characteristics are those of a monodrama. Poulenc, however, refers to this work as opera.

16. Waleckx indicates fourteen leading motifs in the opera and labels them emotively "Exasperated Waiting" motif, at no 1; "Suffering" motif, 5 after 5; and so on. However, the ringing of the phone surprisingly *does not* figure among them. Denis Waleckx, "'A Musical Confession': Poulenc, Cocteau and *La voix humaine*," in *Francis Poulenc: Music, Art and Literature*, ed. Sidney Buckland and Myriam Chimènes (Aldershot: Ashgate, 1999), 320–47.

17. The opera, as opposed to the film, incorporates Cocteau's interruptions of other parties on the line (there are four such phases in the play). This engenders more ringings and more "phonic talk." Rossellini, by contrast, preserves only the bad-line interruption in which they cannot hear each other properly and drops the implications of an operator and another woman who come on the line. For a comparison between the play and the libretto, see Waleckx, "'Musical Confession,'" 325–28.

18. Poulenc himself alludes to this feature of her singing: "The impact of the

following musical response then suggests what she has heard." Poulenc to Louis Aragon, February 1, 1959, in *Correspondance, 1910–1963*, ed. Myriam Chimènes (Paris: Fayard, 1994), letter 59–2 (907); quoted in Waleckx, "'Musical Confession,'" 339.

19. Avital Ronell, "Finitude's Score," in *Thinking Bodies*, ed. Juliet Flower MacCannell and Laura Zakarin (Stanford: Stanford University Press, 1994), 91. For a discussion of this passage, see Lawrence Kramer, "Opera: Two or Three Things I know about Her," in *Siren Songs*, ed. Smart, especially 188–90.

20. The writings of Carolyn Abbate have greatly influenced these ideas. See, for instance, "Elektra's Voice: Music and Language in Strauss's Opera," in *Richard Strauss:* Elektra, ed. Derrick Puffett (Cambridge: Cambridge University Press, 1989), 107–27.

21. My warmest thanks to Vered Lev Kenaan for introducing me to this film.

22. It is not in the scope of this chapter to consider the uncanniness in the doubling of Rossellini's *Una voce umane–Il miracolo* in Poulenc's *La voix humaine–Dialogues des Carmelites*.

23. There was, in fact, someone who prompted the actress (Anna Magnani) over the phone. See Tag Gallagher, *The Adventures of Roberto Rossellini: His Life and Films* (New York: Da Capo Press, 1998), 231–32.

24. The term was borrowed from a practice of a Pythagorean sect which forbade seeing the master and whose worship followed the master's voice. See Michel Chion, *Le Son* (Paris: Editions Nathan, 1998), 201. The term was further developed in opera studies by Carolyn Abbate. See Abbate, "Debussy's Phantom Sounds." See also Marcia Citron's discussion in "Cinema and the Power of Fantasy: Powell and Pressburger's *Tales of Hoffmann* and Syberberg's *Parsifal*," in her *Opera on Screen*, especially 134–36.

25. Chion terms this *deacousmatization*—it robs the acousmatic voice of its omnipresence, as in the famous example in *The Wizard of Oz*. Chion, *Voice in Cinema*, 28–29. See also Slavoj Žižek, *Looking Awry: An Introduction to Jacques Lacan Through Popular Culture* (Cambridge: MIT Press, 1991), especially 125–28.

26. For the phenomenon of the voice on the phone in film, see Charles Affron, *Cinema and Sentiment* (Chicago: University of Chicago Press, 1982), especially the chapter entitled "Voice and Space," 104–31; Chion, *Voice in Cinema*, 62–66; his *Audio-Vision Sound on Screen*, ed. and trans. Claudia Gorbman (New York: Columbia University Press, 1994), 71–78 and 89–92; and his *son au cinéma*, 53–57. Lawrence, *Echo and Narcissus*, especially chapter 4, "The Problem of the Speaking Woman," 109–46. For an account of a different affinity between cinema and the telephone, one that equates cinema's early sound (Vitaphone) with a telephone in that they both stress intelligibility over realism, see Rick Altman, "Introduction Sound/History," in *Sound Theory Sound Practice*, ed. Rick Altman (New York: Routledge, 1992), especially 121–25.

27. In Almodóvar's film *Women on the Verge of a Nervous Breakdown*, which takes its inspiration from Cocteau's play *La voix humaine*, the voice of the other on the phone is further transformed into a recording of that voice heard in its absence on an answering machine. See Linda Willem, "Almodóvar on the Verge of Cocteau's *La voix humaine*," *Literature/Film Quarterly* 26, no. 2 (1998): 142–47.

28. Aside from Cocteau's play, there was no script for the film, and Anna Magnani (the woman) was free to improvise. See Gallagher, *Adventures of Roberto Rossellini*, 231–32.

29. Peter Brunette, *Roberto Rossellini* (Berkeley: University of California Press, 1987), 88.

30. Roberto Rossellini, "Dix ans de cinéma," pt. 1, *Cahiers du cinéma* 50 (August–September 1955): 6–7. Cited in translation in *Roberto Rossellini*, by Brunette, 89.

31. Cocteau, *La Revue du Cinéma* 7 (Summer 1947). Translated in *The Art of Cinema*, by Jean Cocteau, ed. André Bernard and Claude Gauteur, trans. Robin Buss (London: Marion Boyars, 1992), 187. Compare Cocteau's reaction to the film with that to the opera: "I was utterly overwhelmed, because it was completely new, it was a new way of performing the play, of perceiving it. It was neither recitative nor song, it was a musical tragedy and it required not only a singer but a great actress to perform this little opera which had become a very great tragedy thanks to Poulenc." Robert Sadoul (1958), radio interview with Francis Poulenc and Jean Cocteau, broadcast in *Actualités de Midi* (Paris: INA, recorded July 1958); quoted in Waleckx, "A Musical Confession," 340–41. Moreover, Cocteau acted as director and costume and stage designer for the opera's premiere (Ibid., 340–44).

32. Brunette echoes this sentiment when he writes that in *Una voce umane* one is constantly aware of the real woman's presence. Brunette, *Roberto Rossellini*, 90.

33. Magnani performed in the world of the café concert and had experience in the music hall form of *avanspettacolo*, equivalent to vaudeville. See André Bazin, "An Aesthetic of Reality," 22–24, and "Sources and Translator's Note," 179, both in *What Is Cinema?* by Bazin; and Peter Bondanella, *The Films of Roberto Rossellini* (Cambridge: Cambridge University Press, 1993), 49.

34. A vocal close-up, rather than a visual close-up, establishes a disproportion between the degree of intimacy that we are drawn into and the exposure resulting from the enlarged image. Cinema tends to associate the enlarged face of a close-up with the centrality and importance of the voice on the phone. For the idea of filmic vocal close-up, see Affron, "Voice and Space," 104–31.

35. In fact, critics at the time of the film's release stated the film was uncinematic. See Roberto Rossellini, "Dix ans de cinéma," in *Roberto Rossellini: Le cinéma révélé*, réunis et préfacés par Alain Bergala (Paris: Flammarion, 1988), 45.

36. Poulenc himself, in a brief discussion of the place of opera in his time (early 1960s), believes that operas should be composed with an awareness of a public conditioned by cinema: "Opera remains a perfectly valid and viable form in our time. I would go as far as to say that, at present, it is logical for composers to be progressively less attracted to the writing of ballet scores than to opera. . . . But— and I think this should be apparent to all those creating operas today—we must find a practical means of adjusting ourselves to the demands of a public which has been psychologically conditioned by the lively dynamics of the cinema." Francis Poulenc [as told to Elliott Stein], "Opera in the Cinematic Era," *Opera* (January 1961): 11–12; quotation, 11.

37. Here I disagree with Brunette, who writes that "barely noticeable are the sound effects . . . which arise between calls." Brunette, mistakenly I believe,

groups these diegetic sounds with the faint voice hardly heard over the phone. Brunette, *Roberto Rossellini*, 87–88.

38. In mainstream Hollywood practice, characters do not hear the music of their film unless marked within the narrative as diegetic. Rossellini, who is considered the founder of Italian neorealism (and also, as is well documented, the director who broke away from what seemed to many critics to be the style's fundamental traits), has rejected many of Hollywood's conventions. One of Rossellini's stylistic innovations over Hollywood practice was to radically reduce the employment of unmotivated music and to reject continuous background music. It is typical of Rossellini's films, other neorealists' films, and films of the French new wave to inscribe a far richer diegetic world of sounds than that of nondiegetic sounds. Sounds in these films are foregrounded, as is speech, relegating music to a higher degree of artificiality. However, Rossellini does not totally reject the nondiegetic music in favor of source music. Even his early (more clearly stylistically marked) films incorporate music. This does not explain the peculiar appearance of music in *Una voce umane*, however. Indeed, such music cannot be associated with atmospheric, background music, and it raises the question, Why is there music *at all?* Richard Dyer tries to explain this phenomenon by offering three possible avenues for thinking about the awkwardness of music in these films: there was always music in Italian film, as the genre of opera is so important in Italy; it is present for the sake of narrativity; and music is a universal human value. As none of these explanations satisfies him, Dyer continues by distinguishing between the various uses of music by different film composers. Renzo Rossellini supplies the "emotion missing from the image alone," and Nino Rota supplies "the musical culture of the people depicted"; in other words, the difference between the two composers is that "Rota's music refuses the external position implicit in the scores of Rossellini . . . [he] goes some way towards achieving the synthesis of external and internal realism implicit in the neo-realist project." Neither of these descriptions fits the function of music in *Una voce umane*. Richard Dyer, "Where Is the Music in a Film? Or, Why Is There Music in Italian Neo-realist Cinema?" (presented at the Royal Music Association conference "Music and Film," Southampton, England, 2001).

39. The music is a distinctly sounding Italian melody. A more detailed consideration of the appearance of the melody in the film reveals that it is heard in only three places: at the outset accompanying the titles and spilling sporadically into the film's "prelude"; at the conclusion, again with the titles; and once in the body of the film when the woman desperately puts down the phone after speaking with the wrong man. In the first instance, after accompanying the titles for both *Una voce umane* and *Il miracolo*, the melody is heard together with diegetic sounds emanating from the woman's surroundings. When the diegetic sounds spatially expand to include the neighboring apartment's noises, voices, and ringing of the telephone, the music halts. It does not sound continuously. The first ringing of the phone marks the disappearance of the melody. Diegetic sounds also disappear and are replaced by muffled diegetic sounds emanating from the phone conversation. The melody resumes when the woman picks up the unringing phone once again; it halts once again for the repetition of the sound of water, and so forth. In other words, the onset of the film is an

unsystematic juxtaposition of the rich universe of diegetic sounds and the film's single nondiegetic melody. The second (chronological) occurrence of the nondiegetic melody sporadically punctuates her emotional outbursts as she realizes that her lover is lying. The third instance occurs at the very end of the film. In this occurrence the melody is truncated to a cadential chord. The woman and her lover's conversation has terminated, and the woman hangs up for the very last time. The melody follows her final words and slides into the end titles. There is no pattern to the melody's recurrences in terms of its correspondence with other sounds in the film. Thus, the appearance and disappearance of the music throughout the film are equally conspicuous.

40. In *Il miracolo*, music is used more frequently and for longer stretches of time as more fully orchestrated repeating music. Its "unheard" quality results from its function as punctuator, so very synchronized with the visual.

41. Ernest Jones analyzes the legend of the Madonna's conception through the ear and the reasons for the choice of the ear as the receptive organ for the immaculate (aural) conception. See Ernest Jones, "The Madonna's Conception Through the Ear," in *Essays in Applied Psycho-Analysis: Essays in Folklore, Anthropology and Religion,* vol. 2 (London: Hogarth Press, 1951), 266–357.

42. For different thematic connections between the two episodes, see José Luis Gaurner, *Roberto Rossellini,* trans. Elisabeth Cameron (New York: Praeger, 1970), 27–28.

43. My reading of *Amore* gives heavy interpretative weight to the music. In contrast, Lawrence Morton—in a rare reference to the employment of music in Rossellini's films—questions the very merit of Rossellini's use of music. I quote him at length:

> None of Rossellini's films has been distinguished by a score of any merit whatsoever. His talent, great as it is, does not include a sensitivity to music. Apparently he is no more capable of resenting what is bad than he is able to produce what is good. In *Germany, Year Zero* his intentions as a recorder of contemporary history are consistently controverted by his brother's score. For example: The boy Edmund is walking aimlessly through the ruins of Berlin. He is hungry, he has poisoned his sick father, he has been rejected by friends and playmates, he has been defeated in the struggle to maintain with his family a semblance of decency in an environment where decency is almost impossible. The urgency of his flight from home has passed. He pauses to kick a pile of stones. What does the music tell us? Something like this: that Edmund is a spy, that he is concocting a plot to overthrow the Allied military government, that the ruins are full of counterspies watching his every move, and that beneath the pile of stones he has just kicked lie the bodies of Adolf Hitler and Eva Braun. Will Edmund uncover them? I mean by this that the tragedy of the film is interpreted musically in terms of whodunit. (Lawrence Morton, "Film Music of the Quarter," *Hollywood Quarterly* 3 (1950): 289–92; quotation, 289–90)

44. Jean Cocteau, *The Human Voice,* trans. Carl Wildman (Great Britain: Vision Press, 1951); see "Scenery," 17–19.

45. For the elaboration of the idea of death as the outcome of singing as such, see also the introduction and chapter 3 of this book.

CHAPTER 6
FELLINI'S ASHES

A shorter version of this chapter was read in the study session "Between Opera and Cinema" at the American Musicological Society in Atlanta, Georgia, 2001. The epigraph to the chapter is from Wayne Koestenbaum's *Queen's Throat*, 239.

1. The "end of cinema" is Fellini's response to a question posed by Costanzo Costantini: "For some time now you have been saying that cinema is on the brink of collapse, that it is about to end. On what do you base your catastrophic diagnosis?" Quote cited in "The Cinema Is Finished. *And the Ship Sails On*," in *Conversations with Fellini*, ed. Costanzo Costantini, trans. Sohrab Sorooshian (San Diego: A Harvest Original, Harcourt Brace, 1995), 128.

2. See Thomas Elsaesser and Kay Hoffmann, preface, in *Cinema Futures: Cain, Abel or Cable? The Screen Arts in the Digital Age*, ed. Thomas Elsaesser and Kay Hoffmann (Amsterdam: Amsterdam University Press, 1998), 7. See also Vito Zagarrio, "Theseus and Ariadne: For a Counter-History of the Cinema-Television Relationship?" in ibid., 85–104; Tom Gunning, "'Animated Pictures': Tales of Cinema's Forgotten Future, after 100 Years of Films," in *Reinventing Film Studies*, ed. Christine Gledhill and Linda Williams (London: Arnold, 2000), 316–31.

3. Marcia Landy, *Italian Film* (Cambridge: Cambridge University Press, 2000), 359. For a different sense of the death of cinema, one that sees the very *image* in danger of disintegrating and disappearing, see Paolo Cherchi Usai, *The Death of Cinema: History, Cultural Memory and the Digital Dark Age* (London: British Film Institute Publishing, 2001). On cinema signifying death, much has been written. See, for instance, Garrett Stewart, *Between Film and Screen: Modernism's Photo Synthesis* (Chicago: University of Chicago Press, 1999), 153, 186–87.

4. The quote is cited in "The Cinema Is Finished," ed. Costantini, 162.

5. My aim is not to assess opera's and cinema's deaths in relation to theories about the death of art, but to interpret a moment in which the death of opera erupts as cinema's figure for its own death. Jonathan Gilmore writes: "For as long as art has been written about as having a history, that history has been said to reach an end." Historians of art assert that certain art has "stopped" or "is no longer possible or required" or is "politically illegitimate." The Hegelian view is that art has ended for reasons internal to it, as a result of the nature of art itself. For a discussion of the end of art, see Jonathan Gilmore, "Danto, Arthur Coleman: Danto's End of Art Thesis," in *Encyclopedia of Aesthetics*, vol. 1 (New York and Oxford: Oxford University Press, 1998), 500–503; quotation, 500. See also Arthur Danto, "The End of Art," in *The Philosophical Disenfranchisement of Art* (New York: Columbia University Press, 1986).

6. For a different film, one not about the voice of someone already dead but about voices that can no longer be sung by the living, see *Tosca's Kiss* (*Il bacio di Tosca*). The film is made up of interviews with singers and musicians of the Casa Verdi in Milan (an old-age home for musicians). The musicians, mostly singers, remember their days onstage. Some of them perform for the camera, and others listen to their voices emanating from old recordings. *Il bacio di Tosca*, directed by Daniel Schmid (Italtoons Corporation, 1985).

7. Fellini's *Clowns* is analogous in many ways to *E la nave va*. Not only is the

film an attempt to retrieve and show the dying world of the clowns (which in one interview is even confused by an aging clown with the memory of an operatic performance), but the film culminates in a funeral of the greatest clown—in a circus ring—which then turns into a celebration. Even the clown's funeral carriage resembles the diva's funeral carriage in *E la nave va*.

8. The theme of the death of opera takes on other forms. Pierre Boulez expresses his rage at opera's stagnated institutions in his "Opera Houses?" Jeremy Tambling claims that opera's ideological elitist and ahistorical setting attests to its irrelevance—and if this does not amount to a deadly state of affairs, Tambling says it should. See his *Opera, Ideology and Film* and his *Opera and the Culture of Fascism*. There are also those who view opera's lingering on its past and its inevitable incarnation in the technological media as a sign of opera's end. See, for example, Sam Abel, "Opera Through the Media," in *Opera in the Flesh: Sexuality in Operatic Performance* (Colorado: Westview Press, 1996), 163–78.

9. Philippe Lacoue-Labarthe, "The Caesura of Religion," in *Opera Through Other Eyes*, ed. Levin, 45–46.

10. Ibid., 45–47.

11. William Weaver, *The Golden Century of Italian Opera: From Rossini to Puccini* (London: Thames and Hudson, 1980), 242. Quoted in *Puccini's* Turandot: *The End of the Great Tradition*, by William Ashbrook and Harold Powers (Princeton: Princeton University Press, 1991), 3.

12. Sutcliffe, *Believing in Opera*, 416.

13. Ibid., 425.

14. Henry Pleasants, "Opera in Crisis (2)" (1961), in *Opera in Crisis: Tradition, Present, Future* (New York: Thames and Hudson, 1989), 26.

15. Jean Starobinski, "Opera and Enchantresses" (1979), in *Opera Through Other Eyes*, 23.

16. Clément, *Opera, or The Undoing of Women*, 180.

17. The consistency of the ashes was important for Fellini, and he fussed over the pile of powder serving as ashes. Hollis Alpert attests to the grotesque aspect of the pile of ashes: "Fellini ordered several batches of ashes before he was satisfied that he had the right powdery consistency." Hollis Alpert, *Fellini: A Life* (New York: Atheneum, 1986), 289.

18. For a preliminary consideration of the film's music, see Enrique Ochoa, "E la nave va—opera," found at www.cinemaitalia.com/fellini/nave_comm.html.

19. Rudolph Lothar, *The Talking Machine: A Technical-Aesthetic Essay* (1924), quoted in *Gramophone, Film, Typewriter*, by Kittler, 45.

20. Koestenbaum, *Queen's Throat*, 51.

21. Louis-Vincent Thomas, "Funeral Rites," in *The Encyclopedia of Religion*, ed. Mircea Eliade, vol. 5 (London: Macmillan, 1987), 455–59.

22. In the Bible, the Hebrews reserved death by fire as punishment. In the history of the Jewish people, cremation is a figure associated with their genocide. And in the secular legal world, the practice is associated with attempts to eliminate any possibility of detecting the cause of a suspicious death. There is also the gruesome anecdotal side to cremation. I cite one such example: "Although the attendants attempt to remove all of the remains, a small portion will be left inside the cremation chamber, and subsequently mingled with the next body to be cremated."

See "Cremation vs. Burial: Christian Controversy," at www.religioustolerance
.org/crematio.html.

23. Stephen Prothero, *Purified by Fire: A History of Cremation in America*
(Berkeley: University of California Press, 2001), 6.

24. Stephen Davis, "Survival of Death," in *A Companion to Philosophy of Religion*, ed. Philip Quinn and Charles Taliaferro (Cambridge, Mass.: Blackwell Publishers, 1997), 560.

25. See Prothero, *Purified by Fire*, 7.

26. Thomas, "Funeral Rites," 457.

27. Here is the account given in the *Encyclopaedia of Superstitions*:

> From the earliest times the charm of ashes has been a powerful one. People of all nations, civilized and savage, have seen in them the germ of fertility. Not only were the ashes of more or less sacred fires gathered and mixed with the seed at sowing . . . but they were also scattered on the fields after the seeds had been planted, and when it was growing. . . . In most of the Catholic countries of Europe, ashes of the Easter bonfires were mixed with ashes from the consecrated palms and then mixed again with the seed to be sown for the next harvest. . . . [I]n Scotland . . . if scattered on the land, it was held to protect the land from the ill-wishing of witches. So much for the civilized races; what of the savage? It was the custom of some of the Orinoco tribes of Indians to disinter after a year the bones of a dead tribesman, burn them and scatter the ashes to the winds. It was held by them that the ashes thus scattered turned to rain and thus refreshed and fertilized the lands of the family. The Marinios of Bechuana tribes each year sacrifice a human being to their crops. (Edwin Radford and Mona Radford, "Ashes," in *Encyclopaedia of Superstitions* [New York: Philosophical Library, 1949], 21–22)

28. Nicholas Gage, *Greek Fire: The Story of Maria Callas and Aristotle Onassis* (New York: Alfred Knopf, 2000), 377.

29. Renzo Allegri and Roberto Allegri, *Callas by Callas: The Secret Writings of "la Maria"* (New York: Universe Publishing, 1998), 159.

30. Gage, *Greek Fire*, 378.

31. Allegri and Allegri, *Callas by Callas*, 159.

32. Stelios Galatopoulos, *Maria Callas: Sacred Monster* (London: Fourth Estate, 1998), 457.

33. Allegri and Allegri, *Callas by Callas*, 159.

34. Nicholas Petsalis-Diomidis, "Postscript III: The Mirror Cracked," in *The Unknown Callas: The Greek Years* (Portland, Ore.: Amadeus Press, 2001), 575.

35. Galatopoulos, *Maria Callas: Sacred Monster*, 458.

36. Allegri and Allegri, *Callas by Callas*, 160.

37. In fact, it is act 4.

38. Allegri and Allegri, *Callas by Callas*, 160.

39. Galatopoulos, *Maria Callas: Sacred Monster*, 458.

40. Ibid., 459.

41. Gage, *Greek Fire*, 380.

42. Ibid., 384.

43. Petsalis-Diomidis, "Postscript III," 575.

44. Galatopoulos, *Maria Callas: Sacred Monster*, 458.

45. Allegri and Allegri, *Callas by Callas*, 160.
46. Gage, *Greek Fire*, 384.
47. Petsalis-Diomidis, "Postscript III," 575.
48. Gage, *Greek Fire*, 384.
49. Jackie Callas, *Sisters* (London: Macmillan, 1989), 208–9.
50. Gage, *Greek Fire*, 391–92.
51. Callas, *Sisters*, 209.
52. Ibid., 210.
53. It is unclear who dubs the singing voice of Edmea Tetua on the gramophone in her one aria in the film. There are no credits in the film. Christian-Marc Bossèno mentions this fact and also cites a friend of Fellini, the Jesuit father Angelo Arpa, who offers the hypothesis that it is the voice of Callas: "It is a Greek voice: the Greek world is at the origin of thought, culture and European Art. This voice is frightening." See Christian-Marc Bossèno, *Et vogue le navire Federico Fellini* (Paris: Editions Nathan, 1998), 52. Chantal Thomas is the second scholar who mentions Callas. She states, mistakenly, that scattering the ashes over her place of birth was Callas's wish. See Chantal Thomas, "De la plume au panache," *Critique* 40, no. 444 (May 1984): 435.
54. Callas's most frequently performed roles, and in the order of frequency, were Norma, Violetta, Lucia, Tosca, and Medea. See David Kimbell, *Vincenzo Bellini:* Norma, Cambridge Opera Handbooks (Cambridge: Cambridge University Press, 1998), 116.
55. Quoted in "Cinema and Musica: Luchino Visconti. 2) Between the Cinema and the Opera," found at http://filomusica.com/filo15/visconti2.html.
56. A private screening also occurs in *The Clowns*. Here Fellini is waiting to view a film of the greatest clown; he was told there is such a film in the TV archives. This turns out to be a disappointment, as the film is only a few seconds long and silent, and the clown hardly appears in it. Following this scene, Fellini decides to stage a funeral for the clown.
57. In a documentary about Callas (in which Zeffirelli is the narrator) there is a footage of an interview with Visconti and Callas. Visconti tells an anecdote about how he instructed Callas to thank the audience after one of her performances where members of the audience threw vegetables at her. It is clear that Visconti continues to stage Callas even in the aftermath of the performance (*Callas: A Documentary Plus Bonus*, written by John Ardoin, narrated by Franco Zeffirelli [Bel Canto Society, 1978]).
58. In fact, *E la nave va*'s catastrophe (the sinking of the ship, the destruction of the world) is staged as a performance. The onset of Fellini's World War I awaits in respect for the diva's ceremony. The Austro-Hungarian battleship—perhaps a reminder of the battleship returning Callas's ashes to Greece, a political sign turned musical—attacks only then. The onset of World War I is shown as objects slide, as if taken by the movement of Verdi's music sung by all of the film's characters (though in a previous scene, these same singers were already seen to have left the sinking ship). The cannons and soldiers operating them, the tables and chairs of the illustrious dining room, the grand piano—all dance as the floor tilts with the sinking ship. The scene then shifts to a stage and exposes the studio's operations,

thus collapsing the remaining illusion of the cinematic world itself. Following the funeral rite and the onset of the political as musical, the journalist is transported into a future time as he reports on events that have not yet taken place. He finds it difficult to explain or accurately account for the film's different endings. He tells of the rescue of all the passengers following the shipwreck, as if they emerge from the scene of destruction to give a final invisible curtain bow, as if they are the characters of opera rising from their postures of death to our grateful ovations. For the political as musical, see Pascal Bonitzer, "Le rhinoceros et la voix," *Cahiers du Cinema* 356 (February 1984): 17.

59. It is interesting to note Fellini's technique in general, which relates to the diva's voiceless screening. It is the technique of post-synchronization. This technique was shared by other Italian directors to denote a late stage in the making of the film in which the actors' voices are recorded and made to correspond with the movements of their mouths on-screen. In *E la nave va*, furthermore, Fellini uses *foreign* actors for the most part (French, German, and English), their voices replaced by those of Italian actors. Thus, post-synchronization becomes dubbing, reminding us that the actors were not chosen for their voices and that both the singing and the nonsinging actors were treated equally and dubbed into Italian— either into the Italian language or into, predominantly, Italian song. It reminds us that we are not even told who sings Edmea Tetua's part. For more on Fellini and post-synchronization, see Alpert, *Fellini*, 290. I stress that post-synchronization meant that on the set, while shooting the film, the voice heard over and above the voices of all the actors replacing their voices was *Fellini's voice*—directing, explaining, and continually speaking. Fellini often remarks on the director's one tool: the megaphone (an extinct tool). In this sense, Fellini is the film's primary voiceover, a master dubber, the voice standing for all voices. A rough draft of a Fellinian film is, then, an array of very unusual faces speaking in the director's voice. In his later films we often hear Fellini in the final product as the process and materiality are often exposed and made the subject matter of the film. On Fellini's technique, see Charlotte Chandler, *I, Fellini* (New York: Cooper Square Press, 1995), 362. Fellini's method is alluded to in Truffaut's film *Day for Night*, where the actress says: "When I work with Fellini, I don't speak dialogue, I merely count—*uno, due, tre*" (mentioned in "With Fellini," by Linda Polan, *Sight and Sound* 53, no. 3 (Summer 1984): 207.

60. Zeffirelli's work on *La traviata* parallels Fellini's *E la nave va*. In fact, Fellini's film was delayed because of other films made at Cinecittà, including Zeffirelli's *Traviata*. See Tony Mitchell, "Fellini's Ship Sails On," *Sight and Sound* 52, no. 2 (Spring 1983): 80. (It is unclear whether the article is reliable, as names, sites, and even the synopsis differ from Fellini's final version.) See also Costantini, *Conversations with Fellini*, 134.

61. Zeffirelli had already planned a film about Callas in 1979. See the advertisement in *Corriere della Sera*, June 3, 1979.

62. For a detailed interpretation of *Callas Forever*, see my article "The Afterlife of Maria Callas's Voice" (forthcoming).

63. Mentioned in "A Black Goddess," by Peter Conrad, in *A Song of Love and Death: The Meaning of Opera* (New York: Poseidon Press, 1987), 329.

64. For a list of the films offered to Maria Callas, see Barth David Schwartz,

Pasolini Requiem (New York: Pantheon Books, 1992), 552–53.

65. Clément, *Opera, or The Undoing of Women*, 28.

66. Olivier Assayas gives a different interpretation of the diva's name. Her name, depending on its pronunciation, points to the pronouns *mine* (Latin, "mea") and *yours* ("tua," or French "toi") and thus to the spectator and the various protagonists. Olivier Assayas, "Sic Transit Gloria N.", *Cahiers du Cinema* 355 (January 1984): 24. One can also point out that in French "Tetua," when said out loud in a certain way, can sound like "tais-toi" (be quiet), which is, of course, the imperative addressed to the listener by every singing voice.

67. Stephen Snyder, "*Fellini Satyricon*: The Self Inside Vision," in *The Transparent I: Self/Subject in European Cinema* (New York: Peter Lang, 1994), 141. (Snyder is referring specifically to *Fellini Satyricon*.) In Fellini's *Intervista*, we are shown a parade of faces and the files with photographs as part of the film's plot. Choosing the face becomes a subject for the film.

68. Federico Fellini, *Fellini on Fellini*, trans. Isabel Quigley (New York: Da Capo Press, 1996), 103–4.

69. Fellini, in an interview with Vittoriano Vancini. See Vittoriano Vancini, "Arriva a New York 'La nave va' di Fellini," *La Follia di New York*, January 1984, 17. Quoted and translated by Joseph Perricone, ". . . *and the Ship Sails On*: A Reviewing of Fellini," *Literature/Film Quarterly* 15, no. 2 (1987): 83.

70. Alpert, *Fellini*, 284.

71. Costantini, *Conversations with Fellini*, 123–24. Fellini also tells the story of his first visit to the opera at the age of eight. The noise ruptured his eardrum, and he was left nearly deaf for life. Ibid., 7–8. For Fellini's relation to opera, see also Bossèno, *Et vogue le navire*, 68; and Chandler, *I, Fellini*, 193, 223. The death of Nino Rotta, the composer of the majority of Fellini's films, might be another sense of an end resonating in the background, causing opera to be featured not only in the soundtrack but as the subject of Fellini's film.

72. Quote cited in *Fellini*, by Alpert, 293.

73. Quote cited in *Et Vogue Le Navire*, by Bossèno, 75 (the translation from the French is mine).

INDEX